THE FULL CUP

Other Materials Available

✳✳✳

By Dr. Peter S. Ruckman:
* Bible Believer's Commentary Series
* Beginning and Advanced Bible Study Material
* In-Depth Apologetics
* Numerous Pamphlets on Selected Topics
* Variety of Gospel Tracts
* Audio Cassettes
* Video Cassettes

Also Available:
* AV 1611 Bibles
* Study Helps
* Concordances
* Biographies
* Evangelism Material
* Material by Other Authors and Speakers

✳✳✳

For FREE Current Catalogue write:
BIBLE BAPTIST BOOKSTORE
P.O. Box 7135   Pensacola, FL 32534

"THE FULL CUP"

By Peter S. Ruckman
B.A., B.D., M.A., Th.M., Ph.D.

BIBLE BAPTIST BOOKSTORE

P.O. Box 7135   Pensacola, FL 32534

PUBLISHER'S NOTE

The Scripture quotations found herein are from the text of the Authorized King James Version of the Bible. Any deviations therefrom are not intentional.

Dr. Peter S. Ruckman

Note

This autobiography has been written largely from memory. At seventy-six it is not always easy to get all of the names and places spelled right or the exact dates that events happened. If any of these dates need to be corrected, we will be more than glad to make the changes. If any of the persons involved feel they have been misrepresented or lied about, we will be glad to make these changes also. Simply send us the exact way the statement (or date) should be worded, and we will make the changes as necessary. I have numerous eyewitnesses for all of the events that take place after 1970.

Table of Contents

Introduction

This is a very brief history of one sinner among earth's billions of sinners (about four and a quarter billion at the time of this writing). **"There is no end of all the people"** (Eccl. 4:16), Solomon said, so one man's life doesn't really amount to a great deal one way or another. **"We are as water spilt on the ground"** (2 Sam. 14:14). The great men of this world— the military leaders, popes, kings, and "chairmen"—often fool themselves into thinking that "everyone in the world" knows about them. There are perhaps, on this earth today, around two billion people who could not tell you who killed John Kennedy or who killed Michael Luther King Jr. The hundred thousand German boys who died in Siberia as POW's, many years after the war was over, are mourned by no one today but a handful of close relatives. Three and a half billion people couldn't give you the name of ONE of them.

No one worries about the horrors of the Bataan Death March back in 1942. There are probably not TWO people in Africa, Asia, or South America that could give you the names of TWO men who went through that hell. Television has done much to propagate and magnify the "great men" of the earth, but we often forget that two billion of the people on earth don't have television, radio, or newspapers. Nothing could be funnier than going out into the "boonies" of Mongolia or New Guinea and asking someone what they thought of Presley or Madonna, or Johnny Carson or Barbara Walters. We are "here today and gone tomorrow." Ten years after you are dead, there will probably not be more than ten to twelve people who really miss you, and there won't be fifty that think about you more than once or twice a year.

The "headliners" of today (as will be seen from this chronicle) are the nobodies of the future. Occasionally a martyr is remembered longer, but only because a martyr is the best material in the world for propagating a LIE. One good, dead Communist like M. L. King, or International Socialist like Trotsky, or potential Roman Catholic dictator like John Kennedy is worth a thousand Bible-believing pastors and evangelists, to the world system.

This is the history of a Christian minister. He was a little thirty-watt bulb in "the Father's house," which has contained many a three hundred watt bulb. When you read this account you will understand why he never possibly could have attained the spiritual stature of many ministers of the past or even many of his contemporaries. He was a very small light who tried to shine for His Lord once the "current" got to him. He will never be remembered like Moody or Sunday are remembered, and he could not possibly accomplish what J. Frank Norris or Bob Jones Sr. accomplished. His "role models," as a Christian, were John Wesley, Martin Luther, J. Frank Norris, and Bob Jones Sr. As you can tell from the account, these men were not always his "models." For twenty-seven years it was an entirely different "ballgame."

Beauchamp Vick and Dr. DeHaan have been dead for many years now. Lester Roloff and John R. Rice departed years ago, and Charles Fuller and Mordecai Ham have "long gone."

There are probably more than three billion people who never knew who these men were, what they did, or even when they lived. That is how "important" we are. Modern Fundamentalists make a great mistake in magnifying their importance in their own eyes. Each one of them is just one little speck on the bosom of infinity—one little ant in a pile of ants. Not a thousand people in Europe, Asia, Africa, or South America know who Pappy Reveal or Jimmy Stroud were any more than they knew who Glen Schunk or Hugh Pyle were. But as far as that goes, no one ON ANY CONTINENT, since 1970, has mourned the loss of Rudolph

Valentino, Glenn Miller, Helen Keller, Herbert Hoover, Harry Truman, Pope Pius XI, Pancho Villa, or Gene Tunney.

The headliners, later, are just as big a "blank" as those who never get their names in print. The author of *Peyton Place* had twenty-five people at her funeral. I have seen old farm women who died at eighty-three, who had more than two hundred people come to their funeral, and I could not even tell you the woman's name. So who was "Peter Ruckman"? And who cares who he was? After his death he will be missed by most of his children, one fine Christian wife who loved him very much, a couple of hundred church members who loved him for feeding them the bread of life, and an assorted handful of pastors, "laymen," and evangelists (called "Ruckmanites" by the apostates at Bob Jones University, Pensacola Christian College, Baptist Bible College, etc.) who got a blessing from his ministries. Outside of that (and most of these will not feel any loss after a few weeks), "Ruckman" will have come and gone off of this earth absolutely unknown to 95 percent of its population.

What, then, is the point of wasting a few hundred pages to give you the "life history" of such an insignificant character? Simple: mankind can always use a chronicle of the grace of God, and if you ever saw GRACE—absolute and total unmerited FAVOR—lavished on one sinner on this earth, you will see it in the life of Peter Sturges Ruckman—God's joke on Christian scholarship.

He lived twenty-seven years **"alone in the world . . . without hope and without God"** (Eph. 2:12). Then, after being **"accepted in the beloved"** (Eph. 1:6), he went another forty-nine years as the Lord's "junk yard dog," a sentinel placed at the doors of the *Authorized Version* of the Holy Bible to take the seat of the britches out of "godly" scavengers who used the Book to make a living with when they didn't BELIEVE it.

May you enjoy partaking of **"The Full Cup"** that God poured out for one very small, very base, very insignificant sinner, between 1921 and 1998.

CHAPTER ONE

The Silver Cup

It was the year 1921. Valera led in a revolt against the British in Ireland, and the Allies marched back into Germany to collect extortion money. Harding became the twenty-ninth president, and the Catholic IRA murdered its first woman (April 24). The Turks and the Greeks went to war, and Adolph Hitler became the president of the National Socialist German Worker's Party (NAZI). The Communist Lenin got financial help from America (like Gorbachev, Stalin, and Yeltsin), and Mussolini set himself up as head of the Fascists in Italy.

In an apartment house on Franklin Avenue in Wilmington, Delaware, Peter Sturges Ruckman was born (November 19), the second son of John Hamilton Ruckman and Mary Warner Armstrong Ruckman. He was born less than a block from Howard Pyle's art studio. His background didn't have one piece of sod in it that matched another place. The father was from Boston, Massachusetts, the mother from Pasadena, California. Since the distances were too far apart, they settled in (of all places!) Topeka, Kansas (1922).

From Topeka came John Brown to raid Harper's Ferry, the Charismatic movement (Bethel Bible College, 1900), and the CIVIL RIGHTS MOVEMENT (*Brown vs. Board of Education*, 1954).

The mother was from a wealthy home in Pasadena that sported a Chinese cook and a Japanese gardener. The father was a third generation Army officer with a West Point General for a father (Philippine Insurrection) and a West Point General for a grandfather (Civil War). He became a Captain in World War I and was a Colonel by the time of World War II.

Peter S. was born in his living room before the doctor could get there. Someone said, "He probably hit the ground running."

In those days it was a habit (at least for the Armstrongs and the Ruckmans) to give each child a solid sterling silver cup on his first birthday; this cup had the child's full name and the date of his birth on it. No one knows if this was a sort of "born with a silver spoon in your mouth" thing or whatever; perhaps it was done so if the family ran out of money they would have some silver they could cash in on to take care of the baby. At any rate, Peter S. was given a silver cup in 1922. It was about two and a half inches across the top, about three inches high, and bulged slightly at the base. The inscription on it said "Peter Sturges Ruckman, November 19, 1921." It disappeared many years ago.

In the Bible, **"the silver cord"** (Eccl. 12:6) is emblematic of physical life, and when it is **"broken,"** physical life is over. In the same book will be found a declaration that a man can have TWO birthdays (John 3:3–7) ("Born once, die twice; born twice, die once"), so we may assume there are two cups. Peter S. was about to drink from his first cup; he would find at the bottom of that cup that life **"biteth like a serpent, and stingeth like an adder"** (Prov. 23:32). But let us not get ahead of ourselves.

What "Mommy and Daddy" were doing in Wilmington, no one knows, except that mother's sister (Margaret Armstrong) was a businesswoman there who became quite wealthy. Later, she bought a cottage (19 Oak Avenue) at Rehoboth Beach, Delaware, the big summertime resort for Washington, D.C., businessmen. (The place today is a haven for queers.) Mary (Peter's mother) had another sister named Katherine, who lived and died a chronic alcoholic; she burned to death in her bed after it was ignited by a cigarette butt. Mary's brother was Alfred Armstrong, an artist. He also lived and died a chronic alcoholic. Mary followed the family tradition. John Ruckman neither drank nor smoked, although he would sip a cocktail or two several times a year at social gatherings.

General John Hamilton Ruckman

Peter Sturges Ruckman
Johnny Ruckman (standing)

Both he and his wife were Anglicans (Episcopalians), and when they moved to Topeka they attended Grace Cathedral, where "Dean" Day was the "rector." They moved to Topeka in 1922, when a former classmate of John Ruckman got a job opening for John as a civil engineer, working for Alfred Landon. Kansas, at that time, was a "DRY STATE," and remained so long after the repeal of Prohibition.

There are no very early pictures of Peter S. (he got his middle name from a Dutch pirate on his mother's side, the grandfather of Mary's mother. The pirate—"Old Sturges"—was hung at Charleston, South Carolina).

The first picture we have is Peter (three years old) in what looks like a girl's dress, covered with dirt, hair uncombed, shoe laces untied, standing looking up at his older brother who has mounted a brand new tricycle. Johnny (the firstborn) is neatly dressed, cleaner than a whistle, and has on a brand new straw hat.

The next picture is the two brothers at "Aunty Robinson's" (Hartford, Connecticut). They are five and four years old. The older is blond-haired and blue-eyed, a real Prussian. Peter S. is round-faced, dark-complected, with brown eyes and brown, curly hair: a genuine Oesterreicher if you ever saw one.

Nothing "fit."

Topeka, Kansas, for a wealthy Californian and a Master's degree graduate from MIT in Boston, was about as fitting as placing Herbert W. Armstrong and Zsa Zsa Gabor in Mt. Airy, North Carolina, but there they were. In 1924 they moved to 1525 College Avenue (one block from Washburn College), and there they remained until 1942. They were there when the Depression hit, and they were there when World War II broke out.

The year Peter was born a man who had been the Attorney General of Kansas died: his name was C.I. Scofield.

There was not one Bible-believing Christian on either side of the family for four generations, as far as the record goes. There was no Bible reading in the house in Wilmington or Topeka the entire time the family lived there. Mom and Dad Ruckman took the boys to church about once a month; the "rector" preached on the need for one world government, disarmament, integration, Socialism, and a welfare state. He was a Deist like John and Mary Ruckman: no Bible, no heaven, no hell, no new birth, no Second Coming, no blood atonement, and no Deity of Christ. All he knew was "social justice" and "ending man's inhumanity to man." While he tried to disarm the United States, Hirohito, Mussolini, Franco, and Hitler were arming their countries to the teeth.

This was the preaching that Major John H. Ruckman (later Lieutenant Colonel) got from 1922 to 1942. He sat there, with three generations of Regular Army blood running through his veins, and cursed under his breath. Perhaps he could still hear the thunderous voice of his father, General John Hamilton Ruckman, as he paced the floor rattling his sabre (really and truly: he wore a sabre with his full dress General's uniform) and singing: "In the land of pork and beans, happy, sunny Philippines, In that happy, happy land so far away, where mosquitoes sting and bite, and the natives steal and fight, and the soldiers sing whenever they get sore: &**#*!! the Filipinos, #%**#!! cried out the khaki drones! But beneath the starry flag we'll civilize 'em with a Krag, and return us to our own beloved homes!"

Peter S. wound up in the Philippines, but that was many years later.

CHAPTER TWO

The Child and Its Doings

In 1922, the Communist Party was formed in China (Mao Tse-tung) and the Fascists began to fight the Communists in Italy. Mussolini marched on Rome while the German mark collapsed. When Peter S. was two years old (1923), the French marched into the Rhineland, and promptly the Nazi Party held its first congress in Munich. At this time it took 136,000 German marks to make ONE DOLLAR. The Jews in Germany "cleaned up," but only under the watchful eye of a newly budding NAZI Party. The next year (1924) Lenin kicked the bucket.

Peter S. was called "momma's brown-eyed Booflee" by his mother, for what reason only God knows. Like any other baby, he cried, slept, messed up his diapers, and stuck his lower lip out when forced to eat something he didn't like. The earliest recollections he had of life were being bullied by his older brother, and spending time in his grandmother's house on Gilpin Avenue in Wilmington when she baby-sat for her daughter. Grandmother Armstrong was called "Bama" (for some other reason that no one has been able to find out). Evidently Johnny was with Momma and Daddy, for Peter never remembered anyone being there but himself and "Bama." There were four things that survived the pre-school days:

1. A memory of walking into Howard Pyle's studio and looking at pen and ink drawings for Robin Hood, King Arthur, and The Wonder Clock. There were also some paintings for Howard Pyle's Book of Pirates.

2. Toast and bacon every morning for breakfast: crisp bacon and buttered toast. It was the same every morning from 1924 to 1928.

3. "Hokey Pokey Snowballs," which were "Icees"

made of ice scraped off of a twenty-five pound block and sprinkled with flavors (raspberry, lemon, orange, lime, etc.). They were a penny apiece, and the man that sold them carried his equipment in a little cart that he pushed down the sidewalks, ringing a bell as he went. He cried out "Hokey Pokey Snowballs!" ("Cockles and mussels, alive, alive all!")

4. Illustrations in picture books like Kipling's *Jungle Book* and stories from the Bible. The strange thing about it was that Peter found out that he could remember the STYLE of an illustration anywhere from twenty to forty years after he had seen a picture by the illustrator. He could tell when a cartoonist's "understudy" took over a strip after the originator *died* (for example; Seegar for Popeye, Chester Gould for Dick Tracy, et al.).

In the summer time, Peter found himself on the beach at Rehoboth. He learned later that "Aunt Margaret," who owned the cottage there (19 Oak Avenue), let her sister Mary have the cottage every summer from June 15 to the end of August. While "Poppa John" (that is what Margaret called Mr. Ruckman) stayed out in Topeka sweating for a living, Mary and the two boys (and later a younger sister named Marian) would spend the summer at Rehoboth. They were one block from "Deauville Beach," a swanky, high-class private beach for Washington's elite: the Belancas, the DuPonts, the Proctors, the Clappers, et al. Peter's mother took her whiskey and gin with her, and the cocktail parties were numerous. Peter first saw gambling in the living room: poker and bridge. He first saw cigarettes and whiskey in the living room, and he could not repeat today the words of the first song he heard his mother sing.

The permanent inhabitants of Rehoboth were simple Delaware fishermen and truck farmers. They eyed Mrs. Ruckman and her two boys. The saying was that the small boy (Peter S.) could swim before he was two years old. They said that when his mother was drunk on the beach and not keeping an eye on him, often the waves would wash the baby boy up and down, back and forth, in and out of the surf at the water's edge until it got dangerous, and then someone went out and picked him up. With no shoes on his feet from June to August for fifteen years (three years old to eighteen), Peter S. sported feet that looked like flippers. They stopped at a 9½ double E when he was about twenty years old.

In the days before the Depression, he remembered leg of lamb and rice with lamb gravy. He liked spinach, which most children do not like, and very quickly developed a taste for anything RAW. No cooked bananas, apples, oranges, pears, peaches, apricots, grapes, figs, or any other fruit in any other form. Raw apples, raw oranges, raw peaches, raw grapes, and raw pears. No "cobblers" or pies. At a very early age he decided that "candy" was chocolate and nothing else was, and ice cream was "vanilla" and nothing else was. You might say he was DOGMATIC.

In 1924 Coolidge became president. In 1925 Stalin kicked Trotsky out of his command post, and the first issue of *The New Yorker* hit the newsstands. Chiang Kai Shek became the new leader in China, and Hindenberg was elected president of Germany. The Scopes monkey trial took place in Tennessee (July 26), and the ACLU declared that it was "unconstitutional" to teach only ONE theory of creation in the schools. In 1988, they declared it was unconstitutional to teach TWO.

Forty thousand Klansmen marched on Washington, D.C. (August 8), and Billy Mitchell was found guilty of insubordination for telling the truth about aerial warfare.

Back in those days, kindergarten began at five years old, so in 1926 Peter S. showed up in kindergarten; his older brother Johnny was in the first grade. When Peter sat down to play with the blocks and learn the alphabet, a Scotchman invented a machine he called "TELEVISION" (January 27). The inventor, John Baird, said that it "could someday turn every home into a motion picture theatre." That is exactly what happened, and Hollywood's moral standards came in with it. In 1926 Rudolph Valentino died, and the news media began an all-out campaign to restore whiskey, beer, wine, brandy, gin, and rum to the American homes. They said temperance caused INSAN-

Randolph Grade School (1990)

Randolph Grade School (Primary) From the Northwest

ITY and CRIME. In the meantime a civil war broke out in China.

From the time Peter S. got into "grade school" (in this case Randolph Grade School, one mile west of 1525 College Avenue) until he graduated from college (the University of Alabama, 1944), he was in hot water up to his neck. During the first six grades he was in the principal's office so many times they should have made him vice-principal. In those days, "principals" carried paddles eighteen inches long, four inches wide, and three quarters of an inch thick. When they practised "child abuse" your pants often stuck to you for several hours. Furthermore, you wouldn't dare tell either parent when you got home that you had "got a whuppin'," for as surely as teachers in those days could "beat the snot" out of you, you would get another licking at home when "yer old man" found out about it. Dad Ruckman's weapon was an eight foot strap from a steamer locker up in the attic. He would double it and then lay on the stripes while you saw the stars: he was very patriotic. Peter S. was thankful that he averaged only about one whipping a week; he knew he deserved a little better average than that, for he only got caught on about one out of three offences.

In 1927, Lindberg flew the Atlantic alone, Chiang Kai Shek took over China, Sandino rebelled in Nicaragua, and a revolt broke out in Austria. The first "talkie" was produced. Peter S. played soccer, played hookey, and played "hob" anyway he could. He weathered out chicken pox, measles, and whooping cough, wrapped in blankets in a quarantined house, weeks at a time, his sole entertainment being a radio beside his bed. He listened to this radio sometimes as much as fourteen hours a day (WIBW, KFAB, KSAC, WDAF, etc.) and followed Fibber McGee and Molly, Eddie Cantor, Ed Wynn, Lum and Abner, Vic and Sade, Back Stage Wife, Amos and Andy, Stella Dallas, Gangbusters, Little Orphan Annie, the Shadow, Renfro of the Mounted, Jack Armstrong, Jack Benny, and The Lucky Strike Hit Parade through literally months of broadcasts. During an incarceration for scarlet fever the programs ran six weeks. Another time, for pneumonia, they ran two weeks.

There was only one religious influence on his radio at this time. Some Scotchman called "Edward McHugh the Gospel Singer" would come on for fifteen minutes daily, and Peter would listen to him. He remembered nothing of the program but the theme: "If I have wounded any soul today, if I have caused one foot to go astray, if I have walked in my own will or way, dear Lord forgive."

That tune, which he first heard in 1927, did not bear fruit until 1947.

The only other thing "religious" he remembered was a prayer in the Episcopal church that said, "We have not done those things which we ought to have done, and we have done those things which we ought *not* to have done, and there is no help in us, but God be merciful to us miserable sinners." He liked *that* prayer. I guess he liked it because it made sense, but he never thought anything more about it than that.

When Christmas came, for some peculiar reason, he liked to sleep under the Christmas tree. He did this until he was fourteen years old. There was something about lying behind (or under) a fir tree that he liked. There were no thick woods or forests in Topeka, but somewhere in his blood there was an affinity for large forests. He liked TREES and OCEANS; the rest he could do without.

Woody S. taught him how to steal money from his mother's purse and his father's billfold: a little at a time so it would not be noticed. In those days you could get a pint of milk for five cents, a quart for ten cents, and a gallon for a quarter. ("Shave and a hair cut, two bits!" Two bits is twenty-five cents.) The Cadillacs and Packards were $690 to $880, and the Fords and Chevys were around $300 and $400. Baseball and Indian cards (gum with the card) were a penny apiece. A penny sized Hershey bar was about the size of a "fifty center" today.

Just before the bottom dropped out, Herbert Hoover announced that America was near the end of poverty (August 9, 1928). Hirohito was crowned Emperor of Japan (November 10, 1928), Hoover took his oath of office (March 4, 1929), and the first "Academy Awards" were given to Hollywood actors (May 16). On Black Thursday (October 24, 1929) the bottom dropped out of the stock market, and people went to the savings and loan associations to find out they had no savings and "nobody would loan them nothing."

Bankers and businessmen committed suicide; some others wound up selling apples on the streets. For the next five years Peter S. had nothing but MUSH (oatmeal) for breakfast, while Poppa John worked as a surveyor for forty cents an hour. Lunch was reduced to cheese or peanut butter sandwiches with no butter, and now an apple or orange in the stocking at Christmas time was considered to be a delicacy. Peter promptly constructed a map of his neighborhood showing the location of all the cherry and apple trees. At dark he visited them on his bicycle. From this innocent "requisitioning" there came, at a later date, the stealing of automobiles and jewelry.

With the depression came the "escapism" of Hollywood, and with it the substitution of magazines and newspapers for the American people in place of the Bible. Peter S. knew nothing about these things at this time, but hindsight gives a clear picture. The country had gone bankrupt, and instead of turning to God, as they had done before Prohibition, they now turned to Hollywood, New York, Socialism, Communism, and the teachings of evolution.

Peter S. played "Tarzan," climbing the roof of his house when momma and daddy were gone. He nearly burned the house one time starting a fire under the front porch, and on two occasions he nearly broke his back trying to go from "vine to vine" (in search of Cheetah, or Jane, or something), which were tied to oak trees in the yard. The "vine" was clothesline, and it broke—when Peter was about twelve feet in the air. On one occasion, while walking to school (one mile each way, often in ten below zero weather, or over a hundred degrees at other times), he was attacked by a pack of dogs and bitten. On another occasion, two boys "double pumping" in an iron

1525 College Avenue (1990)

**Grace (Episcopal) Cathedral
1925–1998**

swing hit him right between the eyes with the swing. On another occasion later, while stealing watermelons out of a farmer's patch, he ran slap into an eight foot rattler and missed being bit by about a foot. Finally, a three inch "salute" went off ten inches from his right ear and punctured an ear drum.

Ruckman was not "raised." He was "drug up." He learned how to heal himself with homemade remedies his parents never even knew about. Before he was ten years old he was soaking his feet in boiling water at night in the bathroom while the rest of them were asleep. At other times, he was taking bromo quinine pills and covering himself with quilts until he sweat like a horse. He found out that cheese and peanut butter crackers could stop diarrhea, and canned green beans could stop constipation. He was his own doctor. He came home for meals and bedtime, and that was it.

In 1930, the news media increased its campaign to get America drunk again. Now it claimed that Prohibition was the cause of the increase in chronic alcoholism (January 28). Greta Garbo helped things out by asking for a shot of whiskey during her movie about "Anna Christie."

Two hundred people drowned in a flood in the south of France (March 3), one hundred and four burned to death in a Japanese theatre fire (March 10), and two more fires burned four hundred and ninety-nine to death (a church in Rumania and a Federal penitentiary in Ohio). Peter S. was not in the body count. "Out in Topeka" (as Tammy Wynette sang the song in the 1970's), there was only dry Republicanism: "They take the sidewalks in at eight, way out west in Kansas"!

CHAPTER THREE

Problems and Solutions

There is something about Topeka, Kansas, that produces radicals. It was six-foot Carrie Nation who "axed"
the saloons in Topeka (February 1901). There is something strange about a town that can spark a civil war and
cause the destruction of more than seven hundred million
dollars worth of property (1964–1984), and completely
destroy the public school system of the greatest nation on
earth (the Civil Rights Acts: 1954 and 1964). It must be a
rebellion against an ultra-conservatism that produces this
phenomenon.

At any rate, between 1931 and 1939, while the other
nations were preparing to slaughter twenty-two million
of their inhabitants and displace another forty million,
Peter S. was bored to tears. He had seen at least one
movie a week from the time he was six (1927) to eight
(1929)—ten cents for children; twenty-five cents for
adults. By 1929, he had been exposed to All Quiet on the
Western Front, The Big House, The Cisco Kid, Wings,
The Last Command, The Way of All Flesh, and Seventh
Heaven. Not much for an eight-year-old boy, if you compare him with the boob tube generation, but much too
much for a midwestern Republican Kansan before FDR
got into office. The movies were to mold the boy's life
exactly the way television today has molded two generations of Americans. Life was to be seen in "pictures," not
as it actually is. A "dehumanizing" process was beginning: tiny at the start, of course, but destined to produce
an individual who could not accept people as PERSONS:
they were only "people."

When the bottom dropped out in 1929 there were
not many movies to go to. There was no money. In 1931
(when he was ten and his brother was eleven) gangs of

children began to form to find "something to do." They
were not like the "gangs" of the sixties and seventies.
These gangs, at their worst, dumped over outhouses on
Halloween, painted stripes on the statue of a white horse,
or occasionally jammed a toothpick in someone's horn
and then "went on the lam." Their older counterparts,
however, were beginning to form up to "survive" during
the depression, and these gangs spawned GANGSTERS:
Dillinger, Pretty Boy Floyd, Alvin Karpis, Homer Van
Meter, Lucky Luciano, Jack "Legs" Diamond, and Al
Capone.

Problem: nothing to do. It was true that an earthquake hit Burma and wiped out six thousand people (May
1930), another one in Italy did away with twenty-five
hundred (July), and a hurricane in the Dominican Republic (September) took away another twelve hundred. But
Peter S. Ruckman wasn't there. He wasn't in Shanghai
when eight thousand rebels were killed (October), nor
was he in Oklahoma when a tornado sacked nineteen
people. He was in Topeka. He got on his bicycle and
raced the trolley cars at night when momma didn't know
where he was. (They later became rubber-tired electric
"buses.") He totaled two bikes before 1936 and told his
parents the brakes hadn't worked.

Still there was nothing to do. Johnny became sort of
a leader in the gang, but Peter was too short to make a
good basketball player and too light to make a good
football player. The gang just tolerated him. Football
helmets were leather caps, and baseball gloves were gloves
like you throw snowballs with. Topeka could run twenty
below in the winter, and a hundred and ten in the summer. The boys played roller skate hockey on the cement
using a tin can and tree limbs for sticks. Peter S. liked
that game. (He liked that better than any other game, but
he would not get on ice skates for ice hockey until he
was sixty years old [1981].)

The years dragged by. Life was dull. Stalin killed
three million of his own people. Gandhi, in India, started
riots that did away with more than twenty thousand lives,
setting the pattern for Michael Luther King Jr. Thirty-

one people got killed in an Indiana mine explosion, but Peter S. wasn't there. He preached in Indianapolis and Ft. Wayne and Gary and Scherrville many years later, but he missed the explosion. Three hundred fifty people drowned during a water excursion in France (June 14, 1931), and the Yangtze River quietly produced more corpses than there were American casualties in Vietnam: two hundred thousand perished in less than a week (August 3, 1931).

Slowly, but surely, the music of prostitutes, pimps, junkies, and gangsters (jazz) was working its way up the Mississippi to Missouri and Kansas, and later up to Chicago. America was getting ready to go back to the jungle, but at that time Peter S. knew nothing but that life was a "drag."

Since he had no money to go to the movies, he found ways to steal into the theatres. Since he had no money to buy magazines with, he walked up and down the alleys at night with a flashlight and stole magazines out of the garages, where people stacked them up. In doing this, he not only picked up the first comic books (*Marvel Comics, Big Little Books, Wonder Comics, More Fun Comics*, etc.) but also every kind of pornographic literature available at that time: *Spicy Romance, French Follies, Spicy Detective*, etc., along with *Bluebook, Argosy, Adventure*, and the "standards" (*Saturday Evening Post, Punch, Ladies' Home Journal, The New Yorker, National Geographic, Colliers*, etc.). At ten years old (1931), he began to copy pictures out of these magazines, first with pencil and then with a fountain pen. Having seen All Quiet on the Western Front when he was nine years old, he became fascinated with the military. His father had a book by Captain John Thompson called *Fix Bayonets*. It was filled with pen and ink sketches, but Thompson was a real "sketcher"; you couldn't follow his lines, so Peter S. spent most of his time copying Popeye and *Mickey Mouse.* When he got proficient at this, he graduated to *Tarzan, Flash Gordon*, and *Mutt and Jeff.*

Still, life was dull. His father, glued to the radio, would often say, "Well, you certainly can't say we are

Col. John Ruckman's Civilian Office (New England Building)

living in dull times now!" But Peter not only said it, he thought it and believed it. True, an earthquake in Santiago had killed fifteen hundred people (February 1932), and fifty people had burned to death on the French liner Phillipe (May 1932), and not only had an earthquake killed three hundred in Mexico, but a rail crash in Algeria killed a hundred and twenty people, and a hurricane in Cuba did away with another thousand. Some people live a charmed life. Peter was not among the seventy thousand Chinamen that were destroyed by an earthquake (December 1932), and he was not among the three hundred Japanese that got drowned in a tidal wave (March 3, 1933).

He found that by drawing several score pictures you could paste them together and make a scroll out of them. You mounted this on two bread rollers and set them up in a large cardboard box with a "screen" cut out in front of it. Then you turned off the lights, shone a flashlight on the hole, and wound the pictures past the viewer's eyes in succession. Presto! Homemade movies. There were other innovations; you could actually enter a *real* theatre by walking through the ticket line BACKWARDS while the crowd was at the entrance. Another solution was to go early in the morning when the janitors were cleaning out the theatre. You slipped in an exit and lay down between the seats that had already been cleaned. Three hours later, on came the show.

By 1936, the boy had been exposed to The Great Ziegfield, My Man Godfrey, San Francisco, Romeo and Juliet, The Story of Louis Pasteur, A Tale of Two Cities, Mr. Deed Goes to Town, Dangerous, Becky Sharp, The Dark Angel, and forty others. His parents took him to some of these movies so the fare was paid, but this was a rare occasion (about once a month), for money was "hard to come by." The rest of the time he "snuck" into the theatre with some of his buddies.

In addition to these Hollywood displays came all of the cartoons, all of the movies by Laurel and Hardy, all of the Marx brothers movies, all of the Zorro and Flash Gordon movies, and all of the Tom Mix and Roy Rogers

movies. Into the boy's brain box went It Happened One
Night, The Gay Divorcee, David Copperfield, The In-
former, Ruggles of Red Gap, Captain Blood, Mutiny on
the Bounty, The Thin Man, Viva Villa, and A Farewell to
Arms—all the movies that you now watch (1990s) on the
"movie channel" or the "late, late show." You can imagine the condition Peter's mind was in by 1936, for he sat
before this deluge of artificial, Hollywood entertainment
as a potential ARTIST.

He saw Arrowsmith, The Champ, Shanghai Express,
The Guardsman, Dr. Jekkyl and Mr. Hyde, Smiling
Through, She Did Him Wrong, and Lady for a Day. The
problem was, you took "pot luck" when you snuck into a
theatre if you hadn't checked the ads the day before, and
then again, you went many times just to kill time or
watch the cartoons: MICKEY MOUSE showed up in
1932. The boy saw Anna Christie, The Trespasser, The
Devil's Holiday, Cimarron, Skippy, Trader Horn, Little
Women, Five Star Final, Broadway Melody, and The
Valiant.

Hollywood had a message, and it was getting it
across. Its message was simple: preparation for one world
under the Antichrist with no moral standards and the
Catholic church in charge.

True, very little of this was obvious back in 1936,
but it is a **"little leaven"** that spoils **"the whole lump"**
(Gal. 5:9). It is **"little foxes that spoil the vines"** (Song
of Sol. 2:15). What Hollywood was doing ($$$) was
working on human nature by interspersing moral lessons
and sentimental humanism between sex and violence.
Knowing that in the end the latter items would win out.
They had to. They have ALWAYS "won out." Between
Jackie Coogan's tear jerkers and Shirley Temple's cute
little songs there appeared gradually ("eventually" is the
word) belly dancers doing "the bumps and the grinds."
(The Roman circus did not begin by burning people alive.)
Hollywood was preparing to take America back to the
jungle via jungle music and jungle morals. It was done
slowly, one step at a time.

1. "The first time" you saw two single people sleeping in the same motel at night.

2. "The first time" you saw a prostitute you could sympathize with—she was cheerful and "funny."

3. "The first time" the word "hell" was allowed on the screen; the first time the word "damn" appeared on the screen.

4. "The first time" you saw a man slap a woman on the screen.

5. "The first time" you saw a married couple in bed together.

6. "The first time" you saw a woman undressing on the screen.

This eventually ("eventually" is the word) came into your living room via television, where *all* the four letter words are spoken, and sometimes as many as fifty in two hours, and the "plots" became nothing but a series of fornicating, adulterous cocktail drinkers (or government agents) engaged in killing people or going to bed with people. Shirley Temple, Mickey Rooney, Jackie Coogan, Our Gang, Douglas Fairbanks, Gloria Swanson, Clara Bow, Jeanne Harlow, Mary Pickford, Jackie Cooper, Paul Muni, and Myrna Loy were (unconsciously) getting America ready for Madonna, the Beatles, Elvis Presley, John Belushi, and a drug-headed, fornicating culture with the morals of an alley cat.

Another way to beat the doldrums was to walk to the Kaw River, steal watermelons, pitch them in the river, and then swim down the river with them while they cooled off. Out you got on the bank, broke the melons open with your foot, picked up the pieces, and placed them on a tree, leaned your face into them, and chewed them like you would an ear of corn. This was a good boredom killer because one often got fired at with "bacon rind" out of double-barreled shotguns.

The rapture subsided slightly when one of his buddies dove in and never came up. He got hung up on the "stob" of a broken down tree trunk. The only thing that came up was a spiral of blood. Pete's buddy, Jack Alex-

The Kaw River (North Topeka)

ander, ran and got some help; all the help picked up was the drowned corpse of a fourteen-year-old boy.

There was the problem of grades, but he found out he could pass everything with C's and D's with hardly looking at a book. Somewhere, while going through his vast pile of stolen magazines, he had picked up the habit of reading about three hundred words a minute. This increased to seven hundred words a minute by the time he was twenty-one. The only trouble was that when Poppa John got ready to send his two boys off to West Point to follow in the footsteps of their forebearers, Johnny passed the test and Peter flunked it.

Monotonously, time marched on. FDR dropped the gold standard. "Happy days were here again" with gin, whiskey, rum, beer, brandy, and scotch. Adolph Hitler became the supreme dictator of Germany (March 1933). Iraq and Syria clashed and killed six hundred of their people (August 1933), and a hurricane in Texas killed thirty-two people, but Ruckman wasn't there. He didn't preach in Texas until after 1949; when he did, he preached in Amarillo, Galveston, Houston, San Antonio, Fort Worth, Dallas, Arlington, Graham, Beeville, and Monahan. But that was much later. Now he roamed the streets at night looking for "something to do." Life was dull. It was true Bonnie and Clyde got killed (May 1934), and a heat wave in Kansas killed two hundred and three people—but Ruckman wasn't one of them—and an earthquake off of Formosa killed two thousand people and left thirteen thousand homeless. But Ruckman wasn't in Formosa; he was in *Topeka*.

As if in answer to a prayer for excitement, he ran into a certain Bill Phelps (who was killed in a car wreck two years later at the age of eighteen), who got him into female company he had no business getting in with, but he came out "clean" by a miracle. A second "buddy" (they were both older boys) took him down to a red light house on the north end of Topeka (just before the bridge) and tried to get a prostitute to "break him in"; he was too young (thirteen) to know what was going on. If he had been raised in today's sexually obsessed black generation (1970–1990) he would have gone down at once. The same boy (a certain Jerry B.) showed him how to perform acts of bestiality. *Topeka is a strange place.*

But all of Peter's real loves were altruistic and Platonic; he was a dreamer. The movies had put him into a dream world. He could see clearer with his eyes shut than open. His first "crush" (age six) was a beautiful German blond named Louise Weidling; her father was a doctor. This affair lasted almost two years (1927–1929). His next OAO (age eight) was a German girl named Wilberta Garlinghouse; he never held her hand, but was madly in love with her from 1929 to 1932. After her was another Kraut: Harriet Ann Schmidt. He didn't get over her till 1936, although he never dated her.

"Love" was all right, but it was too dull. Running from the police had more "zip" to it. So he ran. On more than one night he heard the siren, and a couple of nights he heard the bullets. Back in those days children didn't have any "rights," and there weren't any "black activists" to prevent a policeman from doing his duty. If you got shot in the back, it was your fault for either:

1. Not ducking,
2. Not stopping,
3. Not hiding, or
4. Not getting away fast enough.

Still, life was lacking something. By the time he had seen four hundred more movies (two a week from 1931 to 1935), life in Topeka was almost unbearable. It was true that twenty-six thousand people were killed in Pakistan while these things were going on (May 1935), and the concentration camps had been opened in Germany. It was also true that another two hundred thousand Chinese met their Maker when the Blue River flooded (July 1935), and the Japanese invading China at this time didn't help matters. Just before Mussolini invaded Ethiopia, a hurricane in Florida "wasted" two hundred people (September 1935), but Ruckman had never been to Florida. Later he evangelized Jay, Milton, Pace, DeFuniak Springs, Crestview, Panama City, Appalachicola, Lake Springs, Lake City, Tampa, St. Pete, Jacksonville, Fernandina

Beach, Haines City, Orlando, Key West, Fort Myers, Ocean City, Fort Walton, Mary Esther, Tallahassee, and Palatka, but that was later—much later.

Seeing that Peter S. was about to turn into a juvenile delinquent, Auntie Robinson in Hartford, Connecticut, graciously paid the way for Peter and Johnny to go to an Episcopalian camp (Camp Mishawaka) on Lake Pokegama in Minnesota. Their younger sister "Totey" could not go, as it was strictly "chauvinistic." When they got there, one brother became a Chippewa, and the other (Peter S.) became a "Sioux."

This, of course, was for purposes of competition.

"In northern lands there lives a tribe well-known to all of you. They roamed the woods and prairies, the lakes and rivers, too. And when the battle's brunt is o'er, and huntin' days are through, the man who brings the bacon home is generally a Sioux! Whoopee! Wahoo! The noble tribe of Sioux, the man who . . . ."

My, what TREES they had at Camp Mishawaka! Giant trees everywhere. Peter S. loved to go out and just sit under them, or lie down under them and look up through the branches. Sometimes he would sneak off from the "tribe" and be AWOL for an hour at a time, just walking through the huge forests. One time he went out in a rainstorm and just sat down in the rain under a giant fir tree. He loved the dripping of the water, the lightning, the thunder, and the gigantic limbs spread over his head. He felt at home in the forest. The forest and the ocean, that was it; the rest of it could be taken or left. He never forgot those northern woods. The first piece of classical music that his crude and primitive nature would respond to was a work by Johann Strauss which he heard about a year after attending Mishawaka. He didn't know the name of this piece at the time, but it struck home to his heart the first time he heard it, and he was almost in a trance listening to it until it was over. The first piece of classical music Peter S. ever had an "ear for" was *Tales of the Vienna Woods.*

Something happened to Johnny at Mishawaka. No one ever found out what it was, but it altered the course

of Peter's life permanently. When they returned, Johnny
cut off all relations with the "gang." He isolated himself
completely, and when he did, Peter was "out," for the
gang had only tolerated him because of his older brother;
none of them liked *him* to start with. Johnny not only
turned down his chance to go to West Point after passing
the exams, but he told his parents he wanted to be a
movie actor. After graduating from high school, he went
to Lawrence (the University of Kansas) but wound up
drafted, as an enlisted man, in England. From there he
returned to the USA with a Section Eight—"totally dis-
abled"—and spent the next fifty-five years with the
shrinks and in the mental wards. Back in 1936 they called
his malady "dementia praecox." It had something to do
with a mother-relationship.

Peter S. was left alone with a half-German Shepherd, half-Collie named "Shep."

At first he confined himself to reading his stolen
magazines and drawing, but again life got dull. If no one
would have him, he would go it alone, but action he
would have, come hell or high water. Life was too short
to be "bugged."

Forty thousand people had been killed in air bomb-
ings in Ethiopia (1936). Another heat wave hit Topeka,
and with it the Midwest buried three thousand people
(July 1936). Then the civil war in Spain broke out (July
31), and Hitler and Mussolini, in full concord with the
Pope, sent in their planes and troops for pre-war maneu-
vers. Bing Crosby was singing, "Everytime it rains, it
rains pennies from heaven," "The Last Round-Up," and
"Where the Blue of the Night Meets the Gold of the
Day," and Russ Columbo (another Catholic) and Rudy
Vallee were sinking back into oblivion. In 1937 Benny
Goodman hit the Paramount Theatre with Jess Stacy,
Lionel Hampton, and Gene Krupa, and New York began
its trek towards becoming the blackest city in the world,
having more negroes in it (1990) than the largest city in
Africa (Johannesburg).

In the movies, the black musicians played with the
white ones, so in the middle of dry, Republican Kansas,

**Where The Chalk Talks Started
1940–1998**

Topeka High (1990): Torpedoes Down This Hall

in the "white section," more than fifteen years before the first NAACP civil rights suit (Brown vs. Board of Ed., 1954), here was Peter S. at the "gut buckets" in his living room, and accompanying him on the "ivories" was a six-foot, two-inch Negro—Frank Slaughter, a star basketball player. They were "jamming"—doghouse, slide pump, licorice stick, the works—at one in the morning, while the rest of the family was out of town.

Looking back over the course, it would seem that the only thing that kept Peter S. from going straight to the slammer at the age of eighteen and staying there was his reading habits. He had become so accustomed to reading that he devoured books like popcorn. He didn't always understand everything he read, but he read habitually, and it was the "habit" of an addict. This constant consuming of ideas and philosophies, cultures and ideals, acted as a sort of check or brake on his downward course. It wasn't that he simply read all of the required literature in school (*Moby Dick, Anthony Adverse, The Deerslayer, The Call of the Wild, The Raven, The Scarlet Letter, Don Quixote, Alice in Wonderland, The Faerie Queen*, etc.), but he tore through *Ivanhoe, King Lear, The Merchant of Venice, Macbeth, Pygmalion, The Grapes of Wrath, Of Mice and Men, Jane Eyre, Wuthering Heights, War and Peace, Les Miserables, The Decline of the West, The Decline and Fall of the Roman Empire, A Streetcar Named Desire, Of Time and the River*, and all the plays of Eugene O'Neill, George Bernard Shaw, Clifford Odets, and Robert Anderson. The works of Ibsen, Moliere, DeMaupassant, Anatole France, Faulkner, Hemmingway, Steinbeck, and Maugham found their way into his hands, as well as Dickens, Thackeray, Shelley, Keats, Wordsworth, and Emerson. But not even all this could completely reverse the direction of the "jet without a stabilizer." The heroes of fiction could not offset the heroes of the Associated Press and *Life* and *Time* magazines.

Pete had a buddy named Jack Alexander who was two years older than he was, and Jack's mother worked at Pelletiers in downtown Topeka. Daily, after school, they would go into the record room there and play the old seventy-eight rpm Victrola records: Stompin' at the Savoy, Let's Dance, The Angels Sing, Bei Mir Bist Du Schoen, My Heart Belongs to Daddy, etc. Peter S. decided to be a dance band drummer.

Problem: where do you get the shekels from? Answer: you take dares. Why *work* when you can take dares? If a kid dares you to do something, charge him for it. Ruckman went to work with a zeal.

PLAYBACK:

"Ah, Ruckman, you ain't got the guts to do it."

"Wanna try me out?"

"Yeah."

"Okay, make it worth my while. I'll let you use a half a brick, but not a whole brick."

"How high can I drop it on you?"

"Not more than ten feet."

"Okay, it's a deal. What's your price?"

"Twenty-five cents."

"Okay, let's go . . . ."

With a couple of witnesses—he had to make sure the kid didn't throw the brick or shove it as he dropped it; it had to be a free drop—they would go to a barn or someone's house and down would come the brick. Blood all over the place, but he got his money. To this day, if someone shaved Ruckman's head he would find at least half a dozen remains of scar tissue where no stitches had been made. After all, you couldn't charge your parents money for a medical bill that you ran up "on purpose."

The last year of Middle School, Ruckman became the town's "daredevil." They came to him from all sides, and he rarely turned down an offer. He got a dollar for diving off of the thirty-foot slide in the pool at Gage Park. He picked up another dollar eating some of the "stickum" off the trees that they put there to kill locusts and grasshoppers. His prize was a piece of dead monkey, which was pickled in formaldehyde in a biology lab: he made two bucks on that one. The day he graduated from Boswell Junior High School he partook of something unmentionable and made a buck fifty.

"Oh, we are the Boswell Junior Highs! To our school we will ever be loyal, whether in work or in play, we will FIGHT all the live-long day. FIGHT! FIGHT! FIGHT!"

CHAPTER FOUR

The First Real Hippy

In July 1937, another hundred Americans died in a heat wave; Peter S. was not one of them. Ninety-five people perished in a train wreck in India (July 17, 1937), and a typhoon wiped out three hundred inhabitants of Hong Kong (September 3). The Nazis rallied at Nuremberg with two hundred and fifty thousand troops, and Snow White and the Seven Dwarfs popped up on the "silver screen." Ruckman saw it; more than ever he felt compelled to fool with color. He began to cartoon with different colored inks and then gradually began to work crayons into his pen and ink drawings. With no formal artistic education, he proceeded "hit or miss."

When he entered Topeka High School (September 1938) he found he was already famous. His notoriety had come from the "*dares*," but in the high school the new gang that was looking to him for leadership was not like the sand lot gangs of Junior High School. They misread the "brown-eyed Booflee." They figured anyone that bold and reckless had to be a veteran knife fighter and a gunslinger as well. He had not intended to take things that far.

In the summertime, he got a job lifeguarding at a private beach club in Rehoboth Beach, Delaware, and during the time after his shift (after sunset) his job was to check drinks at the bar. He watched the Proctors and the Gambles swapping wives, selling Dusenbergs across the table, and passing out on the dance floor. Having become thoroughly adjusted to the scenery, the next Christmas vacation he ran away from home (alone) and spent two weeks in the French Quarter of New Orleans trying to sell water colors in Pirate's Alley. He played drums in

"The Court of the Two Sisters," "Club Bali," and "La Luna," and picked up some more filthy things he had overlooked or missed in Topeka. He was sweet seventeen.

KALEIDOSCOPE:

Crash! The bimbo falls off the bar stool. A man stoops to pick her up. His buddy says, "Hey, stupid, dontcha know better an at? Never help a woman when she's down: kick er!"

"Go on, try one; it'll make you feel good."

"But it ain't got a name on it. What brand is it?"

"What difference does that make? It'll send you, honey, take a drag."

"I don't dig that jive. Look what it did to the saxophonist."

"Whadya mean, dahlin?"

"The tempo! H—! He started A Tisket a Tasket at a walk tempo, and the third time they played it he kicked it off like rain falling on a tin roof."

"Ever sell anything in this dump?"

"Not much. Portraits are where the dough is. Everyone likes to see hisself."

"I can't paint portraits."

"Me either. Here, take a swig."

"You know, if a guy depended on this for a living, he'd starve to death in short order, wouldn't he?"

"Sure thing, man, sure as shootin."

"Well, how the —— do you make it?"

"Booze, man, that's where the iron men are. Bootleg the stuff. Getcha a dry state like Oklahoma and then run the stuff in."

In Pirate's Alley, Peter S. made one of the first mature decisions in a lifetime. He decided that if he was going to be an artist or a musician, he had better develop both talents while working for a "living wage" doing something else.

His excursions to New Orleans and Washington, D.C. (the next Christmas), on his own, "upped" his stock with the gang. The "gang" was Junior Moss, Jack Bonebreak, Cody Morse, Irwin Coulson, Jack Alexander, Lonnie Noeler, Ed Price, George McAffey, George Moore, Leslie Skrinopsky, Gayland Tabot and some others.

What Topeka High needed was a little "action": they got it.

1. You collect a hundred Ping-Pong balls and put them in a cardboard box with the top down. You tie a long, heavy string to this and then place the box upside down on top of the heating unit in the gym. At the next basketball game you yank on the string, opening the box, and down comes a hundred Ping-Pong balls, which are guaranteed to bounce for at least fifteen minutes. No man or group of men could corral them in less time. The first bounce was twenty feet, the next one sixteen, the next eleven, and so on.

2. You steal a combination from someone's locker, and then between classes you take two cats (this was a two-man job), open the locker, throw the cats in, and then slammed the mess shut. Results usually exceeded all expectations. The owner could never be found in less than fifteen minutes. In the meantime, the corridors and hallways echoed with the sounds of primitive battle.

3. You excuse yourself from class and go to the rest room. You then open the door and sail a torpedo down the hallway. (This was a small, round firecracker with no fuse. It went off on impact; it was about an inch and a half in diameter.) The torpedo would roll down the marble hallway (over two hundred feet), drop off of the landing at the staircase, and then explode on the floor *below*. In the marble hallways, lined with metal lockers, it sounded like a thermonuclear bomb. No one could "trace it" because it came from the floor above, and there was no one on the landing. But crime doesn't always pay. About the fifth time, the vice-principal (Stark) seized Ruckman's hand when it emerged from "the john." There was "hell to pay" that day and the week following.

In the meantime, Hitler "anschlussed" Austria (March 1938), a mine explosion killed seventy-nine in England (May), sixty Arabs were shot in Palestine, and

Hitler marched into Czechoslovakia (October 5).

Stark wasn't as much worried about Hitler as he was about "Ruckman," and strangely enough, that is what he usually called Peter S. Occasionally, an adult would use the name "Peter" or "Pete," but the teenagers and pre-teenagers always referred to him simply as "Ruckman." His closest associates ("the brotherhood," etc.) would sometimes say "Ruck" or "Rucky," but never "Pete" or "Peter." From ten years old upward, his name was "Ruckman," and if anything went wrong at Topeka High School, it had to be "Ruckman."

Stark had what he thought was a "capital" idea. He would apply psychology to Ruckman, since "applied psychology" was the big thing in those days. Dewey's and James's Behavioristic Psychology was another big thing; it had been in the NEA since about 1930. Stark decided Ruckman was just a frustrated child who wanted attention and was using "unacceptable social patterns" to attain it. He couldn't have made a worse mistake. (Years later, Ruckman's peers decided that Ruckman was "insecure" and suffering from an "inferiority complex," and this made him carry the torch for the *King James Bible*; they pulled off a worse boner than Stark did.)

At any rate, Stark invited the "brown-eyed Booflee" to draw for the student body. He rigged up (believe it or not) an eight by four foot sheet of plywood with drawing paper, mounted it on a ladder, and let Ruckman draw for a student assembly. Using four sheets of paper as a comic strip, Ruckman proceeded to cartoon a high school student trying to get comfortable at a school desk (the old one-armed desk with the ink well in it) and squirming as in a torture chamber. He finally fell asleep but writhed in his sleep, for he had a nightmare about an executioner coming to torture him further. No one in the student body could have possibly missed identifying the "ax man." It was Vice-Principal Stark. The audience roared, and the Principal had to wipe several smiles off his face so his students would not think he was one of the "two percent" (see below).

The tempo picked up. One night Ruckman was nearly

Topeka High School: Cats In The Locker

The Escape That Failed

decapitated by a bed slat slung down the hallway by a security guard during an attempt to break into a basketball game. Two weeks later he and his gang were ambushed by the police while "breaking and entering," and Ruckman attempted to escape by climbing up the side of a building between the wall and a forty foot chimney. At twenty feet, in the air, a flashlight spotted him, and an angry Fuzz said, "Okay, you punk, c'mon down!" In those days, you came down. The .38's were loaded, and you were allowed one warning shot, and then one in the back.

Then there was that delightful night, while running from the cops, that he was literally "clotheslined" by a clothesline in someone's backyard; not the football maneuver, but the "real thing." Fortunately, his breath was knocked out of him so hard the police could not hear his breathing when they ran by him in pursuit of his buddy. He was *breathless* as well as speechless.

Twice in the next two years "Poppa John" got phone calls from the police. He "followed through" with the strap from the steamer locker.

Vice-Principal Stark was running around in his shirt tails. He called another emergency assembly and gave a "state of the Union" message where he declared that Topeka High was the finest student body in the world except for a disturbing minority which he limited to "two percent." (There were two thousand students in the school, so he figured forty weren't right. It was an over-estimate.) Thereafter when the acceptable "elite" met Ruckman in the hallway, they would say, "Good morning, two percent."

He couldn't have cared less.

The tempo picked up. You couldn't live a dry, Republican life with *"Wire Brush Stomp"* and *"The Flat Foot Floogee with the Floy Floy"* ringing in your ears. The Spanish Civil War ended in March of 1939, but Ruckman "had not begun to fight." The gang was now doing second-story work, sometimes climbing trees to get into bedroom windows. Cash registers were being rifled when the clerk left the drawer opened and turned to look at something behind him that the gang member pointed at. Cars were picked up by one buddy lying prone on a back street and pretending like he had been hit. When the sucker got out of the car, the boys behind the hedge rushed him, took his belt off, tied his shoelaces together, and took off in the car. The *movies* were the classroom for this training. They picked up all the tricks by watching the movies.

Very slowly Peter Ruckman's heroes changed from Hopalong Cassidy, The Shadow, Boake Carter, Richtofen, Jack Dempsey, Gene Tunney, Jack Sharkey, Walt Disney, and Artie Shaw to Dillinger, Pretty Boy Floyd, Alvin Karpis, Homer Van Meter, and Baby Face Nelson.

Endsville came. He had been stealing his daddy's car at night for about four months. This was done by first stealing a key and then waiting a few weeks. Then, at night, he would slip out of the second story window over the front porch, slide down a pillar, and go out to the street. He would put the car in neutral and push it down about thirty feet from the house so no one would hear the engine start. Then, when the electric bus came by he would "crank her up." Jerry Brown had located a gas pump on the outskirts of town that could not be locked up, so they went out there and got a full tank every night and took off.

Jerry would usually have a girl with him and would demonstrate before Ruckman in various places: golf greens, riverbanks, porch swings, etc., but somehow it didn't really "take" with Ruckman. He seemed to live in another world. To him the thrill was stealing the car and the gasoline. Adolescent lust, in the raw, was not like he had seen it in the movies. These girls were not in evening gowns with silk stockings, and there was no thirty-piece orchestra behind the revelling. To him it seemed a bit crass and carnal. "C'mon, Jerry, let's get the —— outta here. Take the broad home and let's get some shinny."

One night he got "the whole ball of wax." Tearing down to Kansas City, Missouri (wet), which was about sixty miles off, he picked up two cases of bootleg liquor, and then, with nothing in particular in mind, he picked up two "underage" girls (one thirteen and one fifteen) and took them for a "joyride" back to Topeka. He passed a patrolman at about one a.m. He knew it because he had trained his eyes to take in the side of a car going past him by peripheral vision. Months of playing "chicken" out on the highways had made him quite proficient. (In "chicken," both drivers come at each other at sixty m.p.h. with the left tires on the white line. The first man to move off the line was the "chicken." This was in 1939, before anyone in America knew what a "hippy" was. Often the running boards would "ring" as the cars passed each other.)

The patrolman passed, headed for K.C., and Ruckman watched his rear view mirror to make sure he hadn't braked to turn. (If he did, the school solution is: both lights off, and a quick turn off the nearest road in the dark. If you can get to a residential district, you ditch Smokey by driving up into a driveway, turning off your lights, and lying down in the front seat.) No brake light, so he drove on. But that night he learned a new tactic: some patrolmen use a hand brake that doesn't light up the brake lights, so you see nothing. In fifteen minutes he heard that terrible siren not thirty feet behind his car. "The jig was up," as they said in the movies.

NIGHT SCENE:

"Here he is, Major Ruckman. We caught him twenty miles east of here. We have two federal charges on him. He was bootlegging, driving without a license, and transporting a stolen car across a state border. We also have him for statutory kidnapping. What do you think we should do with him?"

"He's just a boy. He's only seventeen. He needs a break."

"We've given this boy so many breaks we are broke. We are sick and tired of fooling with him. If you can't straighten him out, it's the industrial school at least."

"Give it one more try, and if he violates the law again, you can press charges all the way. I won't hinder."

"All right, Major Ruckman, he is in your custody, but if he makes one more slip, just ONE more, we are throwing the book at him, you understand? He will be eighteen in eight months, and we won't tolerate any more foolishness from him."

The boy went out in the night with his father. They got into the "stolen" car.

CONFRONTATION:

"Well, I see you already know how to drive. Drive the —— thing."

One mile of silence.

"Whatcha been doin' with 'em, Pete? —— 'em?"

"Nossir."

"You expect me to believe that?"

"Nossir." (His father had taught him that there were only three answers to any question: "Yessir," "Nossir," and "No excuse, Sir!")

Another mile of silence.

"Well, next year you go to Citizen's Military Training Camp. You go four years to get your commission. If the camps close down, you can get the commission in the ROTC—if you go to college. Have you got enough character to try college?"

"Yessir."

They stopped at 1525 College Avenue.

At the door of his room: "All right, Peter, this is the last time, you understand? You are ready for Hutchinson or Leavenworth, and I will not interfere the next time. Do we understand each other?"

"Yessir."

In ten minutes he was fast asleep. It actually seemed like a great load had been lifted off of his back. The tension was gone. He had not realized how "uptight" he had been for about a year. In the morning he was as docile as a lamb.

CHAPTER FIVE

Boot Camp and Money Matters

CMTC was good. He didn't like it the first week, but only because he saw the handwriting on the wall; nobody, like nobody, was going to do "as he pleased" in that outfit. The Cadre were World War I vets. The squad was an eight man squad, front and rear rank, and you said "Sir" when you talked to a corporal. You had "options," of course; you said "Sir," or you spent the day on KP.

You had options at the mess hall: you could take the mess or leave it. The welcoming committee at CMTC in Fort Leavenworth (summer of 1939) was unforgettable. "All right, girls, have a good time and make up your mind to be happy while you're here, because nobody gives a d— if you ain't." A mad flare of rebellion welled up in Peter's heart at this announcement, but just about the time he had made up his mind to turn CMTC into a second Topeka High School, two things happened. One, he got the snot beat out of him in a fist fight with a bird he thought he could have whipped with one hand tied behind him, and two, he saw what happened to the "recalcitrants" who insisted on having their own way. All of the MP's were over six feet tall, and they carried a baton like a pick-ax handle. You did what you were told, or you got beaten within an inch of your life. Some in the Regular Army were beaten to death, and a report was filed to the effect that they had fallen off the back end of a two and a half ton personnel carrier.

The mess hall had no carpet, like it did in the 1970's. It had no chairs, no booths, no trays, and no waiters. You

sat on a bench and ate out of a mess kit. The toast was
burnt, the bacon was raw, there were egg shells in the
powdered eggs, and the coffee could have cleaned out
the inside of a rifle barrel. You had your "options"—two
of them—you could take it or leave it.

The rifle was the old Springfield 30.06, and the
bayonet was six inches longer than the bayonet they is-
sued for the M1 in 1942. You had "wrap-around puttees"
instead of the "combat boot," and KP lasted from four in
the morning till eight at night because it took more than
an hour for the wood stoves to cool off.

On the parade ground of Leavenworth it often
reached a hundred and four degrees in the shade. Peter
saw grown men falling down like leaves from a tree. The
"meat wagon" came around and picked them up. The
Springfield, fired from the squatting position, put him
back on his "haunches." It kicked like a mule. There
were black eyes and broken thumbs where some dogface
got too near the bolt. "The flag is up; the flag is waving;
the flag is down! Ready on the right; ready on the left;
ready on the firing line . . . commence firing!"

He liked it. Somewhere in his circulatory system
there flowed the red corpuscles of the professional soldier; not the artist, not the musician, not the bookworm,
but the "DOG FACE," the "doughboy," the "grunt." It
was exhilarating. For a while he almost forgot that he
had to be in bed at a certain time and up at a certain time,
and wear his clothes a certain way, and walk swinging
the hands "three to the rear and six to the front." The
rifle sounded like a huge door slamming. He had fired
.22's down in the National Guard armory when he was
twelve, but this was different: KABLOOM! KABLOOM!
He was firing "possibles" at two hundred yards. He liked
the bayonet practise. He had never been in a knife fight,
but he had kept a switchblade on his person clear through
high school, and two times he had popped it for action
without the action "jelling." In his last year he carried a
regular four inch pocket knife, for he had learned how to
open the blade with two fingers of one hand before he
extracted it from his pocket. "A knife for the little man, a

club for the big man" was how the adage went.

But the bayonet was "heavy metal." He never forgot the moves, not even after forty-nine years in the ministry: "Come to the guard position . . . HUP! Long thrust . . . HO! Vertical butt stroke . . . HOOO! Horizontal butt stroke . . . HOW! Slash . . . SLAM! Short thrust . . . OOF!" He never forgot his "general orders."

1. "A dollar a day, and the work ain't hard."

2. "Never hurry, never worry, never volunteer."

3. "Stay away from the orderly room. Keep your mouth shut."

4. "If it's movin', salute it. If it's lying' down, pick it up. If you can't pick it up, paint it."

The second year of CMTC he got a little bolder and began to go AWOL at night. This was accomplished by sneaking through the guard posts via a cemetery which lay near his "company street." He would take off an hour after Taps and return at about four in the morning. He got by with it several times, but all good things had to come to an end, so one morning after he had just gotten into the sack (an army cot in a quadrangle tent) he was greeted with the glare of the cook's flashlight. He had been "requisitioned" for KP, and his night's rest that night was from 3:30 to 4:00 a.m.

"Hit the deck, soldier. You're on the garbage detail today."

All he could think of, as he put his puttees back on and staggered out into the company street, was a line from the Rubaiyat of Omar Khayyam: "Arise, varlet, for lo, in the bowl of night, Morpheus hath flung the blazing stone which puts the dusty stars to flight!" It was a doubly bad day because that night he had had his first real sexual encounter ("fornication" in the Book). The girl was already married, but she was taken to a dance by some other GI. After dancing with the other GI she met Peter outside the dance hall and took him home with her. He was sweet eighteen.

On June 15, 1939, the French submarine Phoenix went to the bottom of Davey Jones's Locker with sixty-three aboard. The same month the Nazi's arrested a thou-

Alf Landon's Governor's Mansion (1990)

sand Czechs for the killing of a German policeman. Three months later World War II erupted. On the twenty-third of August, Russia and Germany had signed a peace treaty for the purpose of dividing Poland, and on the first of September Germany invaded Poland. France and Britain declared war on Germany the third of September. The Reich press called for the bombing of Britain, and good old Albert Einstein, in America, wrote to FDR suggesting the use of the *atom bomb* (August 2, 1939). During Peter's last year in high school (fall of 1939 and spring of 1940) the Soviets attacked Finland (and were not tried at Nuremberg for "waging aggressive warfare"), Britain began rationing sugar, meat, and butter (January 1940), and the Roman Catholic Adolph Hitler—under a concordat with the Roman Catholic Pope Pius XII—set up a Roman Catholic concentration camp in Auschwitz, Poland, with a Roman Catholic commandant in charge of it: Rudolph Hoess. The Germans then invaded Scandinavia, Belgium, and Holland (May 1940), and the British Expeditionary Forces got off the beaches of Dunkirk (June 4) by the hair of their "chinny chin chin." On the fourteenth of June, Hitler marched into Paris and forced the French to surrender in the very railcar (Compiegne) where Germany had been humiliated in 1918.

Back in Topeka again, Ruckman made one last effort to break loose from the world system and "nature's course." When he returned from CMTC he gathered what was left of his gang (there were about four left out of fifteen), and they decided that they would run away to South America; catch a "banana boat" out of New Orleans, etc. The boys packed and settled for a rendezvous at a drugstore at eight in the evening, but Lieutenant Colonel Ruckman had gotten wind of things. He called in Peter S., and they talked (or rather the Lieutenant Colonel talked) for nearly an hour. The boys down at the drugstore fidgeted; whatever Ruckman was, he was never "late" doing anything. (They called him "Little Lightning.") That night he never got to the drugstore till eight thirty.

CONFRONTATION:

"Peter, you are heading for a disaster, and further-more I think you know it. I used to work in the oil fields of South America before World War I, and I know the people and the conditions. You have no aptitude for such a trip. If you are not going to be an Army officer, you should be something like a newspaper reporter, a jour-nalist. You have a flair for cartooning, reading, and writ-ing. In South America they will bury you, or you will bury yourself. How long have you been drinking?"

"About three years."

"What do you suppose you will do down there in a foreign country with no friends and probably no income?"

"Oh, I can get a job."

"What kind of a job? Let's see, you have done yard work, you have held a surveyor's chain, you have sold popcorn in concession stands, you have cleaned out bath-houses and done some lifeguarding on the beaches. What have you done beside that?"

"Well, nothing much. I did twenty cartoon strips . . . ."

"You didn't sell them; you couldn't."

"Well, I wrote a book of poems about . . . ."

"You didn't sell them either. There is no demand for poetry. Why don't you go on to college and get your commission? Incomes for dance band drummers and art-ists are practically nothing; you know that, don't you?"

Sure he did. He had spent two weeks in the French Quarter.

"Pete, that isn't all. Those hoodlums with you have no talents at all. Two of them are dropouts. [How did he find that out?] What will they do for a living?"

Silence.

"Pete, I have taught you that the greatest honor any man can have is to be killed in action leading his troops while protecting his country. You have had enough mili-tary now to know what I am about to say."

Sure he had. He had been reading Clausewitz and Von Moltke along with Tom Paine and Dorothy Parker.

"Pete, if you knew that you were about to lead your troops into a certain massacre and you knew that it was unnecessary and you didn't have to take them in, would you give the order? I mean, if you had no orders and could withdraw, would you take them in anyway to attack an objective where you knew you would lose every one of them?"

"Nossir."

"Son, those boys are going to follow you anywhere. To them, you are a General. They would obey you before they would obey their own parents. And you are taking them to certain ruin. You know that, don't you?"

Silence.

"Pete, I cannot stop you, and I feel sure that you are going ahead with your course of action no matter what I say, but I want you to know that I believe the only reason you are doing it is because you want to show me that you don't give a d— what I say. I do not think you are doing it because you think it is the right thing to do."

More silence.

But the point had been carried. Staring at the floor, red-faced, fists clenched, teeth grinding, Peter S. knew he was whipped. Still, he never answered.

"All right," said the Lieutenant Colonel (about to become a Colonel). "Go ahead. But if anything happens to those boys, the responsibility is yours. *You* are the leader. They are going to follow you. You know the motto at Fort Benning in the infantry school: it is 'FOLLOW ME!' They are going to follow you to their ruin and probably an early death. Dismissed!"

Peter turned on his heel and walked out the door. He wept all the way to the drugstore, but he had to face the music.

"Deal's off, fellas, we're not going!"

"Not going? Hey, are you crazy, man? We're packed! Look at the stuff!"

"Not going? We ain't got an hour to get to the railway. Whaddya mean 'not going'?"

"We're not going," he said sullenly.

"What'sa matter, Rucky, losin' your nerve?"

"Naw."

"What's the pitch, then? How come you chickened

out at the last minute?"

"No reason," said Peter S. "You wouldn't understand, anyway."

And they never would. For one time, his father had hit him below the belt, and had struck him with something heavier than an eight foot strap. He had appealed to Peter's ancestoral sense of military honour. It had never been done till then. It worked. He stayed in Topeka, finished high school, and enrolled in Kansas State College (Manhattan, Kansas) in the fall of 1940. Occasionally he came back to Topeka on weekends to "visit," but these occasions were rare—about once a month. In 1941, his father was promoted to full Colonel and received orders for active duty at Bynum, Alabama, an outpost near Fort McClellan (Anniston, Alabama) where work was already proceeding to handle elements used in the atom bomb.

On Peter's last visit home, around Christmas time of 1940, he was walking home through the snow (by himself, as usual. "Whether down to Gehenna or up to a throne, he travels fastest who travels alone" Kipling). He had been out "womanizing" ("fornicating" in the Book) and was coming up College Avenue at about midnight. There were two inches of snow on the ground, and more was lightly falling.

Suddenly he sensed someone behind him. It was that old street instinct that reported the stranger, for there was no sound of any kind on the street. He looked back and saw a shadowy figure about sixty feet behind him. It appeared to be a tall man in a hat and overcoat. Ruckman walked another three hundred feet at the same pace to see if the man was a bloodhound or just a coincidence. At the next street lamp Ruckman went up to the post, dug his hand into his pocket, opened his knife, and waited. If you got directly under a light you were not silhouetted, and the man coming toward you would be visible before he could see you clearly, and the light would be in his eyes. (It is wonderful what you can learn without a college education!)

Ten feet from the light the stranger stopped (he

evidently had been on the streets before, too) and said gruffly, "Dat you, Ruckman?"

"Yeah, it's me," said Ruckman, "who the —— are you?"

The shadow laughed. "Your old buddy, Woody, man! Don't you know me? Dis is Woody, your old buddy!"

Ruckman stepped cautiously forward and sized the shadow up. The last time he had seen Woody Schunight was in the eighth grade. This character was nearly six inches taller, or at least he looked that way.

"It's me, Woodrow Wilson Schunight," said Woody. "Been up in the Windy City, buddy; in the big time."

It was Woody, all right. Ruckman closed the blade in his pocket and offered his hand. They shook hands and then proceeded on up the street.

"What's jiving dese days?" asked Woody.

"Oh, nothin' much. I'm going to college, studying to be a journalist."

"Newsboy! Agh, Rucky, that ain't your style, man. That's square, man. Why don't you come up to Chi and get in the big time?"

"Yeah? Well, what's the big time?"

"Rightcheer! Lookee!" Whereupon W.W. Schunight produced a roll of hundred dollar bills as thick as the end of a ball bat.

Ruckman whistled: "Man, where did you get that moola at?"

"Big bucks, Rucky, an' plenty more where doze came from."

"Whatcha been doin', Woody, robbin' banks?"

"Naw, man. I know what I'm doin'. Got the contacts, buddy. You oughta get in on it. I can set you up, Rucky! C'mon man, can that book stuff. You ain't no college Joe. Let's go up to the big town. I'll set you up good."

"Can't. Couldn't if I wanted to."

"Why not, Ruckman? No big deal; let's go!"

"Can't make it, Woody."

"Look, when was da last time you seen that much dough?"

He had never seen it once. He hadn't seen a roll of one dollar bills that big since 1929, let alone one hundred dollar bills.

"I'm tellin' ya, Woody, I can't make it. I promised my Dad something. He got me out of a tight place. I'm gonna stick it out, at least for another year."

"Well, okay, Ruck. But, boy, you're missing the gravy train, man! See ya in the funny papers."

They had arrived at Fifteenth and College Avenue. Woody moved off through the darkness, a huge figure in a huge overcoat; he turned east and went down Fifteenth Street toward the city. Ruckman went on home and went to bed.

Four months later he read on one of the back pages of *The Topeka Daily Capitol*, "Woodrow Wilson Schunight sentenced." He read the article. Woody had been stealing cars, taking them across the state line, getting them repainted, and putting new license plates on them. He had been arrested, tried, and convicted on four counts, each count bringing him ten years in the penitentiary. Forty years at twenty years old. If Woody served the full sentence, he didn't get out of jail until 1980. And in those days if you got "forty" you served thirty of it no matter what lawyer you had or how good your behavior was.

Time marched on.

CHAPTER SIX

The Student

The Germans blitzed Britain in July and August of 1940. Trotsky (at Stalin's orders) was bludgeoned to death with an axe (August 21). Italy invaded Greece (October 28), and America "drafted" its first military conscript (October 29). As everyone "rang out the old and rang in the new" (1941), Hitler tore through Bulgaria, Yugoslavia, and Greece and into North Africa.

Ruckman was "rushed" by the Sigma Nu fraternity when he got to Manhattan, Kansas, because they needed some "lettermen" to enhance their reputation. They knew he would "letter" in swimming, and he did. He set several records the first year he was there: two in breaststroke events and one in backstroke events. "Ruckman" and "water" were almost synonymous. He felt more at home in the ocean or a swimming pool than he did on land. He had won four first places in swimming meets at CMTC, four at Camp Mishawaka earlier, and then two more, swimming in competition in Gage Park in Topeka. But his sojourning as a "bright star of Sigma Nu"—"Ten thousand brothers wear you, ten thousand others share you; when college days are through . . . ."—ended abruptly a year later.

It was an old tradition for upperclassmen to "haze" the freshmen, and at Sigma Nu this consisted of being ordered to bend over while the upperclassmen beat your tail end with something like the aforementioned paddle of Randolph Grade School (eighteen inches long, four inches wide, and three quarters of an inch thick). Ruckman could "take it" and often did, but there happened to be a slight-built, cigarette-sucking, mealymouthed character in the frat house named Paige Wagner. He was a sadist. He got his eye on a new "brother" named

Donaldson and went to work on him in a fashion that would have elated Wilhelm Boger, Emil Bednarek, Robert Fulka, or Hans Stark (sadists and torturers at Auschwitz: 1941–44). Wagner did not just "discipline" the "scurb" (the term is equivalent to the Marine "maggot") and mete out punishment for various errors; he delighted in beating the young man two and three times a day for sheer pleasure. Donaldson was a handsome, dark-haired young man and just as clean as a hound's tooth. He didn't drink. (Looking back on it, it may have been that he was a Christian, but at that time Ruckman would not have known a Christian from a Moslem.)

At any rate, Ruckman watched the Donaldson-Wagner relationship through a period of about three months. He finally had all he could take. He decided that "pip-squeak" Wagner was just eaten up with jealousy and that he actually got physical pleasure out of beating the "scurb." He had read about masochism, sadism, and the rest of it, naturally, for he had read all of Karl Menninger's books in print, everything that Jung, Pavlov, and Freud had written, and in addition James Joyce's Portrait of the Artist as a Young Man, The Dubliners, and the infamous Ulysses.

One bright, spring day when Ruckman was alone on the roof of the Frat house getting him a little "tan," Paige Wagner showed up, paddle in hand. He should have "stood in bed."

CONFRONTATION:

"Where is Scurb Donaldson, Scurb Ruckman?"

"Beats the —— outta me. Go find him."

"Do you know who you are talking to?" asked Wagner.

"Yeah," said Ruckman, getting up off of his mattress. "I'm talking to a yellow-bellied coward that enjoys beating people he envies. That's who I'm talking to."

Wagner waved his paddle menacingly and slapped it against the palm of his hand. "Bend over, Scurb Ruckman!" he ordered.

"Kiss my —," said Ruckman.

Wagner's mouth opened and his cigarette fell out of

The Roof at Sigma Nu Fraternity

Sigma Nu Fraternity (KSAC)

it. It was five seconds before he recovered his sensibilities.

"You, you . . . !" he stuttered.

Ruckman walked right up to him; they were just the same height (five feet, eight inches) but Ruckman outweighed him about ten pounds. The "brown-eyed Booflee" was eye to eye, chin to chin, nose to nose with the upperclassman, and there, again, was the Topeka street fighter in full bloom.

"One more word, punk. You got it? One more word. You see that rail over there? It's twenty-five feet to the ground. You land on cement. Got it? Just open your mouth one more time—say anything—just ONE more word to me, Wagner, and over you go! Got it, baby?"

Paige Wagner's paddle dropped to his side; his jaw slacked; his eyes popped. He wanted to say something, he tried to say something, but nothing came out.

"Gowan," said Ruckman. "Just ONE word, any word, and Sonny, if you think I can't throw you bodily over that rail, just say the word."

Fortunately for *both* of them, he never said it.

After he left, Ruckman lay down and went to sleep in the sun. What the ——. What difference did it make? If the jerk had said something, he would have chucked him over, and all he would have to tell the judge was that they were play-wrestling and got too near the edge. What the —. No one was there to see it, anyway, so who could prove anything if he did kill the punk?

The punk lived, but Ruckman got "the boot." The "brothers" gave him the "black spot" at the next council meeting, and he moved out into town into a boarding house.

FEEDBACK:

Nothing to do again. The only exciting thing was playing drums in dance bands. The main band was Matt Benton. Ruckman picked up three hundred dollars worth of Slingerlands: cowbells, wood blocks, sock cymbal, high hat, tunable tom toms—the works. Once a dancer was stabbed through the back with a butcher knife at an outdoor pavilion. The band leaves the stand during a drum solo on Miller's *"Anvil Chorus,"* and Ruckman is left to beat out an additional hundred bars before they come back up. The dancers never quit dancing. The bridge goes out under the strings on the doghouse during Woody Herman's stock on *"Woodchopper's Ball,"* but he is so far "out of it" he hits the sounding board five times before he realized his strings are slack. They play Miller's *"String of Pearls,"* Goodman's *"String of Pearls,"* Artie Shaw's *"Begin the Beguine,"* and *"What is This Thing Called Love?"*

Plenty of girls. Plenty of life. Plenty of sin.

"I don't remember the day we met, time and places are hazy yet. I've forgotten just where, but you were there . . . the smoke makes a stairway for you to descend, you come to my arms, may this bliss never end, and we love anew just as we used to do . . . So don't let them begin the Beguine, let the love that once was afire remain as an ember; let it sleep like the dead desire I only remember. You are the angel glow that lights the stars, the dearest things I know are what you are . . . . Skylark, have you anything to say to me? Won't you tell me where my love can be? . . . Small Fry, truckin' by the poolroom, small fry, should be in the school room . . . You belong to my heart both now and forever . . . Yours till the stars have no glory . . . Amapola, my pretty little poppy . . . Down where the trade winds play, down where you lose a day . . . Pardon me, boy! Is that the Chattanooga Choo Choo? . . . Hark to the sound of the strolling troubadours, hark to the throbbing guitars, hear how the waves offer thunderous applause after each song to the stars . . . I'll be seeing you in all the old familiar places that this heart of mine embraces all day through . . . For you're the one and only one my heart really adores, and I'm so glad my window pane is just opposite yours . . . The leaves of brown came tumbling down, remember? That September in the rain. The sun went out just like a dying ember, that September in the rain . . . Now, laughing friends deride tears I cannot hide, so I smile and say when the lovely flame dies, 'smoke gets in your eyes' . . . ."

They played *"Stardust," "Moonglow," "Little Brown Jug," "Sunrise Serenade," "Anvil Chorus," "Moonlight Serenade,"* and *"Tuxedo Junction."* The singers and the lyrics were still mainly WHITE, but the best were BLACK, and long before Kay Starr and Petula Clark began to sing like "niggers," Martha Tilton, Helen Forest, and Helen O'Connell were lisping and dragging the words out.

Hollywood had been at work. Now with the war on they could "pull out the stops." Negro troops were being drafted. Negroes had already been given full publicity (and special favoritism) as musicians in the swing bands and as athletes—supposedly superior to Germans. A great news media orgy took place after Jesse Owens won some events in Berlin in 1938. (It isn't over yet.) "BLACK" was trying to be "beautiful," and slowly, but surely, America was going "back to the jungle" instead of "back to the Bible." Ruckman knew nothing of this at the time, but he had been thoroughly exposed. By 1941, He had seen Citizen Kane, Sergeant York, The Maltese Falcon, Gone with the Wind, Dark Victory, Good-bye Mr. Chips (Hollywood was still inserting sentimental humanism between the murders, spy plots, and half-nude dancers), The Philadelphia Story, The Long Voyage Home, Captains Courageous, Dead End, Lost Horizon, and The Lost Weekend. The last one pictured Ray Miland as a chronic alcoholic. It was a condemnation of alcoholism. You always begin that way: what you wind up with is A POSITIVE VIEW OF CRACK, COCAINE, AND MARIJUANA.

Ruckman had seen so many movies that his mind had been converted into a movie projector: he could literally project any image onto a blank wall, or sheet of paper, or anything else and then "copy" it by "tracing." He began to fill college notebooks and textbooks with sketches. All he had to do to draw anything was summon up the movie he had seen. These included Dark Victory, Mr. Smith Goes to Washington, Stagecoach, Of Mice and Men, The Good Earth, The Awful Truth, Stella Dallas, A Star is Born, all of the Andy Hardy pictures, all of the Abbott and Costello pictures, all of the Roy Rogers pictures, plus The Wizard of Oz, King Kong, Hurricane, Jezebel, The Three Musketeers, Boys Town, The Citadel, Algiers, Angels with Dirty Faces, Little Caesar, Ninotcheka, all of the full-length Disney cartoons, White Banners, Pygmalion, You Can't Take It with You, Grand Illusion, The White Feather, Beau Geste, The White Cockade, The Scarlet Pimpernel, Treasure Island, Viva Villa, and The Road Back. Those were the *main* ones. Somewhere in that mass of Hollywood propaganda lay at least two hundred other films.

Hollywood was slowly but surely moving toward sex and violence as THE themes for *homes* in America. One by one the "bars" of censorship dropped in the name of "art," and just as murder and adultery became socially acceptable in "Grand Opera," gradually people in America became used to watching women slipping in and out of their clothes, married people kissing other married people, visitors being given a cocktail every time they walked into a house, and acts of violence pictured more vividly each time. After all, wasn't "realism" THE TRUTH?

What could be more "real" than two sex perverts engaged in fornication, unless it would be someone torturing a prisoner, or going to the bathroom?

That is where Hollywood was headed. "Realism" was the alibi used for fifty years to produce the modern American "inner city" culture. *The Bible* was never considered to be "real" or to deal with realities; it was an odd piece that Hollywood used as a "prop."

1. It showed up in courtroom scenes where people took oaths.

2. In a Country or Western film it showed up being used in the hands of a former gunslinger (who would shortly return to that occupation), or it would be quoted out of context by a grandmother or mother to her offspring.

3. It would be referred to as "the good Book," but not THE BIBLE.

4. It would always be absent where Bing Crosby or Pat O'Brian posed as Catholic priests.

Radio Transmitter KSAC, Manhattan, Kansas

KSAC, Manhattan, Kansas

Ruckman knew nothing about the realities of *reality*, for the Bible is the only Book that presents all of them in their correct light. The only light he had on "reality," he had gotten from books or movies abstractly, or else in a totally unreal domestic and social setting: the streets of Topeka, Kansas. CMTC was the only touch of real "reality" he had been exposed to, and even this had not been too realistic, for it was not civilian life; it was military life. Ruckman would be twenty-eight years old before he had a car, thirty-three years old before he could live in his own house (after 1940), and thirty-eight years old *before he could write out a check.*

CMTC had done something for Ruckman's stability, at least for a while. The only radical change he made at KSAC, he made after he had been taking his major in Journalism for six months. He got a real taste of his first love (radio), and after broadcasting plays on KSAC, he altered his major to Radio Arts. He had decided that if he didn't wind up as a "thirty year man," he would be a *radio announcer.* However, the thirty year man looked more like a sure thing. The world was at war while he was beating the skins. He was in ROTC and making A's there without even trying.

The reading never slacked. He read Dashiell Hammett and Edna Ferber. He read Dreiser and Pearl Buck. He read Erskine Caldwell, Gertrude Stein, James Thurber, James Hilton, H. G. Wells, and Andre Malraux. He didn't stop with Saroyan, Fitzgerald, or Thomas Wolfe. *Studs Lonnigan, Tortilla Flat, Waiting for Lefty, Idiot's Delight*, and The *Tropic of Cancer* went "down the hatch" like beer in an Oktoberfest. Not even Dale Carnegie was exempted, nor Sheldon (*In His Steps*), although both books bored him to tears. In Sheldon's work the plan of salvation never even suggested itself. Sheldon, an unsaved Liberal, said that a "Christian" was someone who does what Jesus Christ would do "if He were here." By the time the Japanese had bombed Pearl Harbor, Ruckman had read nearly half of the Harvard "Five Foot Shelf" of classics, plus Malraux, Tolkien, Rawlings, Sherwood, Nathaniel West, Graham Greene, Richard Wright, and the usual raft of *Time, Life, Argosy, Colliers*, and *Post* magazines.

Somehow, throughout all of this, he never stumbled over the most important Book in the world. The world's best seller escaped his notice, and it was very strange that it did. With more than nine million books in the Library of Congress, he had not even seen the Book of books. Stevenson, Poe, Scott, Hawthorne, Melville, Thoreau, Whitman, Dickinson, Twain, Johnson, Adams, Frost, Eliot, Hemmingway, Tarkington, Stevens, Crane, and Dreiser were behind him. He had already read everything that Henry James and John Dewey had written to date, but he had never seen a line penned by Peter, James, John, Paul, or Moses.

On June 30, 1941, Hitler put "Barbarossa" into action: he attacked his buddy, Joe Stalin. The Germans had surrounded Leningrad by September and had laid siege to Moscow by October. They got there too late. Napoleon should have taught them long ago that if they didn't get to Moscow before AUGUST they wouldn't go any further. They went further (Odessa, Sevastopol, Stalingrad), but it was a disaster.

On the seventh of December the Japanese bombed Pearl Harbor. All the ROTC units were alerted, and Ruckman was given his choice of staying in that Corps area or transferring to his father's Corps area, which was in Alabama. This would mean junior and senior years at the University of Alabama. He chose to move: the move probably saved his life. The ROTC at Alabama was not converted into ASTP units until 1943. The units at KSAC went off to military camps in the summer of 1942. Ruckman had missed the Bataan Death March, Corregidor, Wake Island, Guam, Guadalcanal, New Georgia, Bougainville, and Kasserine Pass. *Some folks live a charmed life.*

On the way to Tuscaloosa, Ruckman pulled off a typically stupid maneuver. His "womanizing" had eventually tied him up with a young lady from Topeka whom he wished to marry. He bought her a ring (without her knowing about it), and then on the way to Alabama he paid her a "surprise visit" in Oklahoma City, where she was at that time working in a bomber plant. He arrived unannounced in the middle of winter (January 1942), took a cab to her residence and waited. He waited four hours. She came in drunk with a boyfriend and another couple at about two in the morning. She walked right by him in the snow, and if he had not called out she would not have known he was there. She sent her friends inside and then invited him in. He refused flatly and began to struggle with his "news"— the ring. She patted him on the back like a four year old and told him such a thing could not be: she was engaged to the drunk inside the house. He was an older man (about thirty years old), so all the talk about marriage and engagement was impossible. After fifteen minutes she complained, saying she was cold, and went inside the house. He never saw her again. He went back down to a hotel in Oklahoma City, got dog drunk, threw the ring out a window into the alley, and headed on to Alabama, swearing never to trust a female of the species again. From now on he would "play them all for suckers"—at least, that was how they said it in the *movies*.

He arrived in Tuscaloosa in the winter of 1942, a displaced "Yankee," bitter and mad at the world, chockfull of worldly wisdom. He was five feet eight, one hundred and seventy pounds, and so mean he didn't even love himself. He had been on beer for nearly four years and on cigars for nearly two years. He came down south looking for nothing but ACTION: there hadn't been much at Manhattan. As anyone knows, the KSAC football team has a good year when they can average one touchdown per game. It was kind of like what Cooney Mall, their swimming coach, said when asked about a particularly bad season: "Well, at least nobody drowned."

CHAPTER SEVEN

The Artist
As a Young Man

"Way down south in Dixie" turned out to be something different. His first impression of the place was that it was poverty stricken, junky, and "run down." It wasn't until years later that he learned that this was due to a philosophy of enjoying life first and then "makin' a livin'" later. He didn't know it, but he was walking into a sabretoothed bear trap. *The Bible* had survived below the Mason-Dixon Line. He was about to be "witnessed" to for the first time in his life. A christened, confirmed "Episcopalian," Ruckman was about as religious as Bernard Shaw or Bertrand Russell. He had never seen a gospel tract, never heard anyone actually preach a Biblical text, and such questions as "Are you saved?" or "Where will you spend eternity?" were as foreign to him as Babylonian cuneiform to a hot rodder.

He enrolled with a major in Radio Arts and a minor in Psychology. His Radio Arts professor was a retired program director from CBS, John Carlyle, who was himself an amateur artist. Carlyle gave his professional painting easel to Ruckman after seeing some of Ruckman's artwork. "Here," he said, "I think a professional should have it."

On the rebound from the disastrous love affair in Oklahoma City, Ruckman went to work with renewed zeal to "score" as many times as possible. Being an incurable romantic (the movies had done their work), he quickly fell in love again with a young female artist on the campus. She was a dean's daughter and a virgin; Ruckman seduced her. But this time something went terribly wrong. He had picked on a "Christian," whatever that was. Perhaps it had happened at KSAC before, but there was no way of knowing, for those "Christians" (if there were any) had kept their mouths shut; this one didn't. On the night of nights everything was arranged. ("The scene is set, the breezes sing of it, can't you get into the swing of it, lady, when do we start? When the lady is kissable and the evening is cool, any dream is permissible in the heart of a FOOL . . . .") He was a fool, all right (Prov. 10:23), but he hadn't found it out yet.

NIGHT SCENE:

At the crucial moment the girl said (lying flat on her back and looking up at the stars), "Peter, do you believe in GOD?"

That's the way it came out. Seriously, quietly, slowly, and deliberately: "Peter, do you believe in GOD?"

Why would anyone say a thing like that at a time like this? What a thing to ask your date preparatory to "making love" ("fornication" in the Book). What a question! "Peter, do you believe in GOD?"

Without hesitation, he replied, "You're my god."

Truer words were never spoken. His god was SEX. It was later (much later) that he learned all educated Americans had three gods: money, sex, and education—in about that order. His god was lust. His god was self. His highest authority for deciding all matters of ethics, morals, and conduct was his own opinion. He was "in bondage to no man." He was a "free thinker," a "free wheeler," and a "free dealer," and accountable to no one. At least that is how he conducted himself.

There was no more conversation: the girl gave up the attempt to witness. But when the Dean found out what had happened to his daughter he made two moves; first he sent her off to Mexico for a two week vacation, then he contacted a former "steady" of hers who was a naval officer and got them together again. When Ruckman saw his "love life" leave him flat and take off with an ensign, he went out and got drunk again and renewed his Oklahoma City vows: "quoth the raven NEVER-MORE"! Lust and sex were all right, but love and marriage were for the birds.

In the next two years (1942–43) and up to graduation (1944), the young man spent his time either drawing, playing drums in the dance bands ("Tutt Yarbrough and the Stardusters," and "Hal Halberg and the Cavaliers"), studying his courses, reading, going to the movies, getting drunk, and fornicating. He suddenly found himself in an Italian, Roman Catholic company which he had never been in before. His buddies, now, were Nick Trellizi, Tony Bertini, Al Alois, Joe Zasa, and Joe Domnonavich. At the parties were pasta, pizzas, pepperoni, wine, and lasagna. The BTO's kept a scoreboard on the wall for recording their conquests. Ruckman had a reputation the generations of the seventies and eighties would have envied. **"Fools make a mock at sin"** (Prov. 14:9).

In 1942, the Japanese invaded Singapore and then invaded the Philippines. They took Corregidor and Bataan. Thirty-six thousand American and Filipino troops went into captivity. The RAF bombed Cologne (May 30), the Battle of Midway (June 7) was fought, and Rommel drove the British back to Cairo. U.S. troops landed on Guadalcanal (August 7) and in North Africa (November 11). They got their plow cleaned when they hit Rommel in the Kasserine Pass. Montgomery finally routed the Germans after the Roman Catholic Pope decided that Rommel's gas supplies should be cut off (via Sicily and Malta). The decision was made in November of 1942 when the Pope saw the "handwriting on the wall" at Stalingrad. Fatima's "Peace Plan for Russia" was going to "bomb out." The Americans had entered the war against the Catholic Adolph Hitler (and the Catholic Benito Mussolini), and General Paulus was about to lose a whole army (the Sixth Army) at Stalingrad: three hundred thousand men. As Rommel retreated in Africa, atomic fission was obtained (December 2), and both America and Germany went to work to try to produce an atom bomb.

Ruckman was reading Hegel, Spinoza, Nietzsche, Feuerbach, Lessing, Kant, Astruc, Vatke, Kuenen, Semler, Engels, Marx, "Strata" Smith, Darwin, Voltaire, Rousseau, Descartes, Freud, Pavlov, Hume, Hobbes, Strauss,

Comte, Leadbeatter, Blavatsky (Theosophy), Henri Bergson, Ritschl, Sartre, and the Rosicrucians. He missed getting killed at El Alamein, El Alghelia, Tobruk, Dieppe, Midway, Sevastopol, Kharkov, Singapore, Tripoli, Hong Kong, and Cabanatuan. Some people live a charmed life. If "God takes care of fools and drunkards," Ruckman had double protection. Coming from three generations of professional military men (infantry officers, at that), he had missed the "action" described above. He was not even on the Doolittle Raid when the Americans bombed Tokyo (April 18).

In the fall of 1943 the ROTC was converted into the ASTP (*Army Specialized Training Program*), and all of the ROTC students were put into uniforms, placed in barracks on the campus, and marched to and from meals at a special mess hall. The "barracks" turned out to be a converted SIGMA NU fraternity house.

"Time and tide wait for no man." The sun rose and it set. While it rose and set, thousands of prisoners in Buchenwald, Treblinka, Auschwitz, and Monthausen were being whipped to death, starved to death, worked to death, tortured, and executed. When Ruckman got up in the morning to face another day of revelling in the flesh and stuffing his mind with facts, figures, ideas, and philosophies, hundreds and thousands got up in bombed-out cities, shell-racked hospitals, holes in the ground, and barracks with freezing temperatures and faced another day of hell on earth just trying to stay alive.

Berlin was bombed (January 30, 1943). Stalingrad was captured by the Communists with the help of the American taxpayers, who gave Joe Stalin (a bloody murderer) thirty-four million dollars to build "T-34" tanks. The last Jews were wiped out of the Warsaw Ghetto and killed on the spot or sent to concentration camps. The American dead fell in Sicily (July 23), they fell in Naples, they fell in Salerno, they were buried at Anzio, and they were blown apart at Mt. Cassino (August to October, 1943). The Allied bombers burned more civilians to death in fire raids on Hamburg, Germany (July 28), than the atom bomb killed at Hiroshima.

GENERAL
LUDENDORF

GENERAL
MACARTHUR

GENERAL
GUDERIAN

Wartime Pen and Ink Sketches

World War II Pen and Ink Sketches

Ruckman may have been a fool, but he could read this kind of writing on the wall. Potentially, he was a dead duck. His MOS was a Combat Infantry Platoon Leader; they last about twenty minutes after the action starts, if statistics are correct. It would be graduation in May (1944), OCS in June, and then into the holocaust. He probably didn't have ten months to live after the new year came in (1944). There were no illusions about infantry combat; he had been raised in the home of an infantry officer, and he had "cut his teeth" on *Fix Bayonets* (Thompson) and *All Quiet on the Western Front* (Remarque). Combat was not like a John Wayne movie. It was running out of rations, freezing in the snow, crying like a baby after being whipped with shrapnel, bleeding to death before the medic can get to you, getting captured and having your privates amputated, or shell casings pounded through your kneecaps; it was grim-faced, grey-faced slogging through mud with men dropping in front of you and on both sides; it was screaming for your mother in an artillery bombardment (CRASH! "Mother! CRRRASH! Mother! CRASH!), or losing your mind and trying to dig your way into the ground with your teeth. There was nothing about infantry combat that would make anyone call it "The Queen of Battles" unless he was a general officer in the regimental bivouac area playing chess. On his cot at night, the black-hearted scoundrel (and that is what he was; the old-timers called them "blackguards"—1800) was forced to "count his chickens" before they "hatched."

FLASHBACK:

A cot in the flophouse in Salinas, California, 1941. "Ten cents a bed and a can to spit in." Old men hacking, spitting, coughing. One man up screaming with the DT's. Ruckman lying, listening, figuring (as usual): "Peter, old boy, someday you are going to be old, so you better find someone to take care of you. Marry rich, buddy. Get you a rich girl, and when you get in this condition you won't have to live in a flophouse."

FEEDBACK:

Walking down the streets of Manhattan, Kansas,

after a dance, with his speech professor (Troutman), a fifty-year-old bachelor Jew. It is one a.m. He has sent his set of drums home in a cab to the frat house. There wasn't room in the cab for him after the stuff was packed. "I know what you are thinking, Pete, looking at all those lights in those windows. You think those are happy homes. You don't know what is going on in there. I do. I've had a home. Those houses are not as sweet and secure as they look."

Still, it ached. *What* ached? He could not locate it for love nor money. Was he homesick? "Homesick"? He had never had a home. He didn't know what a "home" was. He had come up on the streets like a dog; a stray dog. Perhaps that explained why he loved dogs so much.

In the converted Sigma Nu Frat house (now an Army barracks), Ruckman made the decision. He would find him a nice, clean, RICH girl and marry her. That way if he got wounded she could support him the rest of her life, and if he got killed, then what the ———. What difference would it make, anyway? At least he would have a little touch of "home life" before they blew his brains out. If you didn't get back (and he didn't figure on getting back) at least you would have some "married life" as well as some single life. Why get a half-empty cup in life?

Ruckman figured he would wind up in the ETO fighting Germans. It was true that thousands of his fellow countrymen were getting their brains blown out (and their arms and legs shot off) on Eniwetok and Truk (February 1944), and later (March) more thousands would send home their ten thousand dollars from Hollandia, Saipan, Guam, and Tinian, but he still thought he would wind up fighting Germans; that's what his daddy had done. Fighting Germans is not a pleasant pastime. You don't take Germans "with a grain of salt." They are by far the best infantrymen in the world, and their artillery can put an .88 in your back pocket at two thousand yards. Germans get a kill ratio of about two to one against British or Americans, a kill ratio of about three to one against Italians or Frenchmen, and a ratio of about five to one against Russians or Africans. Germans are something to be reckoned with. "It ain't funny, McGee!"

Ruckman had been dating a southern belle from a small farm in Hale County, Alabama. He had not tried to "make her" because he respected her. She didn't drink or smoke, and she didn't *dance* or go to the *movies*. She was only seventeen years old when he met her; she was eighteen when he married her. She seemed to fill all of the qualifications. Her father owned several hundred acres of good "bottom land" near the Warrior River close to Greensboro, Alabama. The nearest post office was Sawyerville, a wide place in the road somewhere between "Pop Mays" (that was the farmer) and Greensboro. He had two sons and three daughters. As it turned out, all of them were professing Christians, although the girl at Alabama University (Janie Bess) never made any kind of profession to him until 1949, after they had been married five years. In those five years, he never saw her read a Bible, never heard her pray, and never saw her walk through a church door, but she was "clean."

"Mom May" (Janie's mother) was "somethin' else," as they say in Alabama, Georgia, and the Carolinas. She turned out to be of Huguenot ancestry (her maiden name was Quarrels). She had two sisters, and all three of these girls were Bible-believing Baptists. Peter Ruckman was about to walk into a situation that would get completely out of his control and test all of his craftiness, knowledge, intellect, duplicity, and rebellion to the absolute limit. You see, Mom May had been praying for nearly five years that God would make a *preacher* out of one of her boys ("T" May and "Bubba"). Neither one of them had felt the call, but both of them had been sent off to a Christian school for a few months to see if God would call them.

They had been sent to a small, nondenominational school in Cleveland, Tennessee. It was called "Bob Jones College" and had been founded in Panama City (Lynn Haven) back in 1928 by a Methodist evangelist who had been raised as a peanut farmer near Dothan, Alabama (Brannon's Stand).

Strange bedfellows.

A beer-drinking, profane, cursing, cigar-smoking artist and dance band drummer from "Yankee land" was
about to marry into a family of Bible-believing Baptists
in the "Black Belt" of Alabama. (The only drinker in the
family was Pop May, who didn't get saved till he was on
his death bed.) Mom May was a Bible-believing, praying
woman whose sister followed J. Frank Norris of Ft. Worth,
Texas, and this sister (Aunt Rosa) lived in Dixon Mills,
Alabama, the place where Norris had been BAPTIZED
as a boy.

With a clandestine marriage at night in the Episcopal church downtown (March 1944) and a fifteen dollar
wedding ring, two traveling salesmen from a hotel lobby
were called in to witness the service. The marriage remained a secret until graduation time. In the meantime,
Ruckman had him a ready-made, available "shack up"
any time he wanted it. Janie loved him with all of that
emotional and passionate committal that a "first love"
brings. He had married her because he figured he would
never get back from overseas alive.

Wrong figuring.

The trouble was simple. It was so simple that a
complex character like Ruckman could never have believed it, let alone figured it out. The trouble was that a
BOOKKEEPER was present. There was SOMEONE
around watching all of this and recording all of it. That
One had seen the baby come out of its mother's womb on
the couch in the house on Franklin Avenue and had gotten that baby through the diseases, rattlesnakes, police
traps, fist fights, auto thefts, dances, drunken drives, parties, seductions, river currents, ocean waves, bar rooms,
dance halls, theaters, drill fields, and arrests, and that
One was keeping BOOKS. He knew Ruckman's down-
sitting, his uprising, and "understood his thoughts afar
off." Reaping time had to come sooner or later, for it was
the law of life and nature (Gal. 5). Ruckman would live
to reap in the 1970's what he was sowing in the 1940's.
He was marrying for convenience, and it would be a one-
sided marriage till it collapsed fifteen years later. She

would give all—he would *take* all. But The Bookkeeper has a long memory!

When the "artist as a young man" went down to Mom May's, the first question she asked him was, "Young man, are you SAVED?"

Without hesitating he said, "Sure, I'm saved," and walked out of the room. He didn't even know what he had been asked. To him the question was the equivalent of "Are you in good shape?" or "How are you doing?" Many years later he was to ask that question to over two thousand people face to face, and another four million via pulpits, television, and radio.

Pop May sized up Janie's future husband in ten seconds. He said to his family after the young man had visited them around Christmas time, "That Pete Ruckman! He jes don't give a ——!"

Truer words were never spoken.

But there it was: Mr. and Mrs. Peter S. Ruckman, from Sawyerville, Alabama. That was the "home address" he put on all of his mail for the next three years. He never had an inkling when he wrote that Alabama address that someday he was to preach the Holy Bible in Mobile, Birmingham, Anniston, Gadsen, Montgomery, Wetumpka, Greensboro, Dixon Mills, Bayou LaBatre, Satsuma, Selma, Atmore, Linden, Foley, Elberta, Robertsdale, and Grove Hill.

Graduation came (May 1944), and off the ROTC boys were marched to different camps. The infantry units went to the infantry school at Fort Benning, Georgia. As they went, the Allies landed on the beaches at Normandy, and another ten thousand boys lost their lives. The rocket age opened with the first V-1 hitting London (June 1944), and the Allied Forces entered the Whore on the seven hills, where the Pope had been sitting quietly and safely protected throughout his entire debacle. His Vatican City was neither shell-pocked nor bullet-riddled. It was intact; his concordats with Adolph Hitler and Benito Mussolini (who had been run out, July 1943) had not hurt his "testimony" with Churchill, FDR, and Joe Stalin. Neither of the Catholic dictators were excommunicated before or after their deaths, nor was the Roman Catholic dictator of Spain (Franco).

Off to the infantry school went the student: "FOL-LOW ME!"

CHAPTER EIGHT

The General's Grandson

The days of the "ninety day wonders" were over. When they got to Benning the government took for granted that none of them had been "in the field," so ignoring two years of Ruckman's training (CMTC) in the field, the whole crew was put back through "basic" again *before* OCS: this time six weeks of it. This meant that Peter S. had under his belt (at twenty-three years old) two years of CMTC, four years of ROTC, and six weeks of training on "maneuvers" with live ammunition. If ever a man was getting ready for infantry combat, he was; he still had ahead of him another twelve weeks as an officer candidate.

But this time he had to confess it was "interesting." In this war, Uncle Sam meant business; it was not like the debacle in Korea or the farce in "Nam." This time you used live ammo, and the government allowed at least two percent casualties in training as a "margin of error" to insure that OCS produced some real officers. They went out under overhead fire from .105's and .155's, and they saw "skip bombing" ahead of their units. They used live ammo in the assault problems, including live mortar rounds, live grenades, and live rifle rounds. The "artist" began to fade; the "musician" dropped Tschaikovsky, Beethoven, Brahms, Artie Shaw, Tommy and Jimmy Dorsey, Fats Waller, Strauss, Victor Herbert, Stan Kenton, Woody Herman, Les Brown, and Rachmaninoff for a while. From three generations back the blood began to course again in the other direction: KILL OR BE KILLED.
MONTAGE:
a. Major Bronchorst on the platform—one out of only five non-Orientals to wear an Oriental black belt at

that time (1944). "Come to the guard position . . . HUP!" After an hour, the field began to tilt. Everything went black. Spots began to dance before his eyes. On his right and left, and behind him, he could hear the bodies hitting the ground, and that familiar sound of the rifle strap slapping as they hit.

"Keep the point of the bayonet up in the air! Hold it! I said, HOLD IT!" He never passed out, but there were moments where he could see nothing.

b. Down the dirt road (Lumpkin Road), gas mask on, overhead fire. Plane strafing the road, head for the ditch, lie down, get up, hit the dirt, get up, run. The sweat fills the mask up to your lips; you are about to drown in your own sweat. You can't breath in rhythm with the "diaphragm."

c. Out through the bushes at night. "Assemble at THIS pine tree before four a.m.!" Compasses, luminous dials, taking the azimuth. Look out for the "enemy" on the way. If you wind up with flour on you, you are a "casualty." Noise in the bushes. Can't identify it—the tracers are being fired over your head. Oh yeah, I remember what that noise is. RATTLESNAKE! Run for your life! Just like the watermelon patch in Topeka.

d. Expert Infantry Badge: qualified with the light and heavy mortars, light and heavy antitank guns, the .30 and .50 caliber machine guns, the .45 caliber pistol, the M1, and the carbine. In those days they meant business. KILL OR BE KILLED.

e. "Hey, look what Ruckman's mother-in-law sent him! A Bible! Hey, Ruckman's got a Bible! Can you believe that?"

He looked at the thing with four or five of his barracks buddies staring at it over his shoulder and then said, "Ah, nuts, this thing can't stop bullets," and threw it into a trash can. (It wasn't till years later that he learned that that little black book had stopped bullet after bullet after bullet in the Civil War and World War I. A shot in the upper chest could be stopped by a New Testament if it was in that pocket. It happened a dozen times in two wars.) Ruckman trashed it.

Original Pen and Ink Sketch—Made in 1944

Original Pen and Ink Sketch—1944

The Bookkeeper made a note.

f. The stands: name written on a helmet liner. "Ruckman, what would you do at this time with this terrain? What orders would you give your squads in this situation?"

g. The stands: "All right, spot the sniper. Where is he? I'll have him move his hands when you think you've spotted him." Nobody could spot him. He was in a clump of trees a hundred yards off. When they all gave up, in came a man with a K-9 corps "draftee" on a leash. He ran out twenty yards into the field, sniffed, and then froze on point like a bird dog. "Move your hand," yelled the tactical officer. The "sniper" in the trees waved his hands; THE DOG HAD HIM LINED UP LIKE A RIFLE SIGHT.

h. The stands again: "Blamablamablamablamablamblamblam," went the .30 caliber water-cooled. There were two of them spraying the field. "Go boy!" says the K-9 controller, and a German shepherd starts off through the field with a "dispatch." He goes the full hundred yards in tall grass by executing a perfect series of rushes and crouches. When he "hits the dirt" he actually crawls or rolls to another position four to six feet away and then springs up, and with a short rush he gains some ground, hits the dirt again, and repeats the process. No trained human being could do it any better.

i. Small talk: "You take that water outta my canteen, Richardson?"

"Hell no, Ruckman, I've just been lyin' here by the packs."

"It was quarter full. I know it because I been nursin' it all day long. It was hot, but it was H_2O."

"Well, Ruckman, I don't know anything about . . . ."

"You dirty ——, you s.o.b. You smiling ——. You took my water as sure as you're lying there, cause I know when you ran out, four thousand yards ago in the attack!"

That night on guard duty he crawled over to the sleeping form of his buddy Richardson and put a trench knife on his throat. Gently he toyed with the blade. "You ——. You stole my water, you ——!" But he never slit the rascal's throat. Something held him back; it wasn't fear, it wasn't even caution. It was as though there was a restraining hand on him. He sneered at the sleeping form and finally crawled off and said, "The dirty ——. I coulda cut his —— throat from ear to ear, and the —— wouldnta known what got him!"

j. Casualty: CRASH! Overhead artillery, barbed wire entanglements. "Get down, Bailey, you crazy ——. They're hitting a hundred yards up the hill!"

"Aw, —— man, that's plenty of space."

"Yeah, but you might get a short round; get down!"

"Ah, Ruckman, you're always jacked up about somethin'!"

SLLLASSSH! A fragment hits the kid in his left hand, which he was laying on a tree limb about four feet high. The whole hand turns bright red, and he screams. As he heads for the rear, a whistle is heard somewhere, and with fixed bayonets Ruckman joins the "assault" on the "objective."

k. Night scene: marching five miles back to camp after a two thousand yard platoon in the attack with live ammo. (Uncle Sam meant business in those days.) He has broken his ankle. He can't even strap up his combat boots. The ankle is black and red and the size of a croquet ball. He limps painfully behind the column. He is within two weeks of graduation.

"Whatsa matter there, Ruckman? Yer ankle hurtin' ya?" It's the "bird dog" (First Lieutenant Eddie Copeland).

"Nossir."

"All right, then, catch up with the column!!"

"Yessir." He did.

Ten minutes later. "Howya doin', Ruckman?"

"Just fine, sir."

"Little behind the column, aintcha?"

"Yessir."

"Catch up!!"

"Yessir!"

If you can't "endure hardness" (2 Timothy 2:3), how will you ever make a soldier? He would rather die than quit or give anyone the privilege of thinking that he was about to quit. He caught up with the column. The ankle healed, but it healed crooked, and for the next ten years he unconsciously put all of his weight on one leg. Later this forced him to use a brace concealed in his left shoe, for without it his leg would go to sleep; it would eventually effect his back muscles on the left side and even his left arm. But he graduated.

KALEIDOSCOPE:

1. "But you said if we ever wanted to talk something over to come to you about it."

Copeland: "Yes, and I meant what I said, Corporal."

"Well, can't you help Reyes out? I have been with him for twelve weeks. He is one of the best soldiers I've ever seen. He's already had eight weeks of combat in the Pacific."

"Are you tryin' to tell me somethin' I don't know, Corporal?"

"Nossir, but I just hate to see a good man like that wash out. He fires expert on everything. Reyes, in my opinion, is better officer material than half the guys in the barracks."

"Well, Ruckman, I am sure he would appreciate you goin' to bats for him, but when a candidate gets skunk drunk down in Phoenix and then beats up two MP's and a paratrooper, we are going to ship him!"

"Yessir, but he is an Indian, sir. You know how whiskey affects them."

"Sorry, Ruckman, you're wasting your time. I have my orders from the Colonel, and they will be carried out."

"But sir, you gotta admit if a guy like Reyes' size can whip two MP's and a paratrooper, he would make a mighty good . . . ."

"That's all, Ruckman! Dismissed!"

m. Boarder in the next room: a drunken jump master from the old 101st Airborne: "Yeah, Ruck, you oughtta seen the look on their face! Ha, ha, ha! Man, I would get to the door and take the line off and hand it to that bird and say, 'Here, hold this for me,' and I'd bail out! Ha, ha, ha! You oughtta seen his face! Ho, ho, ha, hah, haaah!"

n. Returned GI from Bougainville: "Sure, man, I got the s.o.b. and ground his fingers down to the bone on a grind stone. Died of pain. The —— kicked out before I got to the third finger."

"Well, h— man, do you mean to tell me you get a kick out of hearing some guy scream?"

"Sure, man, what the h—. How would you feel if you heard one of your buddies screaming half the night, and you couldn't go out to get him, and the next morning you come down the trail and find him skinned alive with his —— cut off and stuck in his mouth? How the h— would you feel? Wouldn't you want to hear someone else scream awhile?"

Yeah, well, maybe he had a point there. Live like an animal, and I guess after a while you will think like an animal.

The Allies marched into Paris (August 1944) after several thousand Americans had perished in Caen, St. Lo, Avranches, Mortain, Falaise, and Chambois. The Russian counterattack drove on to Warsaw, and five thousand more British and Germans and Americans went out into eternity after trying to capture a bridge "too far away" (Arnheim, in "Operation Market Garden"). As Ruckman came out of OCS, the V-2's began to hit London, and the "Big Four" (Churchill, Roosevelt, Stalin, and Chiang Kai-shek) got ready to set up the biggest fiasco since the League of Nations. The four gentlemen— three professing Christians (two of them being Episcopalians) and an atheist—decided that a "lasting peace" could be obtained after "the war to end all wars" by setting up a "UNITED NATIONS" (October 9, Dumbarton Oaks). The plan was simple: China, Russia, England, and the USA would ATTACK ANY WOULD-BE AGGRESSOR before they could start a war. All the clowns were not in the circus. FDR praised the conference recommendations and said good old "Uncle Joe" could be trusted. All of the ding-a-lings were not in the bells.

Upon getting his shavetail bars, Lieutenant Ruckman was assigned to the 201st Infantry Regiment, then stationed at Ft. Jackson, South Carolina. They were originally a National Guard unit and had returned from Kiska and Adak in the Aleutians. This meant that at the last minute, when Ruckman was just about to be shipped overseas (and consequently into the Rhineland battle of the Huertgen Forest and the Ardennes breakthrough— the Battle of the Bulge—or into the battles of Leyte and Manila) he had been shuttled aside to train infantry replacements. America was getting near the bottom of the barrel, and when the Germans broke through the lines around Bastogne and St. Vith, infantrymen had to be "requisitioned" from the four corners of America, given accelerated training, and sent into combat overnight. The top brass at Benning took one look at Ruckman's background and instead of sending him overseas to get in on the ACTION, they sent him first to Ft. Jackson in Carolina and then to Camp Rucker in Alabama to train infantry replacements. *Again his life was spared.* Before he finally "shipped out," Dresden had been bombed out (February 1945), Auschwitz had been liberated (January 27), the Russians had entered Berlin, Hitler had committed suicide (April), the battle for Okinawa was over (June), and the United Nations was formed (June 26—the declaration was signed by Secretary of State Stettenius) in order to set up the Korean War, the Berlin Wall, the Vietnam War, the Israel-Egyptian and Israel-Arab wars, plus sixty-five more wars in Cyprus, Crete, Albania, Turkey, Pakistan, Cambodia, Lebanon, Cuba, Nicaragua, Laos, San Salvador, Tibet, China, Afghanistan, Iraq, Iran, Hungary, and other places. The UN turned out to be the greatest warmongering body in the history of mankind. It began with fifty nations in the faggot capital of the world: SAN FRANCISCO.

Quietly, unobtrusively, almost without press notice, the first RACE RIOT in the USA since 1933 broke out in the murder capital of the world: DETROIT (five murders a day in 1989).

FDR, the greatest pro-Communist Socialist America had had up to that time (M. L. King surpassed him later) died, and Harry S Truman took over the reins of govern-

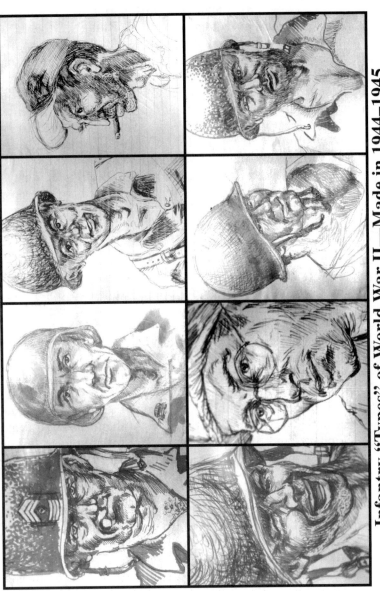

Infantry "Types" of World War II—Made in 1944–1945

ment. It was now the "Big Three" (Truman, Churchill, and Stalin).

Ruckman's first child was born in the Druid Hospital in Tuscaloosa, Alabama on June 27, 1945. He named her "DIANA" after the goddess of the hunt (see Acts 19:27-28). Shortly after she was born, his orders came in. The war was over in Germany (capitulated May 7), so he would not have to fight Germans, but the "Rising Sun" had not set yet, so his POE would take him to the Pacific Theater of Operations. There was a staging area being set up on Luzon to assemble troops for an attack on the Japanese mainland. When Ruckman set sail from Fort Ord (Frisco) on the "Cape Mendecino," Iwo Jima, Okinawa, and Saipan were American possessions.

Then the worst possible thing happened (from Ruckman's standpoint—certainly no one else's). To save the lives of millions of Americans (and it did just that, at the same time saving the lives of millions of Japanese), Harry Truman had Enola Gay (a southern name; it was named after the pilot's mother) drop the bomb on Hiroshima (August 6). In less than a week another one fell on Nagasaki (August 9), and as Ruckman's Merchant Marine "Liberty Ship" anchored in Pearl Harbor—where the whole mess had started—the war with Japan disintegrated right in his face: August 15, 1945.

And there was "Ruckman" (they always called him that; not even his seniors called him by his first name one time out of ten) sitting on the yardarm of the Cape Mendecino, bayonet like a razor, carbine as clean as a hound's tooth, pack and uniform in order, and SIX YEARS OF INFANTRY TRAINING behind him after being raised in a military family. He wasn't going to get to fire a shot. The hospital ship opposite them was shooting off fireworks (flares), the shore batteries were firing antiaircraft rounds up into the clouds, searchlights were waving and probing, flags were waving all along the shore and on the decks of the ships, the convoy now would need no more cruiser and destroyer escorts, some of the wounded on the hospital ship were waving crutches, and those who could walk were jumping up and down on the deck.

But "there was no joy in Mudville. Mighty Casey had struck out!"

The dogface sat on the yardarm, puffing his cigar viciously. He finally threw it down and cursed. Then he sat some more.

FEEDBACK:

"Well, what will you do now? What do you know how to do? Do you think you can go back to spinning platters and making public service announcements after THIS? Six years: two years CMTC, four years ROTC, four months OCS, and nine months training troops. What do you know about anything but KILLING? Do you think you will shake *this* off? What did Paul Baumer say about it in *All Quiet*? I remember what he said: 'We will go back, but people will not understand us. The older men who came with us will return to their jobs and old occupations which they had before the war and take up where they left off. But we will have nothing to come back to. All we learned about life was death. Our knowledge of living is limited to killing. Like salesmen we understand distinctions; like butchers we understand necessities. We are sorrowful like old men and superficial like little children. I BELIEVE WE ARE LOST.'"

After two hours the racket subsided. Most of the troops on the transport went back to their bunks below decks. Ruckman stayed "topside." He gazed over the rail where the lights of Honolulu reflected in the dark, oily waters.

FEEDBACK:

How did Baumer put it? "We shall return, but the coming generation will push us aside; they will not understand us. We shall become superfluous even to ourselves. Some of us will perhaps submit, but never completely, and I fear IN THE END, WE SHALL FALL INTO RUIN."

Sometimes the children of this generation are wiser than the children of light. He was lost, and he was headed for ruin. He had twenty-four years of sin to reap, and these years still lay ahead of him.

"Whether down to Gehenna or up to a throne, he travels fastest who travels alone." Ruckman was a "fast" young man, as they said back in the 1800s. Before the age of twenty-four he had known the life of an artist, the life of a musician, the life of a student, and the life of a soldier. He had hit the ground running and never stopped. Some men, in twenty years, cover the ground that it takes other men fifty and sixty years to cover. The drawback is that you get to the "end" too soon. Elvis Presley had this trouble; so did the Beatles. So did Errol Flynn and Marilyn Monroe. It seemed to be a characteristic of "the jet set."

On the yardarm of the Cape Mendecino in Pearl Harbor, Ruckman swore under his breath that he would have some "action" one way or another. He had "shacked up" in Frisco the night before he had embarked, and he was now making plans to "sample" the Orientals if he ever got there. But this pace would finish him by the time he was twenty-seven. There, in 1944, he didn't realize that life for him would be over in five years, and at the ripe old age of twenty-seven he would be ready to "cash in his chips."

He smoked one more "stogey" and hit the sack.

After a few days in port, the Cape Mendecino headed out across the Pacific. The war was over, but there was an army of occupation coming up, and a thousand details regarding American property and American troops that would take months to settle. The Mendecino, a Merchant Marine, was the proverbial "slow boat to China." It took them five weeks to get from Frisco to Pier Five at Manila. Since all chance of action was gone, Ruckman prepared himself for a first-rate "crashing bore" of a trip. There were no books to read on the ship, but field manuals. Naturally he read all of them: *First Aid, Survival in the Desert, Survival in the Arctic, Automatic Weapons, the Rifle Squad in the Attack, the Rifle Platoon in the Attack, Rifle Company, Battalion, etc., in the Attack, Spotting Enemy Aircraft, First Aid in the Field, Military Decorations, Military Ceremonies*, etc. He read all the books that pertained to him and all the books that pertained to everyone else. LIFE was going to be a drag if he didn't think of something. He got ahold of a watercolor set from an A&R officer who came off another ship and for the first time tried his hand at watercolors; it was a disaster. (He still has [1990] the first two. One was of Pearl Harbor, and the other was of some fishing boats that came up to the Mendecino.)

The ship plowed on past Johnson Island and towards Luzon. Every three days someone would go screaming "Land! Land!" all around the deck, and when everyone came "topside" yelling "Where? Where?" the smart-aleck would say, "One mile *straight down*." About five hundred showed up the first time it was tried, but this trick *trickled* down to about two dozen the fifth time. They crossed the international dateline with some foolishness from the crew (it was a Merchant Marine ship) and finally arrived at Granddaddy Ruckman's "land of pork and beans, happy, sunny Philippines." They took a narrow gauge railroad up to Angeles in Pampangan providence, and there, at a Filipino scout recruiting depot, Ruckman stayed until the fall of 1947. After all the troops and officers were processed, Ruckman was assigned to the depot, and shortly thereafter the 86th Division (from Europe—the Black Hawk Division) moved in. Colonel Richardson was his regimental commander.

Ruckman's job at first was an A&R officer (Athletic and Recreation), but he was quickly removed from this to a DI in hand-to-hand, unarmed combat. He trained Filipino Scouts. He trained them just the way he had been trained: "Do unto others before they do unto you." Dog eat dog, law of the jungle, no holds barred, kill or be killed. When delivering blows to the throat, the eyes, and the "family jewels" it is always **more blessed to give than to receive** (Acts 20:35). If you had seen General Ruckman's grandson in 1945—one hundred and eighty-five pounds, twenty-eight inch waist, cigar in mouth, bayonet in hand, brown as a Filipino, and as mean as a rattlesnake—you would have known that Momma's "brown-eyed Booflee" had "arrived." The boy was no

Heavy Machine Gun (Water Cooled) Squad in Action

Original Pen and Ink Sketch of Combat—Made in 1945

longer a boy; he was a *man*. He was a product of behavioristic psychology, the National Education Association,
Hollywood, the news media, radio, science, philosophy,
and the military: "The choicest product of the brewer's
art." *He was a living DEVIL:* cursing, fighting, swearing,
lying, stealing, drinking, gambling, fornicating, blasphem-
ing, the whole works. He was what the Bible would call
a "fornicating whoremonger"—like Elvis Presley or JFK.

His creators (see the list above) would have simply
called him a "swinger" or "a man about town," or "an
individualist with a permissive lifestyle" or some other
hypocritical alibi for protecting a sinner and giving him
an air of respectability, but there was nothing "respect-
able" about Ruckman. His CO wrote on his report: "This
man is unusually sloppy and dirty for an officer, but he is
a natural born leader, and his platoon will follow him
anywhere. He can obey his own orders and tells his men,
'If I can do it, you can do it,' and then he *does* it. Ruckman has a mind of his own and is often stubborn and
sullen if he does not have a chance to argue with you
over an order. He will obey orders but not without re-
sentment. It is my opinion that if you have an especially
hard, tough, dirty job that has to be done and no officer is
capable of doing it, Ruckman is the man for it." He
didn't even say "Lieutenant": he said "Ruckman."

But he didn't obey *all* the orders. Life had been too
dull. To get things moving, Ruckman had been in contact
with the Hukbulahap (Filipino Communist guerillas), and
for "fun" he was using a one and a half ton weapons
carrier to "rob from the rich and give to the poor." He
was "gunrunning" cots, lanterns, radios, and other supplies at night. There were roadblocks; that was exciting.
There were tracers fired overhead; that helped. There
was always the chance of getting arrested and sent to
Leavenworth; that was interesting. What the h—! He had
seen the Army line up six thousand dollars worth of
Hallicrafter radio sets (brand new) and smash them with
ball-peen hammers; he had seen them line up brand new
two-and-a-half ton trucks, drain the crankcases, and put
cement blocks on the accelerators till the blocks stuck.

Why not help the "po' folk" out! Slaaammmmmm! Off he went! You could accuse him of a lot of things, but standing still wasn't one of them.

Filipino women, plenty of them, right and left. Riot at a dance hall out by Clark Field where paratroopers showed up with tommy guns and blew away some blacks who were getting thick with the senoritas. Night after night, beer and women—women, married or single, it didn't make any difference. Ruckman's wife and daughter were on the farm with Mom May in "Kimbrough bottom," but Ruckman had no ethics, no morals, and no conscience. Life was too short to be bugged.

NIGHT SCENES:

"All right, Swede." (Swede was six feet seven inches and two hundred and thirty pounds.) "You better straighten up and fly right, or I'll sick Rollee Pollee on ya!"

"Who the h— is Rollee Pollee? Do you mean to tell me you know somebody that can whip Swede?"

"Sure as shootin', man. Rollee Pollee can do it, can't he Swede?"

"Yuh, huh, hu . . . ." Plop! (Swede passes out.)

Later, he found out Rollee Pollee was a second Lieutenant at a Reppo Depo in Manila; he was was six feet three and weighed three hundred and twenty pounds.

"Any GI's in here?"

"No, sir," (a Gook talking), "No one in here, bery solly."

The flashlight crosses a dozen faces around some beer wick "candles."

"Well, if you see any, tell them they're off limits and after hours. Stockade if they don't get back to camp quick. Got it?"

"Yessssir, we tell them. We tell them good."

Out went the MP's. Ruckman laughs. Back in the States he had sometimes let his GI's use his bars to get into the officers club, but this was better than that. With his sun tan, his moustache, and his turtleneck sweater he was passing off as a Gook right in front of the ———. (They had a term for an MP that we couldn't repeat.) Besides that, he had picked up enough Pampangan dialect to converse with the natives. Not much Tagalog was spoken yet in Angeles.

SNAPSHOT FOR THE ALBUM: DRILL

Demonstrating disarming a man with a bayonet and rifle. A Malaysian stands up and says, "Dat work all right here, Lieutenant, but in combat dat no work." The man is a six foot Moro from the Malay Peninsula. He was a drill instructor in the China-India-Burma theater in 1943–1945.

"Okay, big boy, show us how they do it in combat," says Peter S. and throws him the rifle with a bare bayonet attached. The Moro doesn't rush; he knows the game. He fences.

("Must commit yourself, Lieutenant! You can't back off forever, Lieutenant. There are four hundred little brown eyes in two hundred little brown faces watching you, Lieutenant. Lose face one time, and you are a dead duck! Quick now, Peter S., no slipups now!")

In he went and seized the rifle. The Gook dropped it and slugged him; he ducked the hook and tripped the Gook; the Gook threw him to the ground. As they fell he tried to pick up the fallen rifle, but the Gook kneed him just in the right place. He felt like puking but had the presence of mind to jam his thumb into the gook's eye. The man grunted and drew his leg back for another kick, but Ruckman had the rifle. Rolling over to get clear of the kick he bounced to his feet and, clubbing the rifle, started down on the man's head. The Moro grinned, raised one hand, and said, "No more, Lieutenant. Das enough! No more."

FILM DEVELOPED:

"What the h--- were you doing rolling around in the dust with an enlisted man? Don't you know that's not 'conduct becoming an officer and a gentleman'?"

"But sir, the man called my hand. I couldn't lose face in front of my troops."

"What the —— were you doing going through the manual with a bare bayonet anyway?"

"Well, sir, I was trying to make things as realistic as possible."

"Ruckman, you're getting to be a pain in the ———.
Now look, your platoon got a unit citation in the parade
last week as the best drilled platoon in the regiment.
What the ——— did you have to go and ruin your record
with this thing for?"

"But sir, the man called my hand. He challenged me
in front of the company. You can't lose face before an
Oriental, and . . . ."

"Are you trying to PREACH TO ME, Lieutenant?"

"Nossir."

"Well, what if you had LOST; what then?"

"Well, in that case I would have stepped down and
let some other DI instruct them."

"Oh, you would choose the officers and assign the
duties in this regiment, would you? What the h— do you
think I'm here for?"

"Nossir, I didn't mean that, it's just that . . . ."

"Here, Ruckman. These are your orders: four weeks
TDY in Paranaque. You can come back after this thing
blows over."

"Yessir."

Paranaque was just outside Manila: Manila had libraries. So it started again. This time it was Oriental. In
he plunged: the Zend Avesta (attributed to Zoroaster),
which was divided into two parts—the *Avesta* and the
Khurda Avesta; *The Book of the Mighty Deeds of Ardashir*
(A.D. 600), the *Mahabharata* (a two hundred thousand
line "poem") containing the *Bhagavad Gita* (the "divine
song"), the *Ramayana*, the *Panchatantra*, the *Jatakas*,
and the *Sukasaptati* (seventy stories of the parrot), and
the *Analects of Confucius*. There followed the *Koran*, the
Rig Veda, the *Sama Veda*, the *Yajur Veda*, the *Atharva
Veda*, and the *Upanishands*, the *Tripitaka*, and *Sutras*.
These were books of "chants, prayers, spells, and hymns."
These books made a great impression on a young man
who was impressed by practically nothing. For the first
time in his life he began to think about God, or at least
something *like* God, if anything like "God" was around.
With his "blood and guts" activities removed from him,
his Huk connections cut, and his "love life" (that is what

a modern Liberal would call it) "out of whack," there was nothing to do but READ and PAINT. He did both. He painted Rizal Stadium and Manila Bay. He painted the Filipino washer women and the boys riding the damulags (water buffalos). His technique improved; he was getting where he could handle water colors.

Instead of bringing him back to Angeles immediately, he got further orders to stay in Paranque and help "survivors" of the Death March and "forty-four pointers" to return home. In those days, they used the "point system" to determine how long a man had to stay overseas. One point per month; anyone with thirty-five to forty points could return in 1945, anyone with thirty to thirty-four could go back in the first half of 1946, anyone with twenty-five to thirty could go back in the second half, and so forth. But there were still some wrecks floating around from 1942. They were collected in two and a half ton trucks and taken to Pier Five. He would never forget the face of one thirty-year-old GI, who didn't look a day under fifty. He was as yellow as a Chinaman from taking Atabrine, and he shook from head to foot as he answered the questionnaires.

When it was over Ruckman said, "There's your duffle bag; shoulder up and get in the truck."

"But Lieutenant, I-I-I can't go b-b-back."

"Like h— you can't. Whaddya mean you can't go back?"

The hands trembled. The tongue licked dry lips. The eyes moved wildly around the tent. "Ah . . . I . . . ah . . . I . . . I been over here too long, Lieutenant! I been over here too long," and he broke down crying.

Something soft got under Peter S.'s combat jacket. It came in like a stranger. "Naw, man, you ain't been over here too long. Lookya here. I'll help ya. C'mon." He picked up the man's bag and helped him to the truck. The man was still crying when the truck drove off. "Reckon his wife divorced him while he was gone? Reckon he's got syph or the clap and can't see his wife? Reckon his mind is gone? How about you, Peter S.? How is it going to go with you?"

Time marched on.

General Tojo committed hara-kiri (September 1945), George Patton was "accidentally" killed (December) after suggesting that the time was ripe to rearm Germany before Russia took Europe over. The Nürenberg Trials began with three notable absentees: ADOLPH HITLER, JOSEPH STALIN, and DWIGHT EISENHOWER. (Eisenhower had given orders [Operation Keelhaul] to "repatriate" more than twenty thousand people who had fled the Russians. They were imprisoned or killed when they got back to the Russian zone. Ike did what Eichmann had done, just not on such a big scale. The UN held its first session on January 10, 1946, and the "Iron Curtain" dropped on Eastern Europe (March 5) and stayed there until the fall of 1989.

Down in Paranque things weren't going much better. A restlessness had now seized Ruckman worse than anything he had experienced in Topeka or Tuscaloosa. It wasn't just that there was no "action"; it was that liquor and women were not curing the ache. What was "the ache"? He couldn't even put his hand on it. He would go down into Chinatown in downtown Manila at midnight, with a trench knife in his boot and his money rolled up in his socks, and look for trouble. But when he found it, it didn't satisfy. He got in a fist fight with his company commander outside of a dance hall in the jungle and knocked the old boy flat and then had him puking. That killed his chances for promotion to First Lieutenant, but he didn't give it a thought. Something else was gnawing at his vitals. *What was it?*

He studied palmistry; he studied necromancy; he studied black magic and white magic and phrenology and ESP and transcendentalism. He practised meditation and "astral projection." Something was still missing. What the h— was it?

Slowly but surely a plan began to form in his mind. The Orientals had convinced him that Buddha began where Hegel had quit. Hegel didn't have the answers. Whatever the "answers" were, they must be somewhere near TIBET. This thought kept at him with a persistence that was completely irrational. He kept thinking, "If I can just get to the source of Buddhism, I can find the answer." THE ANSWER? What was he thinking about? *The answer to WHAT?*

Now the mind turned inward, and with it the artist turned inward. The drinking got heavier and heavier. He would come in after midnight, drunk, and paint with watercolors. He called his pictures "Psychopathic Symbolism." They included "The Fear of Old Age," "The Fear of Death," "The Fear of Disease," "The Fear of the Unknown," "Peace," "Chronic Alcoholic," "The Apathy of the Stars," and "The Unanswerable Question." His classic was two men knife-fighting on a raft in the middle of a typhoon. Both men are in rags, and there is nothing on the raft to fight about. The raft is seen in a flash of lightening about to be engulfed by thirty foot waves, and there on its slippery boards are two men "squaring off" with drawn Bowie knives. It is called "Human Nature" (see the appendix).

The jungle got wetter and wetter, the nights got darker and darker, and the days got longer and longer. What was he doing in the Philippines? He had come here to fight, but the fighting was over. He drank more and more and painted more and more. He had unwittingly stumbled into a warrior's religion: Zen Buddhism. There are two branches of Buddhism (Hinayana and Mahayana) which come from five outstanding Chinese teachers. The schools they had set up were the Dyhana (meditation schools), and from these came Ch'an, the Chinese equivalent of Dhyana; from this came Japanese Zen Buddhism. The word originally meant "meditation." Zen grew out of Buddhism and Taoism and was based on the Chinese *Sutras* and the *Tripitaka* (Triple Basket). Meditation was the means of entering Samadhi (Sanskrit) and (to be short about it) the trick was for the neophyte to attain "enlightenment" (Prajna) by getting free from the cycle of births and rebirths—the constant reaping and sowing and sowing and reaping—that made up "Karma."

Ruckman had to face it, but he didn't want to: what he had to face was the fact that he was miserable and was trying to find a way to escape misery. That was Bodhi Dharma's original intent. Life had poured him out a cup of vinegar. It was setting his teeth on edge. He could have clarified things by saying simply: "I am not happy," but this was much too "simplistic" for a man who had reached the position he found himself in. What was "happiness" anyway? Looking back over the path, Ruckman (as Errol Flynn, Joe Namath, Lord Byron, and a thousand others discovered) could not say he had ever been "happy." He had been excited, yes. Stirred, yes. Troubled, yes. He had laughed his guts out on a couple of occasions, and even rejoiced and jumped up and down on several occasions, but "happiness"? What was THAT?

By now he could kill a case of beer in twenty-four hours without passing out. (His aunt and uncle died as chronic alcoholics and his mother would at a later date.) The pictures got wilder: "Karma," "The Fear of Ridicule," "False Saviour," "Vital Statistics," "The Illusion of Security," etc. Finally, in a drunken stupor, he drew a picture of De Vinci's "Last Supper" with some notable appendages. The glasses were dumped on the table, several wine bottles still stood upright, Simon Peter's feet were sticking out from under the table; John and the Lord were sitting cross-eyed at their wine glasses, Judas was out cold, having passed out on the table, and Matthew, Jude, and others were toasting each other with "Prost!" "Skoal!" "Cheers!" and various things.

Ruckman took this drawing around and showed it to the G.I.'s and company officers. "Ha, ha, ha! Look at that, man. The Last Supper! Ain't that a peach. Ain't that a ripper?" No one laughed. As a matter of fact, no one even smiled. All he got were some red faces and some blanched faces and some frozen stares. "There are some things," said the C.O., "that just aren't funny, Ruckman." But Ruckman thought it was a howl. He had "outdone" the most original of originals. He laughed about it.

Someone else laughed too (Psa. 2), whom he didn't hear.

The Bookkeeper had made another entry.

Ruckman returned to the 86th Division in the summer of 1946, but discovered he had been replaced as a DI. Furthermore, the "point system" had changed. Most of the 86th was going home. They had their thirty points in and the law now was that you could return stateside if you had even twenty-five points. All Ruckman had left was about a year and one month and the way things were shaping up they would probably lower the points again. He might not have to stay over a year.

But here everything stopped. He remembered Paul Baumer (1918), "But here my thoughts stop. There are emotions, feelings, and desires to be sure, but no aims, no goals. If we had returned in 1916 perhaps we could have unleashed a storm, but now we shall go back burnt out, wasted, useless." What was that he said? "And I fear in the end we shall fall into ruin."

Ruckman stuck his nose into Regimental HQ and found out two things. One: if a man wanted to stay in and complete his hitch, or be a thirty-year man, his best bet was to volunteer to go to Japan (GHQ, MacArthur). This was the route to take to "climb the ladder." Two: if he went home, he would still have to finish his hitch (Ruckman's ended June of 1947) unless he "re-upped," in which case he would probably be shipped right back out to Japan or Germany. Ruckman added two and two and got five. He decided to volunteer for Japan. That was the home of Zen Buddhism; in his artistic imagination he fancied going from there somehow through China to Tibet. *"Lost Horizons!"* He did this and in doing it, he turned down his chance to go home in 1947. Instead, he wrote to "Janie Bess," and Diana to pack a steamer locker and meet him in Japan. When he informed his Company Commander of this decision, he had a Bible "pulled on him" for the first time in his life.

The CO of Dog Company was First Lieutenant Self, from Oregon (or Washington, I forget which). He was six feet one and sported a campaign hat, a handlebar moustache and was usually seen with a real live monkey on his shoulder. He wore a brace of 45s, of which he said: "I've only shot two things with these pistols: a German and a pancake." He had gotten mad at some tough pancakes an orderly had served him one time, and he had thrown them out of the tent and "drilled" them. On another occasion, in the middle of the night, Ruckman heard him shoot a lizard in the jungle outside their Quonset hut. The sound effects were marvelous:

"Crash, smash" in the bushes. CHEOWW! Off went the .45.

"Tuckooo! Tuckoo!" said the lizard, who had been keeping them awake for nearly an hour. "Crash! Crunch! CHEOW! CHEOW!" Two more rounds. "Tukoo! Tukoo! CHEOWW!" "Tuk . . . CHEOW! . . . uhoooooooooo . . ." Silence. Then Self crashing back through the bushes.

To this day Ruckman has never found out whether Lt. Self was a Christian, but when Self found out that Ruckman was not going home to see his wife and baby, he sicked the Catholic chaplain on Ruckman; he preached to him about "duties" and said that "duty to country" came after "duty to family." Ruckman got "religious" and said, "What about duty to God?" The chaplain couldn't handle that but he assured Ruckman that "God" wanted him home with his family. Having no family of his own, and having drunk regularly at the officers' bar with Ruckman, the "Sky Pilot" had about as much influence as Vice-Principal Stark.

But the week before the 86th shipped out (or at least those men and officers who had the required points), Lt. Self showed up at the orderly room with a *King James New Testament*. "You're always readin' stuff, Ruckman," he said, "Let me read you something out of this." To this day no one will ever know what the CO was going to read, because Ruckman said insolently, "Ah, put that away! At's a lotta BALONEY." And Lt. Self put it away. Ruckman had just called The Holy Bible "pig meat."

The Bookkeeper made another note.

Lt. Self and company departed.

Ruckman had to make a trip to Manila to get some things for the new A&R officer, so he followed the truck convoy that carried Self and two or three dozen 86th Division officers and men. He stood on the pier as they left and waved to them as they stood on the stern of the

G.I. "Big Time Operator"

ship. Ruckman razzed them; "So long, suckers! I'll tell the Geishas all about you. So long boys. Tell 'em Ruckman said —'em." Lieutenant Self leaned against the stern rail. He didn't wave back. He had a sad look on his face. When Ruckman thought about it, driving back to Angeles, it seemed to him that the "old man" looked like he had been wounded; he had a "hurt" look on his face. Ruckman attributed it to nothing but constipation until years later, when he began to have some experience with Christians who failed their Lord in an undertaking. Self had failed. There was something going on in his mind between him and Someone whom Lt. Ruckman had never met.

Now a ferocious depression settled in. All of his friends that he knew in Dog Company were gone. He was temporarily relieved of all his duties until a flight could be found for him out of Manila, and this turned out to be two weeks in Limbo. Two weeks of inactivity for Ruckman was the equivalent of two years in Hell for someone else. With renewed vigor he tried to dig up something exciting. He went on a ten-day "binge" that contained all the elements of a soap opera, horror story, cops and robbers, and a chapter from James Jones' *From Here to Eternity*. On the last night he outdid himself, as far as "records" are concerned, and after missing getting killed in a brawl in a night club where some character was knocking people out at fifteen feet with a metal ball attached to a chain (Manrikigusari, the Japanese called it), he walked home from Angeles to the Depot. It was long after midnight.

On this particular moonless night the stars were especially bright. There was no one on the road coming or going, and a half a mile out of Angeles he hadn't passed a jeep or a wagon. From his standpoint there was nothing unusual about the night at all. It was just that on this night some peculiar malevolent spirit was taking possession of him; it had oppressed him all the week, but now it seemed to have mounted his back and was gaining weight with every step he took. He was only about half-drunk, but his stride had slackened to a snail's pace. Once or twice he looked up at the stars and sighed. Once or twice he glared behind him as though sensing some ghoul or ghost might be pursuing him. No one was there.

MONOLOGUE:

"What is it all about? Why am I so miserable and disturbed? What the —! What difference does it make? Who gives a — anyway? —'em all, I say; —'em all! Get off my back. Who the — asked you for your opinion anyway? The dirty s.o.b., I shoulda cold— him and taken his wallet. —on it!" Another fifty steps. "Isn't there any end to this —thing? You broke all records tonight, buddy, what the —are you bitchin' about? I can't stand this! What the — is the sense of even trying? Ah, to Hell with it!"

NIGHT SCENE:

He was at the perimeter of the Philippino Scout Recruiting Depot. There was a circle of large bushes around the perimeter and just on the other side of these bushes was a Damulag hole (water buffalo wallow) where the Caribou wallowed in the water and mud in the rainy season. Right now it was bone dry.

"What the —! I need help. Help. That's what I need. Help. HEEELP!" He yelled it outloud. "HEELPP!"

The stars twinkled. There wasn't even a guard at this outpost to investigate.

He stopped in the middle of the water buffalo wallow; it was five feet deep, eight feet wide and twenty feet long. He stood upright, almost at attention, and, taking his overseas cap off, he looked straight up over his head. A thousand diamonds studded the vault of the Oriental midnight. They looked like the glittering bands wherewith an Oriental Sultan clasped the robes of his glory. There was a silence and then Ruckman cried out, "HEEELLPPP!"

He was greeted with more silence. If there was a "Bookkeeper" up there He didn't answer every time someone rang the doorbell; at least not people like Peter Sturges Ruckman.

"Is anyone up there?" called out the Infantry D.I. "Are you there, God? Or whatever they call you?"

Several stars winked merrily at him but the vast host gazed down with absolute, passive disinterest. This was "The Apathy of the Stars" he had painted. He had known about these things without having experienced them. "Apathy" shows a blind man staggering down the center of a large city street alone. There are no cars or people on the street. He is groping along and reaching blindly out ahead of him with both hands as though feeling for something. On either side the skyscrapers rise to heaven. The picture's perspective is "ground level" so you see it from the cement up through the raised foot of the blind man. Everywhere overhead are the stars; silent, apathetic, disinterested—completely detached. The man is alone in his blindness, his misery and his futile attempts to get help.

Ruckman found himself on his knees. He was crying. He wiped off his face with a dirty sleeve and then he began to pound the dirt with his fists. Why? Why? Why? *What was it all about?* He lay down on his belly in the dirt and began to compute. "You wanted to travel, well son, you've traveled. Traveling isn't the answer. You wanted sports, well son, you got the medals and you had the write-ups; that isn't the answer. You wanted to be a "man" did you—you know, a sort of Clark Gable, Gary Cooper, John Wayne, Cisco Kid type; well, here you are, just as macho as Pancho Villa and what do you have? You want love? You got it, and you got two beautiful blue-eyed blonds with it; one twenty-two years old and one about two years old. You want "sex"? You've had enough to last some men for a lifetime. What do you want for a nickel, beans? What did the books say? Didn't they say that "good health" was the greatest gift on earth? Well, you got that too, though you have abused every faculty of mind and body a man could abuse. What now? You wanted liquor, did you? Had enough? You've downed enough Cuba Libras, Rum and Tom Collins, Sidecars, Bacardis, and beers to float a battleship. What now? Your bills are paid, you owe no man anything. You can write poetry, play music, draw and paint—didn't the books say something about "talent"?—and here you are on your face in a mudhole."

He rolled over in the dirt, and looked straight up again. His mind was in a turmoil. He felt if he didn't blow his brains out in a few seconds they would explode anyway. "Heeeeeelp!" he called. This time he croaked it. The stars shone sweetly down; no, it wasn't "sweetly," it wasn't anything. The vast, incomprehensible universe stretched out above him like a thousand oceans over a drowning man. He was on the bottom. "God!" he called out, "God, if You are up there . . . ." He was barely able to continue, " . . . if you are up there You gotta help me! I need help! God, if I mean anything to you. If you are up there and anyone means anything to you, HELP ME! HEEEELLLP!"

He rolled over again on his belly and said between his teeth. "God, if you don't help me I'm a goner." It was a line he had heard in a hundred movies, but it was *the line* for this scenario.

He lay sobbing in the dirt for about fifteen minutes, then got up slowly and brushed the dirt off himself the best he could. Slowly he climbed out of the water buffalo hole and slowly he went off across the drill field to his Quonset hut just inside the "brush." Nothing happened; no one answered. In thirty minutes he was flat on his back and sound asleep. Out in the jungle some lizard sounded off: "Tuckoo, tuckoo!" He didn't hear it.

Outside, the still jungle air remained still, the oppressive jungle heat continued, the jungle stars blinked or remained constant until "Morpheus set the blazing stone that puts the dusty stars to flight." To all accounts (speaking strictly from the objective point of empirical scientific observation and phenomenalism), *there was no God*. There was no anything; just a drunken infantry officer "hitting the sack."

But the Book said **"whosoever shall call upon the name of the Lord shall be saved."** God's time was not Ruckman's time. The Silver Cup was not yet full. When it finally got full it would be turned completely upside down.

Three days later, Ruckman packed up and went back to Manila and on a steamy September night he hopped a converted "Flying Boxcar" to Tokyo. It was his first passenger flight. He was to make more than 2,000 in the next few years, but they would not be to carry a wicked, miserable, sinful, selfish sinner to Tokyo to sample the Geishas; they would be to carry "the BALONEY" to the ends of the earth. The cup was not yet full.

CHAPTER NINE

The Land
Of the Rising Sun

The plane rattled up to Iwo Jima and then landed in Tokyo. The cool, fresh, Fall air was a shock to him when he got out of the plane. He had evidently been in a "sauna" for over a year. His assignment was to be "Music Officer" for radio station JOAK (Radio Toyko). He was billeted in the Yuraku Hotel just behind the Dai Ichi building where "Mac" (General MacArthur) showed up every morning. His assignment was based on his college degree, which had recorded a "major in Radio Arts." To all purposes, he was a civilian. Still desiring to go the full "30" he was, at least temporarily, a civilian. He still wore the uniform twenty-four hours a day and carried a .45 when out on "missions." But there were no bayonets, there were no firing ranges, there were no base stakes or "fields of fire," there was no "fire in the hole" and no "creeping barrages" or "firing for effect." He felt like a fish out of water. He frequented the Kendo and Sumo matches. He studied Karate and Aikiddo. He went to the Kabuki dramas and the Shamisen and Koto concerts. He monitered light opera and grand opera and the ballets and concerts. His faithful servant, Yokoi-San, accompanied him on these trips; Yokoi could speak, read, and write Russian, English, and Japanese. They spent hours with Beethoven, Brahams, Schumann, Schubert, Puccini, Verdi, Rimsky, Korsakov, Mozart, Handel, Wagner, Mendelsson, and the Japanese folk music (Naniwabushi).

But the old animal instincts never departed. Quieted for a few weeks, they arose again, and there he was on the prowl for a "make." This time everything went completely to pieces in even worse fashion than the Oklahoma City incident and the dean's daughter. This time he stopped a young Japanese girl from committing hara-kiri because she had been forsaken by a G.I. lover, and her own people had cast her out. He talked this girl into a "new hope" and did not tell her that he had a wife and family. They got along fine. She cheered up and they even talked about going back to the States together. He got her hopes up high.

(The trouble with all of this stuff is that it assumes there is no God, no Ten Commandments, no accountability to God, no moral standards, no ethical obligations; only "adult consent" and "permissive life styles." The trouble with this stuff is that it is *living exactly according to what is being taught in the public schools now from first grade to post graduate.* True, no one tells you to LIE and no one tells you to SEDUCE anyone, but since both of you are ANIMALS, who got here accidently, since when are you *morally obligated* to each other, or anyone else? Do what "works"; do what works for "you." Ruckman was not an exceptional devil, he was just a normal devil like 90 percent of the American college graduates of today.)

NIGHT SCENE:

"I'm sorry, old boy, it must be dreadfully embarrassing for you and all that sort of thing." (British MP).

"You can't take her. She is not a professional. She is innocent, I tell you. She doesn't belong in this roundup."

"Sorry, Lieutenant, an order is an order, don't you know."

(Sure he knew; who in h— would know better than he would.)

"In she goes with the rest of them!" Slam! went the tailgate.

"But she is not a geisha! Her name is Kinui San and she is a clean girl!"

"Sorry, old top! Cheerio!"

RETROSPECT:

An electric train, plowing through the rain between Katsura and Tokyo. Peter S. is standing holding on to a strap, swaying as the cars rock back and forth. He is the only "white" man on the train. As far as that goes, he is the only "white" man in a radius of ten miles in any direction. Tears swim in his eyes. The dark brown oriental faces survey him cooly. They are absolutely without sympathy or compassion. The rain comes down. It comes down in sheets. It falls on the rice paddies, it falls on the rails, it falls on the cars; it falls on his heart.

"If I have wounded any soul today, if I have caused one foot to go astray, if I have walked in my own will or way . . . ."

Well, he certainly had. That is about all he had ever done for twenty-five years. Tears began to trickle down the cheeks. This was getting to be too frequent. He had just bawled his eyes out not two months ago in the water buffalo hole outside of Angeles. What was happening to him? Was this the infantry drill instructor? Was this the Lieutenant who punched his Company Commander out, sat on him, rolled him over, scissored him till he puked? Is this the second-story man who drove the cars at a mile-a-minute down the highway playing "chicken"?

"We have not done those things which we ought to have done, and we have done those things which we ought not have done and there is no help in us, but God be merciful to us, miserable sinners . . . ."

There it was. *There* was the right word; "MISERABLE."

Ruckman went back to his Buddhism, but then he hit another snag. Here was "The Noble Eightfold Path" and it included "right conduct" and "right speech." He could not proceed another foot, not even with the Zen Master Suzuki in Tokyo helping him out. He had to make things right. He did. He called Kinui-San to the station and in a private studio with Yokoi-San, as a witness, he told her the truth and the whole truth. They both wept copiously. Yokoi sat impassively through about fifteen minutes of it, and then he too began to weep. When it was over and the girl had run out to whatever fate awaited her, Yokoi-San came up to him and embraced him—a matter of honour had been settled—and said, "Lieutenant, Lieutenant, you need to go home. Please, sir, you need to go home." He didn't. He stayed another three months, but in those three months two things happened that finished him off, at least as far as the Army and Stateside were concerned.

FLASHBACK:

A Far East Command Conference, with all the bigwigs present. Ruckman sat in the balcony and watched American Congressmen, Syngman Rhee, Chiang Kaishek, members of the Japanese Diet, and MacArthur call the shots, for the next generation. He saw the ambassadors and attachés with their wives and their cocktails, and heard them joking about "the poor coal miners" in Hokkaido, and what to do with Iwo and Oki (Okinawa). They were going to give them back to the Japanese.

Ruckman, the old ex-dogface, sat in the balcony and burned. This was what he was going to give thirty years of his life to? Why he was a sucker, he was a chump. He and his kind were just pawns on a chess board. They went out and got shot at and died in the mud, rain, snow, and ice for THIS BUNCH. This bunch called the shots. A rage swept across him as he listened to the discussions through his interpreter. After you bail Russia out you let her steal half of Europe? After Patton gives the best performance of any General you have, the news media crucifies him for slapping a defector? You give Iwo back to the people you took it from at the cost of 12,000 lives? Who is behind all of this? He knew. Civilians. He was looking at an Army that was about to be controlled by the news media and politicians. He would not have foreseen Korea or Vietnam at that point, although Korea was "just around the corner," but when it came around the corner Mac would get his: the civilians would sack him.

At that point, Ruckman made up his mind not to reenlist. When his reenlistment came up in June he would not "re-up." He was going to get out.

From then on he was nothing but trouble to his superiors in JOAK and the Far East Command. He went AWOL from the Theatre of Operations at Christmas time in 1946 and lay around drunk on the beaches of Honolulu until he was ordered back. They couldn't court martial him because he had gone over his Colonel's head to get Eichelberger's signature on the order; it was an order to send swimmers to Oahu to compete in the Inter-Pacific Olympics. (Ruckman went and placed second in Breaststroke although he had been "out of the water" for four years and on beer and cigars for the same length of time.)

CONFRONTATION:

"What the —— do you mean going over my head to get to Honolulu?"

"Well, sir, I thought you knew all about it, I . . . ."

"You #!*$!! You knew —— well I didn't know anything about it! Do you realize I can have you court martialed?"

"Yessir."

"Well? Well?"

"No excuse, sir!"

"Ruckman, you !&&$#!#! how long have you been in this man's army?"

"Forty-six months, sir."

"Forty-six months!?! Why you talk like a man who has been in twenty years!"

"Yessir."

"Get the —— outta here. Here is your efficiency report. You were up for First Lieutenant again, but you screwed it up. Do you realize that you have been 'in grade' twenty-six months?"

"Yessir."

"Well, what do you have to say for yourself?"

"No excuse, SIR!"

"Dismissed!"

He could hear the Colonel cursing as he went out the door.

CONTACT:

At the Yuraku Hotel; near midnight. He had been meditating on the Diamond Sutra. Something drove home and made a contact. It was like a spark going across a gap, or a switch breaker slamming. For weeks he had been erasing all conscious thoughts but those on the doorknob (sometimes it was a candle), and then erasing the subconscious thoughts and dealing only with the "sub-liminal level." This had been going on for several weeks. The subliminal level was a place where not only your conscious thoughts but unconscious thoughts quit send-ing in "messages." On this level a peculiar type of "short wave" experience transpired. There were "gaps" in it: ". . . sssssssumm . . . the waves of . . . who know if the . . . zazaza . . . flip, blip, flip, blip . . . unknown to the great . . . static . . . those cliffs by the seas . . . static . . . undergirding a layer of paint . . . zzzzz . . . blink . . . the tree that is tallest . . . static . . . etc." But when the "breaker" hit there was a perfect NOTHING-NESS. He was in a vacuum. Furthermore, he could not locate his sense centers. It was like he was out in the room looking back at his body but the eyes (the organs of sense) were still viewing the room from the chair. It was a "wild scene," as the Hippies said much later, but it was a "good trip" as the Junkies would say later. (Ruckman always ran about ten to thirty years ahead of the pack.)

He was never able to "time" what happened that night for when he resumed his "normal self" he found himself lying in his bed at eight in the morning. He was aware of only one thing. That for some time during that "enlightenment" he had become completely FREE from all worry and care, all sorrow and misery. It must have been something like cocaine or opium, without the ex-pense. Never before had he experienced such freedom, such bliss. This must be what they called "HAPPINESS."

Having believed it was just that, Ruckman decided that Gotama, the Buddha, had "the answers" and now that he had "found the Way," he could return to the States and get out of the Service. (He never knew a real freedom and joy came from a rebirth that was **"NOT BY THE WILL OF MAN"** [John 1:13]. He had to learn that later.)

In the last few weeks before he left, Ruckman found himself very popular with the Japanese men in JOAK. He was invited out time and time again to Sukiaki and Saki dinners. He was always the only American present. Yokoi had spread the word on him so he was now "accepted." When they sat around the Hibachi and began to talk, Ruckman wanted to discuss Bach, Mozart, Beethoven, the twenty-two tone Oriental scale, and remote broadcasts, but every time that there would be a gap in the conversation, one of the Japanese would tell him (through Yokoi-San): "No talk music, Lieutenant. Talk BUDDHA." They knew that about him. He hadn't even told them of his experience in Prasna ("Samadhi" in Zen instead of "Nirvana"). They talked Buddha. They discussed the Shodoka (Song of Realization), the Vimalakirti Nirdesa Sutra, and the Sutras and Shastras of the Vaipulya sections.

On a cold winter day in February (1947) the General's grandson went down to the pier and boarded the USS General Morgan, whose destination was San Francisco. He was through with the military. He had had a full canteen of it, or at least all he could get short of combat; and there wasn't any combat to be had in the immediate vicinity. He sailed away, waving at faithful Yokoi-San, Arima-San, and Okochi-San, who had accompanied him to the ship.

CHAPTER TEN

Falling into Ruin

In the meantime, the Philippine Islands had been declared a free republic (July 1946), Mao had ordered an all-out war against Chiang Kai-shek in China (1946), and the British had stopped Jewish immigrants from returning to Palestine (August 13). In addition to this, a Vietnamese uprising against the French started a debacle that is not over yet (December 28). Nine Nazi "war criminals" were executed: Hitler, Goebbels, Himmler, and Goering all committed suicide, and Rudolph Hoess was left holding the bag as a scapegoat to bear the wrath of Communist Russia until 1988. He was in solitary confinement for more than forty years. The President of the AFL, William Green, having more sense than the congressmen who pass the Civil Rights Acts—warned all of the negroes in the union that they had better look out for Communists (September 15). The warning was that the Communists would use the negroes without really helping them; the warning came on the heels of a Soviet Supreme Federal Court declaring that customers could not be told WHERE to sit when riding in a vehicle involved in "interstate" commerce. The Fourteenth Amendment had begun to erase STATE distinctions, so the Federal Soviet judges could bring the entire nation to its knees before Washington, DC. The General Morgan plowed out through the north Pacific. It would make one stop at Honolulu before docking in Frisco.

The General Morgan was a luxury liner compared with the old Cape Mendicino, and its crew and passenger list was unique. They were the last of the "big parade." More than half of some five hundred passengers were twenty- and thirty-year-old men coming home to "muster out." The rest were men like himself who hadn't re-

enlisted and were going home to get out. He had refused
to "re-up" at the turn of the year and the present Army
regulations stated that all former reservists who wished
to get out of the Regular Army could go back to civilian
life provided they stayed in the Reserve. That was all
right with Ruckman; he wanted "out." Aboard the General Morgan were over a hundred negro troops, plus a
bevy of Red Cross nurses, WACs, and WAVEs; the journey had "possibilities." Walking the companionways one
could see the "payload"; washed-out warrant officers,
bleary-eyed corporals who had been busted from "sergeant," combat leftovers like himself who had failed in
the Armies of occupation and wound up as chronic alcoholics, top kicks and Marine "gunnies" (still immaculate
and "regulation"), and about fifty field grade officers
(Lieutenants, Captains, and Majors). The troop transport
commander was a Major.

Ruckman hadn't been on the ship two days when he
struck up a "relationship" (I believe that is the modern
term) with Helena Soon Kim, a Korean who lived in
Honolulu. They made plans.

At night, lying on a real bunk instead of a hammock
or canvas cot, Ruckman tried in vain to think of what he
would do when he got back. He still recited his "OM"
regularly and practised meditation, but there was no "strik-
ing fire" again as he had in the Yuraku Hotel. Furthermore, "The Noble Eightfold Path" was quickly narrow-
ing to a possum trail or a deer track; he had plans to
commit adultery as soon as possible. Buddhism had NOT
been the answer. It had been some kind of a temporary
expedient, or bridge (or dead end) to get him through a
period of time.

They docked at Honolulu, and then the troop transport commander did a very stupid thing. He gave the
officers shore leave Friday through Sunday and confined
the enlisted men to "quarters." Friday night he nearly had
a riot, and after a few hours he decided that "discretion
was the better part of valor," so he let the GI's off for
Saturday night. They had to be back on the ship by 1700
Sunday even though the ship was not due to weigh an-

chor till Monday morning. Ruckman went ashore Friday, shacked up in the Royal Hawaiian Hotel Friday night and lay around half-drunk on the beach with his concubine. Then he spent a little time Saturday night down in Hell's Half Acre (it is now called "Hotel Street") and returned to the ship Sunday morning at about 1000. He intended to pick up some things and go back to the "Acre" until at least 1700 Sunday night. But when he got to the ship, the major gave him an order. He wanted Ruckman to stay on the docks from 1600 to 1800 and examine every GI returning from Honolulu; they were to be searched for liquor; no booze was to be allowed to be taken on board. The situation was volatile, because the black and white troops were "integrated" below decks. (World War II had let down the bars on more than morality and discipline; America was preparing to return to the jungle, and in the 1960's it did just that.)

"An order was an order," so Ruckman stayed on the pier. He made the incoming men line up, but since all of them showed up at about the same time (ten to fifteen minutes before 1800), he made them wait till the zero hour. At zero hour he lined them up. There were about four hundred of them, a third being black. You could see the whiskey bottles hidden under shirts, wrapped in towels, and bulging through shaving kits. Ruckman made them lay everything at their feet so he could examine it. They stood at attention in ranks.

SMALL TALK:

"Got any booze on ya, soldier?"

"No, suh. No, suh!"

"Open that shavin' kit!"

"B-b-but Lootenant, you ain't gonna, you ain't gonna . . . IS YOU?"

"Zip it open."

With something like tears in his eyes the six-foot black bent over and unzipped the case. The pint, wrapped up in a towel, bulged in the middle of it. The black came to attention staring straight ahead; he was trembling.

"Sure you ain't got no white lightnin' in there, soldier?"

"Yassuh!"

"Okay, zip it up and board."

"Yassuh! YASSUH! Thank you, Lootenant! THANK YOU, SIR!"

He let more than two hundred quarts of liquor go on board. What the h—. These men had earned it. Didn't that dumb troop transport commander know anything about being a GI? To h— with it. Let the boys have a good time and enjoy themselves. Life was too short to be bugged.

For twelve hours after leaving Honolulu, the General Morgan resembled a Chinese fire drill with ducks on a pond trying to dodge lightning. Everything came completely to pieces. The fights that started down on B and C decks quickly progressed from fists to bed slats (Darwin's evolution) and from there to .45 caliber bullets ricocheting off the metal sides of the ship (more evolution). Drunks, who had passed out, blocked exits and companionways. Warrant officers were chasing Red Cross nurses all over the ship. A couple of SP's were too drunk to know what was going on.

Knowing that liquor had gotten onto the ship by some bootleg method, the TTC called Ruckman to account and roared, "Go down and quiet those men!" (All the wimps are not in the ropes.) Ruckman and a First Louey named "Tex" went below decks, but Ruckman refused to open the hatch and enter the compartment. The compartment was in "full swing," and you could hear the shots going off the bulkheads. Ruckman was a fool, true, but not THAT big a fool. But "Tex" was a little "green." He stepped in and hollered, "MEN!" SMACK! Somebody in an upper bunk punched him in the forehead. Tex yanked the guy out and smacked him right back in the mouth. Ruckman slammed the hatch and quickly went back up "topside." Some nurse ran screaming by him with a couple of drunks in full pursuit. Then there followed a classic of classics which would return to Ruckman's mind for more than forty-seven years, it was so "classical."

He ran into the TTC somewhere near the Officer's

Mess and the Major raised both hands in the air—face simply livid—and screamed, "I TOLD YOU TO GO DOWN THERE AND QUIET THOSE MEN!" Ruckman saluted and said, "But sir, there isn't any way on earth anybody could do that without a . . . ." Thrusting his red face to within an inch of Ruckman's nose, the TTC roared, "I'll have you court-martialed if you don't obey that order! I'LL HAVE YOU KNOW I'M RUNNING THIS SHIP!"

He would hear that voice for forty-nine years: "I'LL HAVE YOU KNOW I'M RUNNING THIS SHIP!" He wasn't running water. His ship was completely out of control; it was a floating disaster. "I'LL HAVE YOU KNOW I'M RUNNING THIS SHIP!"

Years later, in the ministry, he heard that voice a hundred times. One could not possibly miss the application if he "kept up with things." The League of Nations had said it. The Popes had said it. Napoleon and Charlemagne had said it. Hitler and Mussolini had said it. The Holy Alliance (and the United Nations) had said it. It was man's eternal boast, his eternal theme; HE COULD RUN THE WORLD WITHOUT GOD. The world he "ran" was a floating CATASTROPHE.

Ahab had gotten Naboth killed, and he went down to TAKE OVER his vineyard because Naboth wasn't around any more. The husbandmen (Matt. 21:38) got Jesus Christ killed and went down to take over his vineyard (Isa. 5) because Jesus was not around any more (they thought!). What men did was mistake the *mercy* and *blessings* of God for *progress* and *evolution*. What God did in history (Zeph. 3:8), they attributed to their own planning. "I'M RUNNING THIS SHIP." The "Ship of State" had been leaking from the top as well as the bottom ever since Cain knocked Abel's brains out. The General Morgan was like a ship with a busted rudder, rusted screws, a fire in the hold, and a mad-man for a pilot. Ruckman almost laughed in the major's face. He thought to himself, "Son, you ain't runnin' nothin' but your mouth!" But he didn't say it.

For punishment, Lt. Ruckman was confined to his

"quarters" the remainder of the trip. He couldn't have cared less.

As the ship entered the Golden Gate, the speaker was intoning, "Now hear this! You will be checked out on TE . . . ." Men were throwing hats, gloves, gas masks, Sam Brown belts, combat boots, mess kits, and overcoats over the fantail. They littered the ocean a mile behind the wake. No one wanted to bother with the stuff; besides, a lot of it had been stolen.

After a short stay at Fort Ord, Ruckman took a train for Tuscaloosa, Alabama. The last night in town (Frisco) he picked a fight in a bar with two sailors over some women; he kicked one halfway across the floor, and both the sailors retired. They left two "dates" in a booth. "Tex" got one, and Ruckman got the other. They slept in town that night. In the morning he boarded the train and headed EAST. The prodigal was returning. No matter how many pages it might have taken to describe his "sojourning," the Bible had summed it all up in less than one short paragraph: **"Not many days after the younger son gathered all together, and took his journey into A FAR COUNTRY, and there wasted his substance WITH RIOTOUS LIVING."** It is amazing how concise and accurate The Book is when describing sinners.

He arrived in Tuscaloosa, and there at the train station to meet him were his wife, several of the May family, and the little girl he had left back in 1945 when she was less than two months old. He was "home."

He didn't feel the least bit "at home." There was an invisible barrier there.

What was it that Paul Baumer had said back in 1918? "I want to feel at home here; I want to think myself back into those former times and again become a part of that which I once knew, but there is a terrible estrangement here. I do not feel at home. I must not think of this. I want to *belong*. I must feel *at home* here. But a feeling of strangeness will not leave me. I did not think that 'leave' would be like this!"

Mom May took one look, and her heart must have sunk down to her shoes. She had been praying for this

wretched profligate for nearly three years, and now, when
he stepped off onto the platform, what she thought she
saw was actually *there*: she saw a hard, tough, bitter,
wicked, vicious young man. If Janie saw it, she said
nothing. She was still in love, and she had been true to
her unfaithful partner the entire time that he was gone.

After scouting around for jobs, an opening came
with Giddens and Rester in Mobile, Alabama. Their station manager (Busby) had just opened up a new radio
station on Telegraph Road (WKRG), and one of Mom
May's relatives got Ruckman "in." With his wife and
child he moved to Crenshaw Street (north of "Five Points"
on Government Street) and went to work as a "morning
shift" announcer and disk jockey. Back he went to Shaw,
Dorsey, Goodman, ragtime, jazz, swing, and "country-
western" music. Spade Cooley, Eddy Arnold, and Tex
Ritter were at the heights of their glory. He read T. S.
Eliot, Somerset Maughm, Tennessee Williams, Van
Druten, George Orwell, Richard Wright, Hermann Hesse,
John Hersey, Thomas Mann, Maxim Gorki, and two dozen
others, and every issue of *Time*, *Life*, and *Look* that came
out.

His drinking slacked off for about three months, but
then it began to pick up again. The trouble was, he had
no roots. He could not "find himself." He joined an
announcer's union, lost his job at WKRG, and went to
work four weeks with the AFL in the Chickasaw ship
building works as an apprentice electrician. An
announcer's job opened in Pensacola at WEAR (Irving
Welch), where Russell Hirsch was program director, so
he went down there. By the summer of 1948 he was
getting write-ups in national magazines as a DJ the qual-
ity of Bob Poole (WWL, New Orleans) or Arthur Godfrey.
A bigger station (WABB, Chandler and Hearn of the
Mobile Press Register) hired him, and he moved back to
Crenshaw Street in Mobile.

In the meantime, England barred the Jews from returning to Palestine (after reneging on the Balfour Declaration), and the UN proposed to partition it (August 31,
1947). India—due to Martin Luther King's idol (Ma-

hatma Gandhi)—had turned into a killing ground with a hundred and fifty thousand casualties arising from his "non-violent, civil disobedience." Palestine was finally partitioned, and the Arab terrorists began a slaughter campaign that continues today (1998). Gandhi got assassinated, fourteen people got killed in Jerusalem (January 4), another seventy got killed in Iraq after a riot (January 27), and the Egyptian army killed another twenty-five in Cairo (April 5). Ruckman still lived and breathed. *Some folks live a charmed life.* In the middle of May (1948) Israel proclaimed itself to be an independent, sovereign state with Weizmann as its first president. The matter escaped Ruckman's notice completely, although it was the greatest event that had happened on this earth since the Resurrection. Later, he discovered that all the casualties and political complications of World War I had been for one purpose and one purpose only: TO PREPARE THE LAND FOR THE JEWS. All of the casualties and complications from World War II had served only ONE constructive purpose: they had PREPARED THE JEWS FOR THE LAND. (There was a Book somewhere, that Ruckman had never picked up, and IT was "running the ship!")

He went back to the beer bottles and began to fool around with oil paints. His watercolor technique had matured and had reached a point where it did not improve any more until the 1970's. Mom May prayed for her son-in-law. She had already one divorce in the family and didn't want another one.

Ruckman taught Janie how to sing popular ballads; he accompanied her on a guitar. Finally he landed her a job singing in a night club. That came to an end in the winter of 1948 when he accidentally ran into a *Mobile Press Register* big shot drinking at a table with the "wrong woman." Ruckman came up, unsuspecting, and greeted the man and his "wife," but it was not his wife. Error. ("So solly!" "Dreadfully embarrassing for you, old top, and all that sort of thing!")

A week before Christmas (1948) Ruckman came home from work *drunk*, as usual. The Russians had block-

aded Berlin (June), Whittaker Chambers and Alger Hiss had gotten caught for spying, Manchuria surrendered to Mao (October), and Pope Pius (October 23) had already tried his best to destroy Israel as a nation and "internationalize" the city as a religious shrine for Catholics and Moslems. (He never did recognize the state of Israel before or after 1949.)

Ruckman shuffled up Government Street and stopped before a small manger scene outside of a Catholic church (the Church of the Little Flower). It was cold and "Christmassy," and everyone was saying "Merry Christmas" and so forth. As far as Ruckman was concerned, the whole thing was "Bah, humbug!" For some reason he stopped at the manger scene; it was probably because they were playing a little recording there of his favorite childhood carol, "O little town of Bethlehem, how still we see thee lie. Above thy deep and dreamless sleep the silent stars go by . . . ." The silent stars go by. *The Apathy of the Stars.* "Yet in thy dark streets shineth the everlasting light, the hopes and fears of all the years are met in thee tonight."

There he stood: five feet eight, a hundred and sixty-five pounds, thirty inch waistline, moustache, light grey suit, black shirt, yellow necktie, four cigars in each shirt pocket, eight beers under his belt. The record began to play, "Joy to the world, the Lord is come. Let earth receive her King! Let every heart prepare him room, and heaven and nature sing . . . ."

What was it all about? "Joy to the world." What was that? What was this "joy"? Everyone laughing and smiling. He had been fighting with his wife for eight months, and she didn't even know what he had done in the Philippines and Hawaii and Japan. "Joy to the world"? H—, he didn't have any "joy." *What was "joy"?*

A big tear ran down the bronzed face and trickled off onto the yellow necktie. Good salary? Sure: he was making eighty dollars a week (and back in 1948, that was worth four hundred dollars in the 1980s). Good health? Not a stomachache or a toothache or a headache in a year. Family? Healthy wife and child. Talent? He could play drums, guitar, bass fiddle, and harmonica, and he could write poetry, cartoon, sketch, and paint. WHAT WAS WRONG? He felt like a condemned criminal before his own conscience, but when facing his past he felt like he had been robbed by criminals. *The criminals were his teachers.* Someone had deceived him; they had led him into a blind alley. Another tear coursed down his cheek. Ruckman was "under conviction" and *didn't even know it.*

On a sudden impulse he walked around the scene and up the path to the door of the parish priest's house. Without knocking, he opened the door, marched right into the living room, and confronted a young priest. Miracle of miracles, the "father" was reading a Bible! Without so much as a "good evening" or "pardon me" or "how are you?" Ruckman asked, "What does the good Book say, Father?"

Absolutely "out of character." This was the Book he had called "baloney"—pig's meat.

The "Reverend" looked down and read the next verse, (or at least from the same page where he was reading.) It said, **"Let the wicked forsake his way, and the unrighteous man his thoughts: and let him return unto the LORD, and he will have mercy upon him; and to our God, for he will abundantly pardon"** (Isa. 55:7).

Ruckman sat down hard (it was more like collapsing) into a chair.

DIALOGUE:

"What's the trouble, young man?"

He told the priest the "trouble," but he told him all the details (as they do NOT appear in this autobiography). The priest's face paled. He had heard all kinds of stories, but nothing like THAT one.

"You are in real trouble, young man," he said, "REAL trouble."

"You're telling me? What the h— can I do about it?"

"You'd better pray."

"I don't know how to pray."

"Well, you had better pray anyway."

"Well, what should I pray?"

"You had better ask God Almighty to HELP you."

"Okay, I'll do it." So he got up and went home and lay down in bed and said, "God help me" and went to sleep. The next day he was fired from WABB. The boss was afraid that he would talk about the nightclub incident.

And that "tied the rag on the bush." Ruckman went out and got stewed again; he came home and sat his wife down, and gave her the whole gruesome, miserable history from June 1944 to December 1948. He told her to take Diana and get on back on the farm where she belonged and forget him. He was going to "hit the road." She argued with him; she did not want a divorce.

Finally he said, "All right, I'll go back to Pensacola, and if I am able to get work I'll send for you and Diana." She didn't want that either, but had to settle for it. (She had heard that line before when he went to Japan.)

When the new year came in (January 1) he was "riding gain" and back at the turntables (the Old Gate's console) in WEAR as a DJ. He was playing in "hillbilly" bands at night as the drummer. The drinking picked up. He played drums for Bill Hendrix and his "Gulf Coast Serenaders" and Buddy Pelham's "Top Rail Wranglers." They played in "posh" joints—"nothing but the best"— The Gulf Seafood and Oyster Bar, Jack's Place, The Peppermint Lounge, The Green Gables, The Coral Club, The Diamond Horseshoe, etc. Nothing but the best: Cowboy Copas, Bob Wills, Hank Williams, Tex Ritter, Eddy Arnold, Moon Mullins, Ernest Tubbs, and so forth.

Back to the wallow; back like a dog to his vomit.

A chemical plant blast in Ludwigshafen had just killed two hundred and fifty people, the Yangtze flood had left three million people without homes (August 1948), and race riots in South Africa had done away with a hundred lives, but Ruckman lived on. The Communist Chinese armies took possession of Peking, and in America construction began on a thirty-nine story, 5,400 window monstrosity which would occupy seventeen acres in Hell City, USA: New York. (New York was called "Stink City" by its sanitary department and "Death City" by its police force.)

Ruckman wallowed in the wallow. He had no intention of ever getting his family back together again this time, but as far as that goes, he had no intention of doing anything else, either, except perhaps drinking himself to death. He was twenty-seven years old, but he had lost all interest in life. He couldn't even tell you what "life" was. All he was acquainted with was **"the pleasures of sin for a season"** (Heb. 11:25), and the viper's bite at the bottom of the cup. He had reached the terminus forty-three years before his allotted **"threescore and ten."** He was no longer interested in anything. He was burned out. *"Burned out" at twenty-seven.*

CHAPTER ELEVEN

The Overlooked Book

He was sitting in the Bell Cafe on Palafox Street, drinking beer. It was about ten p.m. There was nothing unusual about the night, except that he had stayed a little longer and drunk a little bit more than usual because of the company. Two Filipino sailors (now in the U.S. Navy) had shown up, and they had engaged him in some "pleasantries" that had lasted a while. One of them was originally from Angeles. Somewhere around beer number six, the conversation turned to Formosa and the Chinese army. They told Ruckman that there was a real need for American officers to train Chiang's army, and that DI's in hand-to-hand were few and far between. One of them, who had been on Formosa (Taiwan), swore that he knew of the need for such officers. He said the pay would be eight thousand dollars a year, plus room and board, uniform, and so forth. In the 1980's that would have been about thirty-two thousand dollars a year plus benefits. Somewhere around beer number eight the Flips got up and left.

Ruckman sat alone in the booth. The restaurant was still filled with cigarette smoke, although a crowd had thinned out somewhat since nine p.m. Three booths down, a couple of floozies were trying to get his attention. He had lost interest in THAT also. He dropped his gaze to his beer and then slowly surveyed the scene. The Nickelodeon (juke box) was playing Nat King Cole; it had played Petula Clark, Kay Starr, Vick Damone, and Peggy Lee before that. Same old music.

Same old music, same old smoke, same old crowd, same old beer, same old loneliness. Ruckman felt like he was two hundred years old: he looked forty. Would he go back over the pond and try again'? H—, no. It was too

— far. He wasn't going back there again. Slant eyes, brown skins. Go through that mess again? He remembered the water buffalo hole in Pampanga. No, not again. Maybe a war would break out, and he would get into the action. Chiang hadn't been run out of China yet, but he would be shortly. No, not that. Not the bayonet drills all over again; not trying to "save face" before the Gooks.

He stared blankly around him. He was twenty-seven years old, but he had never owned a car or even lived in a house since he was nineteen years old. He couldn't even write out a check. He had no bank account. He had two suits of clothes, an overcoat, two pairs of shoes, a sweater, some shirts and pants, and underwear. What was he good for, anyway? All he knew was how to kill people. Do you want to know what to do at *night* when an unseen assailant is waiting for your muzzle blast and you're waiting for his? Yell, with your mouth right on the ground; he can't tell which direction it is coming from and he'll fire first. Do you want to see him on a moon-lit night when he is in the shadows? Look to the right or left of him. Don't look straight at him. Now, what could you do with THAT in civilian life?

He couldn't fix a car; he couldn't have even fixed a lawn mower or a toaster. He could cut a string tied around a tree at fifteen feet by throwing a hatchet at it. He knew how to garotte a man, and he knew that if you stabbed him between the collar bones near his jugular he would bleed to death in twelve seconds; it had been timed. Isn't *that* practical? Tie a cable at about one hundred and forty degrees to the road and when he comes down it at night, on the cycle, it will guide him into the ditch at forty m.p.h. Put a wire at ninety degrees across, and sometimes you can decapitate him. Amazing what knowledge can do for one, isn't it? He had never borrowed money at a bank, he had never filled out an income tax form. What was he good for? Well, when a big one comes at you, you crouch and come up with hands crossed, blocking outward. You kick as you come; if he kicks before you do, you already have a trap for his foot. If he delays he will wince when the kick hits his groin; then your hands will be inside his—Kureneko (four fingers spread out with two on each side) to the eyes. I don't care how big he is; a blind man can't do much in the way of counter-attacking.

To h— with it! He wasn't going. Let the Gooks train their own Gooks. He gazed around the room. The waitress said, "Can I get you something else?" and he grumbled, "No, gimme the check." While she wrote it out, he finished number eight. He crumpled the check and looked around the room one last time.

Time was up.

His time had run out.

Time to pay the piper.

Time to pay for the party.

He didn't care if the clock passed midnight, or not. He made up his mind. There was nothing sensational about it. No "Farewell, cruel world," and all that jazz. Just short, sweet, and simple. Put the muzzle in your mouth; that's the way the Japs did it. No misfires. If you put it on your temple, sometimes the bullet ricocheted or it didn't go in straight. Right up on the roof of the mouth, that would "cut the mustard." He would blow his brains out. He had thought about it before, but now it was more than a thought; it was a resolution. He would steal a pistol from somewhere. Stealing a pistol out of someone's house would be as easy as eating a bowl of cornflakes. He would get one that night, or in the morning, and end it. It wouldn't matter. No letters to his wife or anyone else. To H— with it. To H— with the whole d— mess!

He got up and went to the register. He was about third in line. While he stood there, he puffed on his cigar and fingered the check. Finish it. That was the ticket. He had tried everything, and nothing had worked. Wind it up. "Pop off," as the Limeys say.

At that moment, a voice just as clear and distinct as a radio announcer's said, "YOU NEED TO GET A BIBLE."

He turned to see who had said this to him. There was no one there. He was the last in the line. Ruckman shook his head and attributed it to "hearing voices." He turned back into line and fished for some dollar bills to pay for his beers. There it was again, slow, quiet, but absolutely distinct. "YOU NEED TO GET A BIBLE." He turned again; again no one was there. Ruckman said to himself, "Too many beers," but that didn't do the job. Blankly, like an automaton, he paid his check, but his mind was elsewhere.

FLASHBACK:

"Now, look, that wasn't you. You know YOU. Remember Samadhi and the Sutras, Shastas, Vedas, and the Puranas? Yes. Well, what was *that* voice? Did you ever hear THAT one before?"

No, he hadn't. It wasn't his conscious voice, for certain, and it did not resemble any of the subconscious, or even subliminal levels he had tested. This voice was Something unique. Where could it be coming from? What was its source? "You need to get a Bible." Who could be telling him that? Why would he need a "Bible"? What could possibly be in that Book that he hadn't read a dozen times, in other books? Could it be that he had missed something? *Missed something?* Wouldn't he be a fool to blow his brains out if there was something yet he DIDN'T know about? What if this unknown Book had some "answers" in it? What then?

He had gone out the front door of the Bell Cafe. The pavement shone with a red light, reflected off a neon sign over the Rhodes Furniture Store, on his right. Across the street next to the San Carlos Hotel, stood St. Michael's, the Roman Catholic church. "YOU NEED TO GET A BIBLE," the voice persisted.

"All right," said Ruckman out loud, "if I need to get a Bible, I'll get a Bible. An order is an order." (Back in high school someone had told him to go to Hell, so he had gone down to the French Quarter in New Orleans; that was the nearest place he could find to it at that time.)

So down the street, at eleven p.m., went Peter S. Ruckman, looking for a "Bible." Naturally, everything was closed. In a half-drunken search, he walked up on the porches of several houses, going down Garden Street (westward), looking into the windows. At last, he looked into a window of a cheap boarding house, and there, lying at the bottom of a bed, half-hidden by a pile of old newspapers, was a very old dimestore *King James Bible;* it had no front cover. The occupant of the room was passed out cold, lying face down on the bed. Ruckman jimmied the lock, got into the room, and stole the Bible. He then went on to his own room, turned on the light, got up on the bed, and held the Book up on his knees. He then said to himself, "Now, if this Book is more than any other kind of a book, wherever I open it it will speak to me personally." (He said this because he had noticed that that was one of the characteristics of the Hindu and Buddhist literature. What he didn't know was that he had an Oriental Book in his hand: every writer in it was a *Shemite.* Furthermore, he had now in his hands a copy of the oldest book ever written on this earth: the book of Job, written before 1700 B.C.)

Ruckman closed his eyes, opened the Book, placed his finger at a passage, and then opened his eyes and read. He read Ezekiel 28:2–3. The words hit him like a jackhammer. He nervously skipped verses 4 and 5 and landed on 6–10. Upon completing verse 10, he threw the Book across the room under the dresser. He sat on the bed in a state of shock, but he recovered himself quickly and said, "Why you stupid nut, what are you getting upset about? It's just a — book. What the H— are you getting upset about a *book* for? It's just print on paper. It can't hurt a flea. I'll go over and try it again." He went over and picked the Book up, came back to the bed, and repeated the process. When he opened his eyes this time he read Deuteronomy 28:20–24. He threw the Book across the room again, and went out and walked two miles to a joint that was still open, and got stoned. When he came home at two a.m., he passed out until eleven a.m. the next morning.

Now began the strangest combat that ever took place in Pensacola, and perhaps the United States as well (and maybe the whole world). It was never filmed, never broadcast, never put in print, and never published by anyone.

What began was a duel between a man and a Book. For four weeks Ruckman would come in, drunk, open the Book and read it. Every time he did, the Book would do everything but skin him alive. He used to stagger in, look in the mirror, hold the Book up in front of the mirror, and then say, "C'mon, tell me somthin' good about myself! There must be SOMETHING good about myself. Tell me ONE GOOD THING!" Open would go the Book. Pop! **"There is not a just man upon earth, that doeth good and sinneth not."** Pop! **"Every man at his best state is altogether vanity."** Pop! **"And I will cast abominable filth upon thee, and make thee vile,"** Pop! **"Can thine heart endure, or can thine hands be strong, in the days that I shall deal with thee? . . . I will make thy grave; for thou art vile . . . . The LORD shall smite thee with madness and blindness . . . . And thou shalt grope at noonday, as the blind gropeth in darkness, . . . The LORD shall smite thee in the knees, and in the legs, with a sore botch that cannot be healed, from the sole of thy foot unto the top of thy head . . . . moreover all these curses shall come upon thee, and shall pursue thee, . . . so the Lord will rejoice over you to destroy you, . . . And thy life shall hang in doubt before thee; . . . In the morning thou shalt say, Would God it were even! and at even thou shalt say, Would God it were morning! . . . Depart from me, ye cursed, into everlasting fire, prepared for the devil and his angels: . . . Ye are of your father the devil, and the lusts of your father ye will do . . . . having eyes full of adultery, and cannot cease from sin; . . . Fill ye up then the measure of your fathers . . . . Ye serpents, ye generation of vipers, . . ."**

Not once did he stumble on John 3:16 or John 5:24, or John 10, or Matthew 11:21–24. It was "thunder and lightning stewed down to a fine poison" everytime he opened the Book. In four weeks he lost twenty pounds and was reduced to a nervous wreck.

In a panic one night, he broke into the parish house at St. Michael's and seized "Father" Sullivan by the cassock and cried, "You got anything real, Father?"

The Catholic priest smiled and knocked the ashes off of his own cigar and said, "Well, that all depends on what you're looking for, my boy."

"Well," said Ruckman, sitting down, "I've been half-way round the world looking for it, and I can't find it. I'm tired of sports, I'm tired of travel, I'm fed up with men and women, I'm bored with books and music and art. I'm up to here with everything. If there is ANYTHING 'real' in this life, I want it. YOU GOT IT?"

Sullivan smiled and said, "What you need to do, my boy, is join the church!" So from early February to the middle of March, he took convert courses from a Jesuit priest who had graduated from Loyola. At the end of four weeks, Ruckman knew the priest only knew one or two things that Ruckman didn't know, but what Ruckman knew that he didn't know would fill a library. But on they went: the perpetual virginity of Mary, the sacrifice of the Mass, extreme unction, the assumption of Mary, the ex cathedra fiats of the Pope, Trappists and Dominicans, absolute contrition, the seven sacraments, penance, and so forth. Ruckman went to Mass, crossed himself everytime the Angelus rang, and flipped the beads. He wound up wearing the ashes on his forehead all day on Ash Wednesday, and he took the palm leaf home on Palm Sunday and laid it on the shelf. He began to give alms to beggars, and was "tithing" into the coin box before his conversion to Christ. If "religion" could have saved anyone, it would have saved Peter S. Ruckman. He was a good Catholic. Still, there was no emotional rest or peace of mind.

He hated the Book and feared it, but he could not quit *reading* it. One night he came in and opened up to Revelation 3. There he was informed that he was **"wretched, and miserable, and poor, and blind, and naked."**

He laughed and slammed the Book shut and said, "Well, now THAT'S a lie! I may be wretched and miserable, but I sure as H— am not blind!''

The next morning he broke his glasses, and it took two days to get them fixed. He couldn't read the copy

Illustration for the Book of Revelation (Revelation 17)

well without them. He went back to his flophouse, opened the Book, and found the same passage and read again.

"Well," he said (to the Book), "I'm not *naked*, that's for sure."

The next day one of the two suits that he had (and it had just gotten back from the cleaners) disappeared right out of the radio station where he had hung it on a rack. It never showed up again, and to this day no one knows what became of it. Back he went to the terrible Book, opened it up, and glaring at Revelation 3 he said. Well I'm still making sixty dollars a week. I ain't *poor* yet! and slammed the Book shut.

He never should have said that. The next night, while playing in the dance band someone stole his billfold: he had saved up part of three weeks' pay and kept it there. He never found the billfold or the money.

He fasted, he prayed, he tithed, he "Hail Mary"-ed till she hailed back, he attended Mass; he still kept taking the convert courses, and he even gave up beer and whiskey for "Lent." But there were no terms of surrender; no quarter was given. Everytime he opened the Book it poured in the shot and shell: **"Behold, ye are of nothing, and your work of nought: an abomination is he that chooseth you . . . . ye shall cry for sorrow of heart, and shall howl for vexation of spirit . . . . and ye shall leave your name for a curse unto my chosen, for the Lord God shall slay thee, and call his servants by another name: . . . And mine eye shall not spare, neither shall I have pity: I will recompense thee according to thy ways and thine abominations that are in the midst of thee; and ye shall know that I am the** Lord **that smiteth . . . ."**

Terrible combat. You couldn't locate your enemy. You couldn't see your enemy. You couldn't fire back. When would He wipe you out? How would He do it? "Conscience makes cowards of us all." So now Peter S. was engaged in a battle he had no heart for; his conscience recalled every item from the first time he stole a penny from his mother's purse to the last woman he had committed adultery with. The Book never let up: **"Cursed** be the man that trusteth in man, and maketh flesh his arm, and whose heart departeth from the LORD . . . . I also will laugh at your calamity; I will mock when your fear cometh; When your fear cometh as desolation, and your destruction cometh as a whirlwind; when distress and anguish cometh upon you . . . . ye have done worse than your fathers; . . . Therefore will I cast you out of this land into a land that ye know not, . . . I will not shew you favor . . . . I will make thy grave; for thou art vile . . . . The LORD shall send upon thee cursing, vexation, and rebuke, in all that thou settest thine hand unto for to do, until thou be destroyed, and until thou perish quickly; because of the wickedness of thy doings, . . . the LORD shall smite thee with a consumption, and with a fever, and with an inflammation, . . . And thy carcase shall be meat unto all fowls of the air, and unto the beasts of the earth, . . . They shall bring thee down to the pit, and thou shalt die the deaths of them that are slain in the midst of the seas . . . . go down, and be thou laid with the uncircumcised . . . . with them that be slain by the sword . . . ."

His "random" selections never landed one time on 1 Corinthians 13, Romans 10, Ephesians 1, or a dozen other places. It was "hell on wheels" for nearly two months.

Then one Saturday night, in early March, the "boys in the band" asked him to play an all-night stand; seven p.m. to midnight at the Coral Club, and then one a.m. till five a.m. at the Green Gables.

"Naw," said Ruckman, "I can't make it. I'm off beer for Lent and we always get drunk everytime we go to that dump."

"Aw, c'mon, Ruckman. Don't go gettin' religion! C'mon, man, good pay! Two bucks an hour!"

They finally talked him into it. They went and played both joints and sampled some women between the "sets." He came home drunker than a hoot owl, at about six in the morning, set his alarm for "Mass" and went to sleep. He opened one eye at ten a.m. and slapped the alarm off and went back to sleep. He did not get up till six-thirty Sunday evening.

He walked into the bathroom, turned on the light, and began to shave. One look in the mirror, and his mouth dropped open. There were red bumps all over his face, and some of them looked like they had pus in them. A man that had lived like he had lived could only think about one thing. But before he could think about it long, a voice—the same one that had arrested his attention in the Bell Cafe—said, **"I shall smite thee from the crown of thy head to the sole of thy feet with sores and blemishes and thou shalt know I am the Lord God Almighty that smiteth!"** He dropped the razor in the basin and ran back into the bedroom and got down on his knees by the bed, for a one-man prayer meeting. The room was already getting dark. And there on his knees, with the sweat now popping out on his forehead, the debauched libertine reviewed his past. While he did it, the same quiet voice said, "You're going to Hell." It came out just like that: *"You're going to Hell."*

He looked around the room. Just as he had suspected, there was no one else present to whom he could "refer" the message. It was *him*: he was going to Hell. Ruckman stared into the dark, and that old Topeka motion picture projector (chapter four) rolled off the footage. He thought of where he had been, who he had seen, who he had talked to, what he had said, and what he had done; and he said out loud to himself, "Yessir, Peter S., old boy, if any man was ever going to make Hell, YOU are going to make it. If there ever was a candidate, YOU are it!"

The voice said, "You've got to find Christ tonight."

Well, *"Befehl ist Befehl"* (an order is an order), so up he got. He threw on his shoes and pants, and without tying his shoes, buttoning his shirt, or shaving, he ran out to the street into a light spring rain. He didn't know where he was going, except that "Christ" must be in a church. So he ran down Garden Street to "A" Street and turned up "A" Street, intending to go east to St. Michael's. But the second block up, "A" Street sported a small brick

Missionary Alliance Church, and on the front of the church
was a neon sign that said, "GOD LOVES YOU." It was
after seven p.m., and as Ruckman approached the building in the gathering darkness, he heard the sound of
congregational singing inside. He came up to the building and peeked in the half-open doorway. "Go on in and
get on your knees and find Christ."

"DON'T BE A FOOL, GO ON BY!"

Another actor had "stepped out of the wings" or
something. This was a new voice; it wasn't *his* either.
The new voice said sarcastically, "What do you mean,
'God loves you'? Why, if God loved you, he wouldn't
send you to hell, now, would He? Go on by!" He went on
by.

The Voice said, "If you don't find Christ tonight,
you are never going to find Him." He ran down to St.
Michael's and tried to get in, but it was locked. He ran
up Palafox to Wright Street and tried the First Christian
Church; it was locked. He ran east on Wright Street to
the large stone Methodist Church at the top of the hill. It
was open, but evidently the Sunday night congregation
was so small they were meeting in a backroom behind
the auditorium. As he walked up the steps in the rain, he
could hear something like a choir practice. By now, he
was soaking wet.

DIALOGUE:

"Now, you go in there and go down that aisle and
get on your knees and find Christ."

"Don't be a fool. What if somebody comes in? They
all know you in this town. You've been announcing here
two years. Look at your shirt and your pants. You don't
have a shave. Don't be a fool!"

*"If you don't find Christ tonight, you will never find
Him."*

He started in. He got halfway through the lobby and
ran back out. The aisle looked a hundred yards long.

*"Go back in. Go down there and get on your knees
and find Christ!"*

"Don't be a fool! You're just gettin' over a hangover. This isn't real. You crazy nut! What are you doing

out here running around in the rain, anyway? Go home and sleep it off!"

He started home to sleep it off. He got to the bottom of the steps, and then for no reason he could find, he turned, went back up the steps and into the building. Down he went to the altar and fell on his face. He was there for thirty minutes, and not a man, woman, or child put a foot in the auditorium while he was there.

Back in some room in the "plant," a small group of Christians were rehearsing a number, or else singing at a "fellowship." They were singing "Rock of Ages." As Ruckman knelt there, numb with sin, mute with ignorance, and exhausted with life, he heard the words: "Should my tears forever flow, should my zeal no langour know, all for sin could not atone: Thou must save, and Thou alone. In my hand, no price I bring, simply to Thy cross I cling!"

Ruckman tried to pray. He didn't know how to pray. All he knew was, "Hail Mary" and "Our Father," so he just poured out what was left of his soul.

MONOLOGUE:

"Lord, I'm tired. I'm wet, and I'm cold. Lord, I can't take any more of this. I am so tired, so very tired. I don't know where 'home' is. I don't know how to get back to You. But I am so d— tired. I've been beaten, cussed, lied to, stolen from, shot at, and here I am drunk and I don't have any money and my family is gone and I'm tired. It's cold and dark out here, Lord. Lord, will you please take me back? I mean, take me 'HOME'? Where is HOME, Lord? If I came from You, I want to come back. I've had enough of this; I can't take one more minute more. I am a miserable sinner, I have hurt people all my life, and I am hurting myself, and I hurt. I hurt. I'm so d— tired. Please take me home: let me come home!"

The choir intoned: "When I've drawn life's fleeting breath, when my eyelids close in death, when I rise through worlds unknown, and behold Thee on Thy throne. Rock of Ages, cleft for me, let me hide myself in THEE!"

He got up, blew his nose on his sleeve, wiped his

tears off of his cheeks, and went on out to walk home in the rain.

The sarcastic voice said, "Sleep it off. You're losing your mind, Rucky. See a shrink next week and get things straight. Sleep it off." So he did. He went back to the "pad" and "slept if off."

But at five thirty the next morning, it was "something else." He had to get up that early to get the transmitter warmed up so WEAR would be on the air by seven A.M. It allowed him time to get dressed, walk about a mile and a half, and "breakfast." But when he started down the street, he began to hear chimes (church bells). *There are no church bells ringing at five thirty from any church in Pensacola.* That isn't all; these bells were accompanied by some "humongous" choir that sounded like ten thousand voices. They were singing "Praise the Lord!" and "Glory to God!" and "Alleluia!" and "Bless the Lord!" Ruckman weaved down the street like he had not yet slept off his hangover. He shook his head like a man trying to get water out of his ears after submerging. No dice. The singing and the bells continued for nearly ten minutes. He never found out what they were, or where they came from.

He opened the station. Sometime before mid-morning, Hugh Pyle came into the studio. He was pastor of the Brent Baptist Church in north Pensacola, just outside the city limits. He had spoken to Ruckman before, but Ruckman had never paid much attention to him. This time, however, Ruckman watched every move he made while broadcasting.

"Now, you see that preacher in there? He is what you would call a 'man.' If you don't think so, just check his water when he comes out . . . ."

OLD SARCASTIC:

"Now, you see that little, skinny, anemic sissy sitting in there? He's never drank anything stronger than buttermilk. What the h— could he know about anything?"

"Now, if you don't believe that man has what you call 'guts,' why don't you just check him when he comes out."

**Illustration for the Book of Revelation
(Matthew 23:27–28)**

Illustration for the Book of Revelation
(Matthew 13:13–15)

He decided to check him. As Brother Pyle walked by the door of the control room, Ruckman said, "Hi, preacher, whaddya know?"

DIALOGUE:

The slightly built, sandy-haired young man turned and looked him right straight in the face and said, "I know the Lord Jesus Christ. What do YOU know?"

Well, that was a nasty turn of events. How did one answer THAT?

"Well," said Ruckman (not to be paralyzed by anybody), "I don't know Him."

"Would you like to know Him?" asked Pyle.

"Sure," said Ruckman without hesitating.

"Well, what are you waiting for?" asked the preacher.

What was he WAITING for? Man, what a stupid question! He had been trying to find the answers for most of his life, and he had been working like a dog to know something about Christ for more than two months.

"What do you mean, what am I waiting for?"

"Come here," said Hugh Pyle. He led the way back into the record room which lay between the control room and the vestibule. And there, surrounded by Bing Crosby, Frank Sinatra, Perry Como, Vic Damone, Peggy Lee, Nat King Cole, Red Nichols and his Five Pennies, Artie Shaw, Benny Goodman, Stan Keaton, Tommy and Jimmy Dorsey, and Duke Ellington, the preacher produced a New Testament: *King James 1611 Authorized Version.*

"Do you believe this is the Word of God?" asked Pyle.

"Yep," said Ruckman, "that's it!"

[My, how things had changed! Three years ago he had called it "baloney." But it is amazing what simply READING that Book will do to "broaden your outlook" from the prejudices of an "isolated mentality" that one gets from the news media and a college education. Ruckman knew what the Book was: it was a "two-edged sword." It would cut you till you bled to death. He did not understand it, but he knew two things about it that were true.

1. Men were against it because it was against them, and

2. People didn't like it because it knew all about them and told it.

He himself had experienced that typical scholar's frustration, which he was to meet at much closer quarters in a few months. Someone said to a Bible-correcting scholar, one time, "If you don't believe it, why don't you let it alone?"

His honest reply was, "IT WON'T LET ME ALONE."]

"Yep," said Ruckman, "that's it."

"Do you believe that you are a sinner?"

"Oh, — yes. I know I'm a sinner."

"Do you believe that Christ died for sinners?"

"Well, I suppose He did."

"Do you believe He could save a sinner?"

"Well, I suppose He could."

"Do you believe He could save YOU?"

"Beats the H— outta me. I don't know."

"Would you be willing to ask Him to save you?"

"Sure." "All right, take my hand. " He did. "Now bow your head." He did.

"Now, in your own words, ask Jesus Christ to save you."

"But I don't know how to pray."

"That's all right. Just go in your own words the best way you know how."

Okay, here goes. God, I know I am a — sinner, and I want you to save me, and if you don't save me pretty — quick I'm going to Hell just as sure as —."

He looked up from his "prayer." Hugh Pyle was smiling.

"Did you mean that prayer?" he asked.

"You're — right, I meant it," said Ruckman indignantly.

"Well then, if you meant it, you are *saved*!"

"I don't *feel* any different."

"You're not supposed to feel any different."

"Well then, how the — do I know I'm saved?"

"You just KNOW."

"No, I don't."

"Yes, you do."

"I DO NOT!"

Hugh opened his Testament to 1 John 5:13 and made Ruckman read it. "There," he said, "God says if you believe on His Son you know you have eternal life. Now, do you believe on the Son?"

"Yes—sure I do. But I don't think . . . ."

"What do you mean, 'think'? It says here, 'That ye may know. ' Do you know, or don't you?"

"Well, ah . . . ."

"You don't think GOD IS A LIAR, DO YOU?"

"Oh no, no, no, NO! I don't think God is a liar!"

"Well, God said that if you did not believe the record He gave of His Son, you made God a *liar*. In the record God said, **'that you may KNOW you have eternal life.'** Now, do you have eternal life, or do you not?"

This was the proverbial "rock and a hard place." Ruckman had never had so much trouble with anybody before. Alongside Pyle, Paige Wagner, Colonel Richardson, Eddie Copeland, Lt. Self, and the TTC were pushovers.

"Well," Ruckman stutterd, "all right, all right. I KNOW." But he still felt like he DIDN'T.

Two weeks later he did know "for sure," and that assurance would stick with him for forty-nine years (1949–1998). That is six years past the date of this writing.

That week, Brother Pyle checked on Ruckman's marriage situation. He let Ruckman know that the first step in his new life would be to be reconciled with his wife.

The next week a package arrived in Pensacola from Sawyerville, Alabama: it contained a *Scofield Reference Bible* with Proverbs 3:5–6 printed on the flyleaf. It was the best advice he had ever received in a lifetime. He read the Bible for nearly four hours Thursday, four hours Friday, and four hours Saturday. Slowly he began to get some light on the passages he had been reading; most of them were aimed *doctrinally* at Israel, but there were still dozens of them that dealt with the individual depravity of sinners like himself. Although he still could not locate the books in either Testament without the help of an Index, he did begin to see that there were other things in the Book beside damnation and judgment. There was security and life in the Book.

Saturday night came around, and with it came his last "convert course" from Father Sullivan at St. Michael's. He was planning on being "confirmed" in the morning (Sunday). But as "fate" would have it, this time when he went to see the priest, he took the *Scofield Reference Bible* with him. He saw nothing incongruous about this because he still fully intended to "jine the church." He had no idea what Roman Catholicism was really all about; to him it was just another "church" like the Baptist church or the Anglican church. (My, what he had to learn!)

In he went; down they sat. After thirty minutes, Ruckman said, "Father, when I first came in here a few weeks ago you said you had something real for me. I'm ready to join the church."

"Good," said the Jesuit priest, "we will arrange confirmation services for you in the morning." There was a pause, and then suddenly Ruckman produced, from under his raincoat, THE BOOK. The priest unconsciously shifted in his seat.

"There is only one thing that really bothers me," said Ruckman. "This business about worshipping the Virgin Mary: I can't find that anywhere in here," and he thumbed suggestively through the pages. He didn't even know where the New Testament began. "What is all of that worshipping Mary stuff?" he asked.

DIALOGUE:

"Well, do you remember when Christ was on the cross?"

"Yes." (He did, but he could not have found it in any of the four Gospels without looking for it.)

"Well, do you remember when He said, **'Son, behold thy mother'** and **'Woman, behold thy son'**?"

"Yes," said Ruckman, vaguely remembering something or other like that.

"Well, doesn't it stand to reason if the Son of God is dying, then His last few words are going to have more significance to them than, 'just take that woman home'?"

"Well, yes, I guess that makes sense."

"You see, Ruckman, what He is saying here is, 'Anyone who becomes my son—a son of God—has to have Mary for their Mother' and, 'Mary, anyone that follows me is your son.' Got it?"

"Yeah, but what is this worshipping Mary bit?"

"Oh, we don't worship her; no, no, we just honor her, like YOU DO YOUR OWN MOTHER, understand?"

"Oh, ah . . . ah . . . yeah, sure."

THE VOICE:

"Open the Book and look down."

He opened it, and it fell open at John 19. He looked at it and read verse 30. "Uh!" he said, "Why, here He says, **'It is finished.'** If He is dying, His last few words must have more significance than, 'My life is just over.' He must mean, 'everything's all over'! He must mean SALVATION IS COMPLETED!"

The priest stubbed out his cigar with about three times the pressure it would take to do it, shifted in his chair again, and said, "Put that away, Ruckman; you've been reading that too much. It's bad for you to read the Bible if you don't understand it."

THE VOICE:

"Look down." He looked down and flipped a section and found himself reading 2 Timothy 3:16–17. "Look here," he said, and read it out loud. "What does that mean?"

Sullivan shifted again, bent forward, and said, "Well, that's true, but there are many other good books beside the Bible.

The Bible says, many other things **"should be written"** besides what is in the Bible. Yes, the Bible is good to read, but it doesn't say *other* books aren't good, too, does it?"

"No," said Ruckman absent-mindedly, while turning to the last book in the Bible.

THE VOICE:

"Look down." He looked down and found his eyes had landed on Revelation 22. "Why, it says here that, **'If any man shall ADD unto these things, God shall add unto him the plagues that are written in this book,'** What does that mean?"

Sullivan slammed a drawer shut on his desk, reached for another cigar, and said, "Put that away; you're reading it too much! It doesn't say every single word, Ruckman. You take it too literally! It just said, **'THINGS.'"**

THE VOICE:

"Look down."

He looked down and saw verse 19. (He was just as astonished as the priest, because he couldn't have found either verse in less than fifteen minutes, and maybe not then.) He read aloud, **""And if any man shall take away FROM THE WORDS OF THE BOOK . . . God shall take away his part out of the book of life'**! What does that mean?"

"PUT THAT BOOK AWAY!" shouted the priest as he bounced to his feet. "What you need to do is read some GOOD BOOKS!"

Whereupon he proceeded to shoot out the door like a rat going out of a sewage pipe. Ruckman sat and waited. He sat in his raincoat, with his Bible open on his lap, and his half-smoked cigar in his right hand. A red light was flashing somewhere in his poor benighted mind: it was not from the Rhodes Furniture store, across the street. "Good books? Good books?"

THE VOICE:

"Don't you smell something fishy going on here?"

Him, read some *good books*? What books would these be? He had read Dickens, Shelley, Keats, Thackery, Byron, Scott, Wordsworth, Emerson, Tennyson, Kipling, London, Poe, Melville, Shakespeare, Goethe, Moliere, Rousseau, Voltaire, Zane Grey, Tolstoy, Hugo, Kant, Schelling, Fichte, Hegel, Nietzsche, Menninger, Pavlov, Poe, Jung, Marx, Darwin, Paley, Huxley, Haeckel,

**Illustration for the Book of Revelation
(Nahum 3:4–8)**

**Illustration for the Book of Revelation
(Daniel 8:25)**

Maughm, Hemmingway, Steinbeck, Dos Pasos, Anderson, Shaw, Ibsen, and fifty more! "YOU NEED TO READ SOME GOOD BOOKS"? Like what? The Shastas, the Koran, the Analects, the Book of Mormon, the Puranas, the Vedas, Cervantes, Abelard, Anselm, Homer, Aquinas, Duns Scotus, Sartre, Hobbes, Hume, Descartes, Ovid, Spinoza, Dante, Aristotle, Milton, Plato, Anaxamines, Boccaccio, Zeno, and fifty more? "Something is wrong here," said Ruckman to himself. Something was SNAFU.

Back came the priest with five volumes on "How to Study the Scriptures" by St. Thomas Aquinas. *He had already read them.* Sullivan put a fatherly arm around his new convert and guided him to the door.

"You know, Ruckman," he said, "I don't think you are quite ready for confirmation just yet! Let's wait another week."

"Okay with me," said Ruckman, and headed for the door. He was planning to catch a bus and go out to Hugh Pyle's church to something or other called a "Youth for Christ" meeting. As they went through the vestibule, Sullivan said, "Your wife phoned up today and said you are thinking of going to Bob Jones University. Is that correct?"

"Well, I don't know," Ruckman said, "I've been thinking about it. My mother-in-law knows the place; I never heard of it. But I got four years of free education coming on the GI bill, and I could go up there and get a Masters in Radio Arts for nothing."

"What on earth would make a man like YOU want to go to a place like that?" the priest asked.

"Beats the H— outta me," said Ruckman. "My wife and my mother-in-law say that no one drinks up there, and no one smokes, cusses, or dances, and no one goes to the movies. Sounds to me like a *clean place*. I never been in a clean place in my life. I think I'll go up there and see what it's like."

They were at the door.

"Did you ever hear of Loyola University?" the priest asked.

"Oh yeah, sure."

"You know, that's where all the brilliant intellectuals go."

Flash! Flash! Now a bell began to ring somewhere; it wasn't a church bell—it was more like an alarm bell. Where had he heard *that* line before?

They stepped out on the small porch into the early spring night. It was drizzling (as usual) in the "Sunshine State." The priest stood on the top step smoking his stogey, and Ruckman stood on the bottom step smoking his stogey, and carrying the six books under his arm: one by God and five by a demon. At this juncture, Ruckman became so startled that he lowered his head and just stared at the ground so the priest could not see the excitement in his eyes. The Voice had just said, "Now, watch it, Pete! I'm going to show you something. Here it comes: don't miss it!" The priest rambled on, perfectly unaware of Ruckman's state of mind.

"Have you ever been down to New Orleans?" he asked.

("NOW GET IT, Pete, Get it. Listen close!")

"Sure," said Ruckman, "I've been down there." You bet he had. He had cut his teeth down there in Pirate's Alley before he was out of college. He couldn't go into any details about it, however, for THE VOICE was so startlingly real that he was taken up with listening to it. ("Here it comes, Pete: GET IT!")

"Did you ever go down into the French Quarter?" asked the priest.

"Yea, I've been down there."

("LISTEN! Don't miss it!")

The priest inhaled and looked up into the night sky and said, "You know, that is a fine old people down there in the French Quarter. Of course, they are a little bit IMMORAL, but they've KEPT THE OLD FAITH!"

And he exhaled. Ruckman, standing two feet below him, looked up in time to see the smoke coming out between two gold teeth in the front of the priest's mouth. The effect was absolutely awesome, for the red light from the neon sign on Rhodes Furniture Company (across the street) illuminated the smoke. It filtered up past the priest's eyes in red strands that wavered like snakes.

THE VOICE:

"Do you see THAT, Pete? That is not a priest; it's a DEMON!"

"Good night, Father!" said Ruckman, and he tore out across the street, headed for the bus stop by the post office.

As he crossed the median, he remembered the cigar. He looked at it. He had been smoking since he was eighteen.

THE VOICE:

"He gave that to you. It's probably unclean, too. You'd better get rid of it."

He started to throw it away but didn't.

THE SARCASTIC INTRUDER:

"It's your last one, you might as well finish it.

THE VOICE:

"What's the matter, don't you have enough will power? Throw it away."

THE SARCASTIC INTRUDER:

"We know you got will power. What are you trying to do? Show off? Go on, finish it, it's going to be your last one anyway."

He took two more puffs and threw the cigar into the gutter. It was the last one he ever smoked. He never inhaled tobacco again for forty-nine years, unless it was someone else's in a plane or restaurant. Fifteen minutes later the bus came by, and soon he found himself out beyond Brent Lane, in the first Bible-believing Baptist church he had ever been in in his life.

The thing that impressed him the most was *the music*. For the first time in his life he saw a mass of teenagers, clean cut, happy, smiling, singing hymns. The hymns were not like the Catholic Ave Marias and dirges and chants. The words were about heaven, eternal life, joy in service, and the "Good News." Here was something he had missed. His education had turned out to be only *partial*.

It was appearing that his liberal upbringing and his "avant-garde" activities, plus his liberal college educa-

Brent Baptist Church, Pensacola, Florida (1965)

tion and more than liberated "lifestyle," had actually made a narrow-minded bigot out of him. What he saw and heard at Brent proved that his real problem was an "isolated mentality."

The preacher preached; the invitation was given. It was the first gospel sermon Ruckman had ever heard in his life. It was the very first time the Biblical "plan of salvation" was made clear. When the invitation hymn was sung, he didn't need two stanzas to know what to do. They never got through the first stanza. Somewhere between "But that Thy blood" and "Oh, Lamb of God, I come," he came down the aisle and took the pastor's hand and said, "I will accept Christ as my Saviour." *He had assurance about salvation the moment he put his foot in the aisle.* As to whether the "great transaction"— the planting of the "incorruptible seed" of the new nature—had taken place in the Methodist church, or the record room at WEAR, or just now, he knew not. It made no difference. He had eternal life now, for certain, and he KNEW IT. He knew it beyond the shadow of a doubt. One other sinner came down the aisle with him that night; a twelve-year-old GIRL. What a pair they made, standing side by side, shaking hands with the church members who were congratulating them on their "decision"!

The congregation was now singing, "Blest the tie that binds our hearts in Christian love," and as Ruckman stood there shaking hands with these smiling Christians— many of them converts from the ages of five or ten years old—he thought he was shaking hands with angels. If you had told him that many of the elderly women there were gossiping about each other, or that some of the teenagers were necking in cars in the parking lot, or that some of the deacons were stealing bonds and falsifying the treasurer's reports, he would have been ready to fight. (How it would come back to him a few years later when a man gave him a ten dollar bill after a service! He asked the man why he had not put it into the plate, and the man said, "Preacher, in this church if I put it in the plate, it probably wouldn't have gotten to you." He had much to learn about the Lord's "sheep.")

Brent Baptist Church, in those days, was outside the city limits, and the buses didn't run out that way after six p.m. All of Palafox (and what is now Highway 29) from Brent Lane northward was pecan orchards, farmland, bushes, grass, and pine trees, with a few live oaks. There was no Cordova Mall or University Mall, and Nine Mile Road didn't have four stores on it or two restaurants. There was no "Car City" and no string of motels (Ramada, Holiday Inn, Eight Days Inn, etc.) on the highway. Ruckman had to hitchhike back to town. No one offered him a ride when he left church, although the truth of the matter was, probably no one knew that he was "on foot"; most twenty-seven year old men, in those days, had a car.

He walked along the highway in the moonlight. The old nature asserted itself immediately. "Fine bunch of Christians THEY are! Wouldn't even give you a ride. Hypocrites! 'God bless you' and all that jazz! Shaking your paw off, and wouldn't even give you a ride home! That's 'Christianity' for you!"

The last word was not through his gray matter before a car stopped right in front of him; it backed up, and a man yelled at him across the passenger's seat, in front, "Want a lift home, Ruckman?"

"Sure," he said. He couldn't say more because he was too embarrassed to be caught with such thoughts in his mind. He got in.

It was a man and his wife in their forties. As they went on down the highway, the man said, "I was in church tonight, and saw you accept Christ as your Saviour. You'll never regret doing that!"

"No, you won't," chimed in his wife. "That's the best decision you ever made in your life."

"Yeah, I guess so," said Ruckman, and looked out the window where the moon was shining down on the trees and on the buildings of a fertilizer plant. Old man Adam said, "You gotta lotta room to talk. Gotta car and got your wife with you. I'm on foot, and my family is shot to H—. Yeah, you gotta lotta room to talk."

The man went right on talking, without knowing what Ruckman was thinking. The next thing that popped out of his mouth was this: "Yessir, Brother Ruckman, I accepted Christ when I was a boy, and let me tell you something. I never had any mother or daddy; I was raised in an orphan's home. But I accepted the Lord Jesus as my Saviour when I was nine years old, and ever since then I've been just as happy as a dead pig in the sun!"

"All right," said Ruckman inaudibly, "I'll shut up. I'm through arguing." It was the first time he had really talked to the One who had saved him. (He figured he was talking to himself, because he thought he was still alone. He did not know yet that his body was **"the temple of the Holy Ghost."**)

That night, back in his "flophouse," he knelt by the bed. A thousand confusing, conflicting, irritating, and disturbing thoughts ran through his head. "What if you lose it? What if you never got it? How do you know all this is real? It's all in your mind: you're simply losing your mind like your brother Johnny lost his. How can all of this nonsense be true? It's just religion; you're just 'getting religion.' You'll be over it next week. What about Janie? She'll never come back, and if she comes back, how will you live together when you don't love her and never did? What do you know about loving anybody? How do you know God loves you?" And on it went.

But now some peculiar voice—some voice that sounded like that voice down on the street outside the Bell Cafe ("You need to get a Bible")—would slide in between the menacing questions and say quietly (oh, so quietly), "It's all right now, Peter. It's all right now."

After this happened about four times in a space of thirty minutes, the tempest began to subside. Someone was speaking, "peace be still" to the waters of that troubled and tormented soul.

"It's all right now, Peter. It's all right now."

And it was. If he could have looked ahead and seen what the future held—poverty, near starvation, ostracism, slander, threats, desertion, divorce courts, split custody cases, and even suicidal thoughts again—he might have backed out, but the great God had "in love, thrown a veil across the way," and all he could see, now, was a dark room and a stolen Bible that lay on a bedspread. It was the thing that had brought him to this point. One Book— one very old, cheap, dimestore Book with no front cover, small print, "the words of Jesus in red," and no reference notes, footnotes, or concordance.

The handsome *Scofield Reference Bible* (less than two weeks old) lay on the dresser. *He would read it through twenty-four times in the next twelve months.* This was the Book he had called "pig's meat" (baloney) in the Philippines. He already had two copies of it. Before he got through, he would have ten copies of it in English, three copies in Greek, two copies in Hebrew, one in Spanish, two in German, two in Welsch, one in Dutch, one in French, and one in Latin. Kneeling there in the dark, all he knew was that "it was all right now." He didn't know that the old, archaic, Elizabethan *King James* dime store Bible was going to be not only his bread and butter and hobby and interest, but his guide, his counselor, his income, his occupation, his LIFE, and his only hope on this planet.

One Book. With more than nine million books in the Library of Congress, one sinner had found the ONE BOOK that could change a man's life completely, and turn him around one hundred and eighty degrees, and keep him going in the other direction without drugs, medical care, money, education, friends, family, counselling, hospital help, or science. Here was ONE BOOK, and it was going to rid him of his smoking, his cursing, his drinking, his lying, his dirty jokes, and his confidence in himself. This ONE BOOK was to convert old Peter S. of the Topeka alleys, old "Ruckman" of the French Quarter of New Orleans, old Lt. Ruckman of the infantry drill fields, old drunken "Peter S. Ruckman" of the dance bands, into a PUBLIC SERVANT who would entertain little children with chalk talks, play a tuba in a Christian orchestra, and preach the gospel in Germany, Austria, Russia, Mexico, Korea, India, Canada, Hawaii, and the Philippines.

"What hath God wrought!" (Num. 23:73).

CHAPTER TWELVE

The Babe in Christ

Bob Jones Sr. used to say that every convert, when he is first saved, is a baby. He needs "milk" for nourishment (1 Pet. 2:2). The longer a man waits to get saved, the more of a baby he is. So many things have to be "unlearned" that a younger man would not have to unlearn. At the speed I had traveled, I was not about to "unlearn" overnight what an average man about fifty years old would have to unlearn if he had just gotten saved. A number of things happened in quick succession in the months of April, May, and June. And while these things were happening to me, the Communists took Nanking and Shanghai, the Berlin blockade ended, and in Vietnam, Bao Dai entered Saigon in an attempt to rule a divided country. Twenty thousand people were left homeless by floods in China (July 1949). Fifty-four people died in a plane crash in Puerto Rico (June 7), and one hundred and fifty people got killed in riots in Bolivia (May 29). I wasn't in Bolivia or Puerto Rico. I was in Sawyerville, Alabama.

First of all, an attempt was made at reconciliation. Pastor Pyle met with Janie and myself and went through the Scriptures with us. We knelt together, prayed together, and I wept. *Janie did not.* She now professed to have been a Christian the whole time (1944–49). Without one bit of evidence to prove it, she claimed she had been saved when she was a little girl. I took her at her word; there was nothing else to do. I was a brand new Christian and didn't even know how to handle such problems. But there was ink on the crystal ball. She had not gone to two services with me when she became furious at my suggestion that she should use her voice to sing hymns "like so-and-so" (I pointed out a girl in the choir who sang a "special" that night). Janie "came apart," and I saw at once the damage I had done between 1944 and 1949 would probably never be repaired. She was now jealous and suspicious of ANY move that I made in any direction. Looking back over it, I could not blame her. No woman could have had a sorrier man for a husband than Janie Bess May. The trouble was, now I was saved and, according to the Book, **"a new creature"** who was **"in Christ."**

Aunt Rosa invited me up to paint a baptistry for her pastor, a certain Roy McCallum from Ft. Worth, Texas. While painting it (Dixon Mills, Alabama) I had a chance to hear J. Frank Norris's Bible teacher, Roy Kemp, lecture on the book of Revelation. He illustrated it with cartoons (very poorly drawn) mounted on strings around the walls of the church. I took one look and made up my mind I could do better. Hugh Pyle egged me on. He gave me a bunch of reproductions of cartoons by E. J. Pace, who cartooned for *The Sunday School Times* for years. I studied them; I figured I could do better. (I was hooked and didn't know it.)

When I knelt in McCallum's baptistry to paint and held out my rags, brushes, and "turps" and asked God to bless them, He said quietly—it always seemed to be quietly—"Do you remember that picture you did in the Philippines?"

Did I remember it? I reckon I did! Christ and John drunk, feet sticking out under the table, some of the disciples cross-eyed, and others passed out on the table . . . . yeah, I remembered it.

"Yes, Lord," I said, "I remember it."

"Do you see any reason," He said, "why I shouldn't just take off your hands at the wrists, right now?"

I gritted my teeth and closed my eyes tighter, and (still holding the brushes out) I said, "No, Lord, I can't give you one reason why You shouldn't do just that."

I waited tensely, expecting any minute to feel something like a shell fragment sail through the air and cut off my hands. Nothing happened.

About ten seconds later the Voice said, "All right,

go ahead and paint." I did. I did for the next forty-nine years. I painted twenty baptistries, illustrated six books, did more than four thousand chalk talks, produced thirty portraits for the Christian Hall of Fame, and then turned out a 205 paintings on the book of Revelation. God knew how to "get blood out of a turnip."

Roy Kemp baptized me and my wife in the creek at Dixon Mills. She complained after it was over that I had not gone down into the water *with* her, and I hadn't. I went ahead of her, and I suppose my reason for doing it was I didn't think she would get baptized, for she had professed to be a Christian before we met. I could not imagine anyone going through what I went through and then delaying baptism for five years.

In June, I resigned my position at WEAR, came back up to the farm in Sawyerville to live with my wife and daughter, and enrolled at Bob Jones University. They had just opened on a new campus in Greenville, South Carolina. On the farm, I read the Bible through at eighty pages a day; twice a month. I had not gotten through it the second time when I began to get some powerful "impressions" about the will of God in my life. I could no longer discern any "voices" leading in these matters; it was as though the voice of God had switched from something operating on a sub-atomic sound level to a *Book*— the Book that had started me out on this "whatever it was." The impression I kept receiving was to the effect that I should go and witness to my mother and father, immediately. I now realized they were lost and headed for Hell, and I became more burdened about them every time I put my nose in the Scripture. That isn't all; God began to call to my mind what I had done back there in the 1930s and 1940s. I owed my parents something. Every time my eye crossed **"honour thy father and thy mother,"** I would get a pang of bad conscience.

So I drove up to Rehoboth Beach, Delaware, where my father (now a retired Colonel) had settled down. Janie and her brother (Bubba) went with me. We drove all one day, all the next night, and all the next day, coming into Rehoboth Beach in the afternoon. Instead of using the old "Annapolis Ferry" from Washington, DC, we came across the big, new Chesapeake Bay Bridge out of Virginia. I drove up to the little cottage at 19 Oak Avenue, and there in that tiny "living room" (it was about ten by twelve feet) I got on my knees before my parents and begged their forgiveness for the way I had lived in Topeka. They were both very nervous, but both freely granted me the forgiveness. However, when I began to witness to them about my conversion they both suddenly tightened. (Of course, my "witness" left much to be desired. I really didn't know how to witness. All I knew was my mommy and daddy were headed for a Lake of Fire, and I wanted to see them saved. That is about all any real new convert knows. I blubbered and I squalled, I was so burdened.) They didn't accept any of it. Dad's reaction to "I just don't want you to go to Hell, Dad!" was "Well, son, don't take it so hard. We can see a doctor in the morning. Johnny has a good psychiatrist up in Dover." They thought I had lost my mind. To the contrary, God had just given me the first SOUND MIND I had since the day I was born.

After two or three days of futile attempts to win them to Christ, I returned to Alabama. In those three days, Mom and Dad had tried every way they could to get me interested in the "old life" of Rehoboth, where I had been a beach boy, a lifeguard, and a bar-checker. Nothing "clicked" any more. The ties were completely broken. Much as I loved the ocean I did not even enjoy the swimming. The "magic" was gone. The "hot spots" of this world become mighty commonplace when one gets acquainted with the Lord Jesus Christ.

I returned to Sawyerville and went back to reading the Bible: eighty pages a day. With it, I read Clarence Larkin's *Dispensational Truth*, a book that Janie's brother (T. May) gave me from the days of his schooling in Birmingham when Mom May was trying to make a preacher out of him. I read Larkin through five times in three months. In September, I shipped off to BJU to get a Master's degree in Radio Arts. I had four years of paid education coming from the GI bill, so I could now enroll in post-graduate school and get a Ph.D.

Without a car, and with little or no money to do anything, I purchased a forty-foot plywood trailer (second hand) that had no bathroom, no hot running water, and no refrigerator; and for the next five years I hauled ice by the block for the ice box in it, heated water in a pan on a kerosene stove in it, and used a community bathroom in the trailer court. My income was thirty dollars a week. I picked up a few bucks (a pitifully "few" bucks) working with Unusual Films as a "story board" man for the Christian movies and as a radio announcer for WMUU, the university's new radio station. Bob Pratt was the program director.

While I made these moves into the "new life," an earthquake in Ecuador killed six thousand people (August 8), forty-eight people perished in a plane crash in the Azores (October 28), and four thousand more were killed in floods in Guatemala (October 19). Over in Rome the Vatican claimed to have found Peter's bones (August 7), the author of *Gone with the Wind* got killed (August 16), one hundred and forty-nine people got killed in the month of November in plane accidents, and a fire burned another two hundred and seven people to death aboard the Noronic (Toronto, September 17). I wasn't one of them. I was at Bob Jones University when Mao Tse-tung set up a military dictatorship in China (as Stalin had done) under the hypocritical profession of it being a "People's Republic."

Korea was about to be invaded. If I had "re-upped" in Tokyo instead of coming home, I and my wife and daughter would have been north of Seoul when the Communists came in. The shipping orders for my wife and daughter (which went out in the winter of 1945) were assigning us to a military base in KOREA. Thus, I had escaped certain death in combat TWICE: once when I was sidetracked from being shipped out in 1944 (World War II) to train infantry replacements, and then again in 1947 when I had gotten bitter with the service and decided to come home. *Some folks live a charmed life.*

You've got to admit that any young man raised in

an infantry officer's home who manages to escape being
killed during a period of history that recorded the violent
deaths of over *one hundred million people*, when he was
part and parcel of that history, is a very fortunate young
man. Stalin and Lenin together had murdered more than
fifty million Russians; Mao did away with at least ten
million Chinese. World War II got rid of twenty-two
million people; Korea and Vietnam together snuffed out
the lives of another two million; the revolutions and civil
wars in India, Pakistan, Cuba, Nicaragua, San Salvador,
Lebanon, Cyprus, Iraq, and Iran had accounted for another three million; another one million had been killed
in tidal waves, floods, earthquakes, conflagrations, fam-
ines, and accidents.

Certainly I wasn't any more worthy to live than
ONE casualty in the list, and certainly LESS worthy
than, say, ninety-nine million of them. But there I was; a
student at BJU in 1949.

I thought about these things, if no one else did.
Looking back over my life and examining it (in the light
of truth, righteousness, and holiness) it scared me. I knew
that if a man like me lived to see *forty*, it would be a
miracle. I didn't deserve thirty years on this earth, and I
was now twenty-eight. My firstborn son came into the
world (May 26, 1950), and when I paced the floor outside the "display window" in the hospital (Greenville,
SC), I nearly sweated blood. I knew what I deserved, and
the thought that God might now reward me "according to
my works" (Rev. 2:23) filled me with a terror I couldn't
describe. I prayed like I never had prayed before in my
life, and when the boy showed up healthy, hale, and
sound, I was crying and shouting at the same time. What
a luxury! A healthy baby boy! What a miracle of kindness! What a gift to a miserable, wretched, depraved,
godless sinner who had broken every rule in the Book!

Still my conscience would not let up on me. I said to
myself, "Peter, ol' boy, you may be saved, but you'll
never live to see forty if God requires HALF what you
owe Him." I planned for a very, very short life. I never
expected to see 1970. The last thing I ever expected to

hear on this earth was ten little boys and girls calling, "Hey, Grandpaw!"

The problem at BJU was, I had been thrown in with a typical BJU-PCS, twentieth century "Christian": a smooth, effeminate, slick, passive intellectual who was absolutely without one MILITANT trait about him. Putting me in with Bob Pratt was about like hitching up Tiny Tim and Larry Czonka to the same plow, or perhaps Woody Allen with Mike Ditka. We did not get along. The real trouble lay much deeper; God had called me to teach and to preach, and I wasn't going to BJU to learn how to teach or preach; I was going to help a new radio station get on the air and get a Master's degree in Radio. God didn't want me in Radio; *He wanted me in the pulpit*. But in these days things were still in the fog. I was still in that grey area where a long-confirmed sinner is coming out of it "cold turkey," and nothing is sharp and clear. Furthermore, I knew nothing about "Christians." I had never lived with them. I had never studied them as a "species."

My wife and I were arguing constantly. She would go to sleep while I read the Bible to her and then would wake up and start talking about the past. I warned her, time after time, to "let sleeping dogs lie," but to no avail. If she could forgive, she could not *forget*. The subject of my past infidelities would surface time and time again; every time, in fact, that an argument came up about *anything*. And there was nothing about Janie's situation that helped matters. She was pregnant with my first son, David Farrior, and living in the small plywood trailer with no transportation, very few friends, and a diet that would hardly keep a sharecropper alive. She had little to live for. The gap between us widened with the passing of the months. I would tell her, "Don't bring it up. Don't kindle the fires again; you'll get BURNT." She went right on. Several times she talked about divorce.

Finally, Pratt had all he could take of me, and the feeling was mutual. Matters came to a head when Billy Graham was invited to hold a revival in Homer Rodeheaver Auditorium (on the campus). In those days, Dr.

Bob Sr. and Billy were still in fellowship, and he had not started on his vendetta against Billy; nor had John R. Rice. Graham came; the students had orders not to attend the services so there would be room to seat the crowds that came from town. I decided I would hear him anyway, so I hid myself in an upstairs control room to one side of the stage, and when Billy began I was seated on a stool in the "wings," about ten feet over his head. My "booth" was a small room where some floodlights were mounted in brackets. I heard Billy preach. The Holy Spirit was so thick in the auditorium it looked like a fog. Thirty people got saved, and at least two hundred came forward for other decisions. The thought overwhelmed me: "That is what I want to do! I want to win people to Christ. I want to be like Billy Graham! I WANT TO BE AN EVANGELIST!"

Half-truth. The devil was **"more subtil than any beast of the field which the LORD God had made"** (Gen. 3:1). God wanted something else from me, but "evangelism" was at least a step in the right direction.

During the invitation, up in my light booth, I was kneeling and crying out to God. I said, "Now, Lord, I am not getting along with Pratt. I cannot 'see' him and he cannot 'see' me, and I know I am right. That guy knows nothing about radio at all, he has no experience, and we are bumping noses all the time. I cannot handle it. You must handle it. God, I know I am right! I WANT JUDGMENT BETWEEN ME AND BOB PRATT!"

That was the last time I ever prayed a prayer like that. Three days later I was called to the "orderly room" to be confronted by Dean Edwards, Theodore Mercer, and Bob Jones Jr.

CONFRONTATION:
"Now Ruckman, what is the matter with you, anyway?"

"Whadya mean, 'What is the matter with me'?"

"Well, you don't speak to anyone. You have been here three months, and you never speak to anybody."

"Why, sure I do. I speak to people."

"All right. How many people have you spoken to TODAY?" (It was about three p.m.)

"Oh, I don't know. Several."

"How many? How many, actually?"

"Well, rats, I don't know. I'm not used to shootin' the bull with people. Most of my life I've just saluted them. But I speak to people."

"How many TODAY did you speak to?"

"Well, let's see . . . ah, THREE."

There was laughter in the room. "Three!" said Bob Jones Jr. "Why, I speak to more people than that walking from here to the Dining Common." (At that time the Dining Common was less than a hundred feet from the Administration Building.) "Well, of course you do," I said. "After all, you're the big cheese around here—King Kong. Everyone knows you; you're the founder's son. Of course everyone is going to speak to *you*."

At that moment there was a gruff voice from the other end of the room. Bob Jones Sr. had been listening to the whole conversation. He had been standing behind a portable screen at the end of the room. Now he walked up to the group, and fixing his eyes on me he said, "YOU DON'T FIT."

"Whadya mean, 'I don't fit'?" I asked stubbornly. No "Bob Jones" was going to bluff me. Who the H— did he think he was? Bob Jones, Sam Jones, Jim Jones, Bill Jones, John Jones, et al. "One of the Jones boys," as far as I was concerned. I didn't know Billy Sunday from chocolate sundae or Bob Jones from Bobby Jones (a golfer).

"You don't fit!" repeated the founder of BJU. "I spoke to you outside coming in, and you never even looked up!" (I had been sitting on a cement bench with my wife and daughter, just outside the Ad building a few minutes before.)

"You never spoke to ME," I said, without batting an eyelash.

"I DID, TOO!" roared Senior.

"You did not," I insisted. Before everything exploded, Bob Jones Jr. intervened and said, "Did you really speak to him, Daddy?"

"Well, I spoke to his little girl," said Senior, a bit mollified, "Same thing."

"You didn't speak to me," I repeated.

"But—!"

Junior interrupted Senior: "That's all right, Daddy, I'll take care of this."

The older man retreated to the other end of the room, turned his back on us, clasped both hands behind his back, and began to mutter to himself. I found out later what this "muttering" was. *He was praying.* And from that moment on the "situation deteriorated rapidly" (to cite an old infantry expression). Something (or Someone) got hold of me and nearly shook my teeth out. Mercer and Edwards were saying something, but I wasn't getting it. Bob Jones Jr. said some more things, but they weren't coming through, either. I began to snuffle for no reason at all and then got mad enough at myself to kick myself for doing it. I felt like a perfect fool. Who in the world was I to break down in tears before this bunch of sissified greenhorns who never tasted anything stronger than iced tea? Why, I had been reamed out by experts! I had stood at attention before Sergeants, Majors, Colonels, and Captains who had vocabularies that would make Eddie Murphy sound like St. Francis, but here I was just all torn to pieces about something. *What was it?* I never found out that day. All of us knelt in prayer, and ten minutes later I walked out and took my wife and daughter back to the trailer.

The next week I was fired from the radio station.

Seeing my Radio degree going up in smoke, I decided there was no use staying at BJU any longer. I would leave and get my Master's somewhere else. I got prepared to check out. But "a funny thing happened on the way home." I walked by the trailer of a tough, young, converted Catholic named Glenn Schunk: he was from Indiana and had served three years in World War II, in the infantry, as a saved witness for Christ. When I walked by his trailer, he stepped out and said, "You're Pete Ruckman, aren't you?"

DIALOGUE:

"Yeah," I said. "That's me."

"You're a new Christian, aren't you?"

"Yeah," I said. "How did you know?"

"Easy," said Schunk, "you got a face like a KILLER." (He had my number.) I didn't answer. Suddenly he asked, "Did you ever preach on the street?"

"Naw, I ain't never preached on the street."

"Would you be afraid to?"

I bristled. "Ruckman" afraid to preach on *the street*? Ridiculous. "No, I ain't afraid."

"All right. I'm taking three other guys with me this weekend up to Spartanburg to preach on the street. Will you go along and try it?"

"What time?"

"Be here at the trailer at 12:30 noon."

"I'll be there."

I showed up and went up to Spartanburg and preached on the street. I learned how to pass out tracts, and I led my first two souls to Jesus Christ. The first one was a young negro man walking down the street in a residential section, and the other was a white truck driver about thirty years old, sitting in the cab of his truck. I had first been **"made a partaker of the fruit"** (2 Tim. 2:6). It tasted like nothing I had tasted in any beer joint, cocktail lounge, dive, restaurant, bar room, juke joint, or disco from New York to Manila or from Tokyo to Miami. I had picked up the "bread" that many Christians **"know not of"** (John 4:32). In one day I made up my mind to drop all of my Radio courses and *stay* at BJU and enroll in the School of Religion—as a FRESHMAN. I had no "transcript" with "credits" under the heading of "Religion." I could apply, of course, my whole undergraduate curriculum to anything else—calculus, trigonometry, organic chemistry, physics, biology, mid-Victorian poetry, medieval history, abnormal psychology, etc.—but it was Freshman Bible all the way; I was about to come clear through college again.

Bob Jones Sr. stood back and watched with interest. He thought that I would drop out "for sure," as he had seen many others do. He was surprised to find me still on the campus after being fired, and several times he spoke to me directly, and I spoke back. Our respect for each other was growing. From now on, I listened to him like a wire tapper plugged into a CIA circuit.

But once the first Old Testament and New Testament Survey courses showed up, more trouble cropped up with them. I had not been in one week of classes before I began to get my doubts about the whole Bible curriculum. The problem was two-fold. In the first place, I had read the Bible through nearly eighteen times by the time I got into the classes (along with Larkin's work); in the second place, I had studied under a Jesuit priest from Loyola, and now I began to remember some of the sessions. Something about the teaching of Afman (now at Tennessee Temple), Kruschek, Whitte, Paine, and others strongly resembled something that the "School of Religion" called "ROMAN CATHOLICISM."

"Irenaeus says this . . . ."

"Eusebius tells us that . . . ."

"A better translation should be . . . ."

"A more accurate rendering is found in the *RSV*." (They were selling *RSV* New Testaments, not just the *ASV*, in the cam-pus bookstore in 1950.)

"The best and oldest manuscripts say . . . ."

"The most authoritative scholars believe . . . ."

"The *ASV* has a more accurate reading here."

"The historic position on the passage is . . . ."

Red lights flashing again: Rhodes Furniture Company? Warning bells sounding. I went back and checked Scofield's notes on the sun in Genesis 1, and the **"sons of God"** in Genesis 6. Someone was wrong. The Bible said the earth was here *before* the sun was here, and the **"sons of God"** in Genesis 6 were in Job 38—they were NOT "the sons of Seth." Who was in error: Scofield or the Book? I noticed that half of Romans 8:1 shouldn't have been in my Bible, and the reference to **"water"** in John 3 was somebody GETTING SPRINKLED WITH WATER in Ezekiel, according to Scofield. Well, I knew better than that, even if I was a "babe in Christ." *C. I.*

Scofield was wrong. If Scofield, Pettingill, Gaebelein, and his company could be wrong, couldn't Origen, Eusebius, Jerome, and Augustine be wrong? How would anyone know which one was *right*? Surely, but certainly, I was being placed in the position of having to choose between the words of *men* and the words of *God*. IT WAS THE FACULTY AT BOB JONES UNIVERSITY THAT WAS PUTTING ME INTO THIS POSITION. I had come to the school with THE BOOK, and I had come to it *believing THAT BOOK* was the word of God, containing God's words to me. I was being talked out of my belief, or at least someone was *trying* to talk me out of it.

I wrestled with this problem. I lay the *ASV* down beside my *AV* and looked at Acts 9:5–6, 1 John 1:7–8, 1 Timothy 3:16, Luke 2:33, Luke 24:50–51, and Acts 1:3. Both versions could not possibly be correct. Someone was either subtracting from the word of God (*ASV*), or someone was adding to it (*AV*), and I had already been through that business with Father Sullivan, toe-to-toe, face-to-face, at St. Michael's. The Book had said, **"Call no man on earth your Father"** (Matt. 23:9). Sullivan said to call him "Father." The Book had said the **"one sacrifice,"** forever, was good **"forever"** (Heb. 10:12). Father Sullivan said, "Every Sunday morning at eleven a.m." The Book had said **"one mediator"** (1 Tim. 2:5), and that One was a MAN; Sullivan had said there were several, and one was a woman. When I had pinned the priest right down, the answer I got every time had been the same. You were to let the CHURCH give you the correct interpretation. I had not been saved thirty days before I got THAT one figured out. The Catholics had been recommending TWO CONFLICTING AUTHORITIES to me (the Bible and Tradition) for the purpose of creating a THIRD AUTHORITY which would arbitrate between the two and settle their differences. This made the THIRD AUTHORITY the final authority, actually *nullifying both the other "authorities."* The Catholic church was God Almighty when "push came to shove." Their *profession* was a joke, for it was nothing but an expedient to set themselves up as GOD.

Here was the faculty at BJU. "The *AV* says THIS, but the *ASV* says THIS." Which one was right? "The *AV* here reads . . . but the best and oldest manuscripts do not have this reading in them."

Old Erich Marie Remarque (speaking as Paul Baumer in *All Quiet on the Western Front*) used to say that infantrymen "have a fine nose for such distinctions," meaning that they could tell the essential from the sham IMMEDIATELY, by virtue of the fact that their LIFE depended upon grasping such distinctions, IMMEDIATELY. The professional "Golden Pheasant" (German soldier's term for a "chicken" or "hot dogger" among the officers) could be spotted almost before he opened his mouth. Vast acquaintance with con men, gaffed dice, stacked decks, Buddhism, army officers, musicians, bookies, bums, artists, crooks, bootleggers, cops, and killers had sharpened my sense of perception when it came to MEN. I saw what was going on immediately. I WAS BEING RECOMMENDED *TWO CONFLICTING AUTHORITIES* SO THE SCHOLARS (*THE SCHOOL AND THE FACULTY*) COULD PLAY "GOD."

I haven't changed my mind about that matter in forty-nine years.

The way to mess me up is the "challenge." I never could resist ACTION, and I certainly would have dropped out of BJU the first year of "Religion" if it had not been for a challenge from an old timer there: Dr. Charles Brokenshire. He could speak, read, and write about eight different languages, and he had graduate degrees from schools on the Continent. "Brokey" was THE intellectual at BJU. He was a baby-sprinkling, Five-Point Calvinist, for as anyone knows BJU has never been a Baptist school and is not one *now*. They were, and *are*, interdenominational.

One day in "Brokey's" class, the old man was expounding on "the parable of Dives and Lazarus" (Luke 16). This went against my grain two ways. In the first place, I knew it was NOT a parable, and in the second place, I couldn't find old "Dives" in the Holy Bible with a flashlight or a searchlight. After going to some length to prove that "Dives" was another language for "rich man," Brokenshire asked for questions.

CONFRONTATION:

I questioned him. I raised my hand and said, "Doctor, why do you keep calling this a parable when it is not?"

He cleared his throat and said, "Well, Mr. Ruckman, what makes you think it is not a parable?"

"Well, sir," I said, "Jesus doesn't say it is a parable. Every time He gives them a parable, the text says, **'And he spake THIS PARABLE to them'** or **'He spake a PARABLE, saying . . . .'** Luke 16:19 is not prefaced with these words."

Dr. Brokenshire coughed and rearranged some papers on his desk. (How strangely the action resembled Father Sullivan in his office at St. Michael's!) "Well, it is a parable," he said.

"Then why," I asked, "does Ezekiel say that people will call the truth about Hell just a 'parable'?"

Dr. Brokenshire stamped his feet under the table and cried, "What do you mean by THAT, Mr. Ruckman?"

"Well, sir," I said, "when Ezekiel preached on Hell," and I read out loud Ezekiel 20:47–48, "those who didn't believe it said," and I read Ezekiel 20:49.

Brokenshire stamped his feet under his desk like a six-year-old child who is about to have a temper tantrum. "Mr. Ruckman! Mr. Ruckman!" he screamed in a high-pitched voice, "HAVE YOU EVER STUDIED GREEK OR HEBREW?"

"No, sir."

"All right, then. I suggest that you keep quiet until you know what you are talking about!"

"Yes, sir."

All of the class (who had been staring at me) smiled and looked at each other knowingly, and then returned to their textbooks. "There!" they said to themselves, "that takes care of THAT character."

Guess again. It would take a lot more than that to take care of Ruckman. I wasn't about to be "taken care" of by any Bible-perverting blockhead engaged in making a liar out of God Almighty because he knew "Hebrew and Greek," not even if he drew a salary from "The World's Most Unusual University." I sat back in my desk and studied the professor. I thought to myself, "So that's how the snow drifts, is it? You have to know Hebrew and Greek, do you, to spot falsehood? Well, bless my soul, I'll just take Hebrew and Greek, and we'll find out what's what!" On the spot I made a decision to spend the rest of the GI bill at Bob Jones until I had mastered Hebrew and Greek. That fleshy decision was based mainly on spite and stubbornness, but God used it. I stayed and studied Hebrew under "Brokey" and Greek under Dr. William T. Brunner until I found "the pig in the poke," and honey, let me tell you, *I FOUND HIM.*

"THAT TAKES CARE OF RUCKMAN," DOES IT?

It took more than that to "take care" of Ruckman before he was saved.

CHAPTER THIRTEEN

On the Battlefield: Combat at Last

I could sum up the years at Bob Jones (four years of regular school sessions with two years of accelerated semesters in the summer) as some of the best years of my life. I read the Bible through about once a month during that time. I submerged myself in it. Naturally, my "heroes" changed. Not only did my heroes change, but my company changed: whereas I had been up to my neck in Roman Catholic Italian "buddies" (Trelizzi, Chiccine, Zasa, Alois, Bertini, et al.) I now found my closest friends were Protestant Germans (Schunk, Klingman, Dievendorf, Trim, Warnock, Kleipper, Bruhn, et al.). It was almost like taking a trip up from Rome through the Brenner Pass and Austria, arriving in Bayern.

I no longer cared anything about Audie Murphy, Art Wermuth, Max Baer, Artie Shaw, Joe Louis, "Pretty Boy" Floyd, Clark Gable, Dillinger, Benny Goodman, "Baby Face" Nelson, Bonnie and Clyde, and Lindbergh. The new "role models" were John Wesley, Sam Jones, Bob Jones, Martin Luther, J. Frank Norris, Billy Sunday, General William Booth, and Billy Graham. When Jesus Christ shows up, the heroes of this world become mighty commonplace. Once the Holy Spirit takes up residence in the body of the believer, characters like Washington, Lincoln, Napoleon, FDR, Wilson, Wendell Willkie, Castro, Mao Tse-tung, Marx, Gorbachev, Freud, Lenin, and Einstein are seen in their true light: Romans 1–3 and 1 Corinthians 1–3.

The Christian life proved to be anything but dull. I took to the street preaching like a duck takes to water. There was something challenging about it, like drilling troops out in the open fields. Soon I was taking along a small aluminum easel and drawing while I preached. I went out every weekend and preached somewhere on the street Saturday morning and Saturday night. In a period of four years this list would include nearly fifty towns in North and South Carolina, Tennessee, Georgia, and Alabama.

One Sunday morning service on the campus at BJU convinced me I was in the "wrong pew": I was right back in Rome with the robed choir, the clerical collars, and the whole rotten mess. I left and joined Pellham Baptist Church in Pellham, South Carolina, where Harold Sightler was pastor. (He was forbidden to preach at Bob Jones, and students were forbidden to go to his church. After BJU went to pieces around 1960 and had to appeal to Baptist churches to get a student body—*while remaining interdenominational*—he was invited in.) In the meantime I got into "shouting" and "running the bases" at an early age.

As a matter of fact, I "cut my baby teeth" in the ministry in the mountains of North and South Carolina. My first "offering" for a weekend meeting was $3.30. I was prouder of it than any money I had ever made in my life, for it was the first pay I ever received for doing what God told me to do. In the winter of 1951 I bought my first car. It was a black, two door Chevrolet coupe. I was twenty-eight years old.

Another child was born in Greenville (April 15, 1952): she was my second daughter, Priscilla. When I graduated I had three little ones in the plywood trailer, and although the first two years were rough at thirty dollars a week, the last years showed some signs of "making a living," for I had preached in so many places that my name was "in circulation." The last year and a half at BJU I preached in a church somewhere every Sunday in the year, including all summer long. I was even offered a chance to become the State evangelist for the Southern Methodist Church, which had not yet gone into apostasy. My street preaching got all kinds of publicity, and Church of God pastors invited me in, as well as Nazarene pastors and Pentecostal pastors. Some of my friends at BJU took pastorates in Methodist and Presbyterian churches, and I preached in them also. Hugh Pyle got up an ordination committee for me in 1950, and I was ordained as a Southern Baptist minister in the largest Southern Baptist church in the Escambia Bay Association. Hugh Pyle was the "moderator" of the association at that time. But the Southern Baptists were slow about having me in, and one couldn't blame them. I was "growing in grace," but my sermons still resembled a drill instructor bawling out infantry replacements. Bob Jones Jr. couldn't stand my vocabulary, which, although it had sloughed off the "damns," "hells," "s.o.b.'s," and "such like," was still the vulgar Koine of the street. *It still is today.*

I learned my Bible "on the road," because no one at BJU knew it well enough to teach it to anyone. If I had gone to BJU to learn the BOOK, I would have gotten the worst disappointment a new convert ever experienced. Being interdenominational, there were three Biblical truths they could not teach as DOCTRINE:

1. That a born-again believer is eternally secure.
2. That water baptism is only for believers, and then only by immersion.
3. That Jesus Christ would come back BEFORE the Millennium.

None of these items were considered to be "Fundamentals" in the heydays of city-wide revivals (Sam Jones, Moody, Sunday, and Bob Jones Sr.), so they were never in the BJU creed. In order to "stay afloat" after 1970, BJU had to cater to the Baptists, but from 1930 to 1955 they did not. In 1980, they just about had to call their school a Baptist school but still didn't dare do it for fear of losing some "old friends and associates." In 1985, they had to reach out and embrace *The Sword of the Lord*, which published a BAPTIST directory of BAPTIST churches and BAPTIST pastors, without an Anglican, Methodist, or Presbyterian showing his face.

I ran into the J. Frank Norris crowd while holding revival meetings in local Baptist churches, and I soon got the "lay of the land." There were two kinds of Funda-

mentalists. One might call them the "uppity-uppity Fundamentalists" and the "Texas Fundamentalists." The
uppity-uppities were the Princeton, Presbyterian, War-
field, Machen, A. T. Robertson, *ASV, NASV* crowd, and
the Texans were the independent, Premillennial, J. Frank
Norris, *King James Bible* crowd. I quickly made up my
mind which side of the fence to get on. I bought some
cowboy boots.

These were days that one could look back on and
cry for joy. How unlike it was to looking back on 1933 to
1949!

KALEIDOSCOPE:

a. Driving down the highway at night with a PA
system hooked up that could carry ten miles. **"Prepare
to meet thy God!" "In such an hour as ye think not
the Son of man cometh!"**

b. Preaching to a man driving ahead of you at fifty-
five m.p.h. and then putting a Charlie Fuller, Old Fash-
ioned Revival Hour quartet on the portable turntable, and
giving the man an invitation, still at fifty-five m.p.h.

c. Snowed-in at a mission station in the mountains
of St. Charles, Virginia. Driving over Big Stone Gap in a
blizzard with no chains.

d. Making "gospel bombs" and dumping them out
all over railroad tracks, where work crews picked them
up literally "by the hundred."

e. Preaching in barber shops and pool halls, men
getting saved right on the spot.

f. One time I preached on the cleared-off floor of a
skating rink at eleven thirty at night, and four people got
saved.

g. Preaching to the chain gangs; they got saved.
Preaching in the workshops, peach sheds, gasoline stations, even one time on the roof of a projection board of
an outdoor drive-in theater.

h. They got saved. Twenty, thirty, forty, fifty, a
hundred, two hundred, and on and on.

i. Personal work in the hospitals, door to door across
the countryside, into the county jails, into the Federal

Mrs. Ruckman At BJU—Bob Jones Jr.'s Residence

Illustration for the Book of Revelation
(Acrylic)

penitentiaries (Atlanta and Wetumpka and Atmore). They got saved.

j. One time I set up the board in the waiting room of a railroad station where two hundred troops were lying on their duffle bags ready to ship out to Korea. Forty of them got saved.

The Communists in North Korea invaded South Korea on June 25, 1950, and I was contacted by the Army. I was given a choice: I could either stay in the Reserves and keep my commission, if I reported back for active duty in ninety days, or else I could get out (and drop my commission) as long as I was subject to being drafted back in as a private within thirty days after I "mustered out." By faith, I signed OUT and dropped my commission, and by some miracle the "emergency" never got bad enough in thirty days to get back in.

In the meantime, the UN decided to fight in Korea, and good old "Dugout Doug" MacArthur was the chump chosen to pull off the "police action." In July and August of 1950, the Americans were almost run out of the country and were killed by the thousands, but in September the Marines landed at Inchon and "liberated" Seoul. In November, the Chinese Communists entered the war and drove the UN troops back to the thirty-eighth parallel, where they fought in the winter of 1951. In April of 1951, Mac was fired by the civilian Harry S Truman. The trouble was simple: *America had lost her guts.* Rather than win the war and risk war with China, America chickened out and settled for "coexistence" with the Communists. A truce was signed in November of 1951, but air strikes went right on, and the bloody fiasco was not over until April 1953. Hundreds of American POW's disappeared and never showed up again. America had just lost her first war. She was about to lose another one.

But this time I was "on the battlefield *for my Lord.*" As the old song said: "In distant lands I trod, crying, 'Sinner, come to God!' I'm on the battlefield for my Lord!" I led a medical doctor to Christ in Greensboro, Alabama (Dr. Norman), who began a sign ministry that was responsible, in a measure, for the salvation of Bob

Harrington (the Chaplain of Bourbon Street). I led a lawyer to the Lord in Panama City. I led a lumber man to the
Lord in Foley, Alabama. I was about to lead two dozen
Catholics to Christ in personal work, four Campbellites,
two Seventh-day Adventists, two Jehovah's Witnesses,
and a "lay reader" for the Episcopal church. I learned the
Book "on the field." I learned it by tangling "one on one"
with Catholic priests, laymen in the Knights of Columbus, Kingdom Hall booksellers, Campbellite elders, Mormon "apostles," and Five-Point Calvinistic Hard-Shell
Baptists. When they "stumped me," I would go home and
search the Scriptures till I found the answers and then
make my own "reference Bible" with cross-references so
I could handle the problems if I ran into them again. The
faculty and staff at BJU were absolutely powerless to
equip me for the firefight. All they had were opinions
about someone's opinion, who "preferred" someone's
preference over someone else's opinion. The more I studied the more I witnessed, and the more I witnessed the
more I studied, and the more I did this the greater became the "communication gap" between me and the faculty and staff.

I couldn't get along with "Junior" at all. We didn't
see eye to eye on *Wine of the Morning*; we didn't see
eye-to-eye on casting problems, or script problems, or
anything else. When I was ordered (as all students are) to
attend all of "The Artists Series," I contramanded the
order by telling him the truth: I had monitored and broadcast dozens of symphonies and operas, and I knew what
was in the majority of operas—ADULTERY and MUR-
DER. Jones Jr. was what we call a "hothouse intellectual," a sort of pseudo-artist like Truman Capote or Andy
Warhol. He had no personal experience with art or music
and no experience with *life*. He was an excellent AC-
TOR, but that was about the limit of his talent. His writing was mediocre, he couldn't play one single musical
instrument, and he couldn't draw flies or paint a barn. He
completely overlooked the greatest Christian paintings in
the world—the Protestant, German and Flemish painters
of 1800 to 1900. The Bowen Museum was stuffed with

Roman Catholic tripe. It was "valuable," of course, but *spiritually* it was about as valuable as "The Last Supper" or the "Mona Lisa." Jones Jr. was too sissified for me: I liked his daddy. (Infantrymen have a fine nose for such distinctions.) The old man was rough, rude, crude, and aggressive. Like anyone else, he had his sins and his faults, but he was a straight talker. He put it over the middle of the plate, waist high. He was in my ball park, not his SON'S, and THAT created a bad situation, for the son KNEW IT.

You learn these things in the infantry. For every Patton there is an Eisenhower. For every MacArthur there is a Westmoreland. For every Truscott there is a Lucas. For every Charlie Fuller there has to be a Dan Fuller. For every M. R. DeHaan there has to be a Richard, and for Bob Jones Sr. there had to be "Junior." It was Martin Luther and Melanchthon all over again, as surely as you lived and breathed. Combs and Henderson cannot replace Rawlings and Vick. Graham cannot fill Billy Sunday's shoes, and Jennings and Afman trying to simulate Lackey and Roberson is just too FUNNY for words.

FLASHBACK:

James McGinlay and Bob Shuler at the yearly Bible conference. Homer Rhodeheaver himself—trombone in hand—leading twenty-five hundred people. Trips into the hills of Georgia with Big Bob Perssons (six feet three inches, three hundred pounds): sinners saved right and left—two hundred, three hundred, four hundred. Drunks getting saved in Rescue Missions (Memphis, Kansas City, St. Louis, Charleston, Jacksonville, Mobile, Pensacola, etc.). A man slashing his wrists with a razor on the street, a man unloading a .38 on his way to killing his ex-wife, a man threatening to cut off my head, a man threatening to blow me away with a pistol, a man kneeling in a living room crying out to God for salvation, a man storming out of church in the service yelling "You d— fool! You're crazy as H—!"

Perils in the city, perils in the country, perils in the air: the stabilizer on the plane freezes; it can't land. The landing gear is stuck and won't come down, and they

don't find out about it till they are ten feet off the run-
way. Two cars pass on a one way bridge at thirty m.p.h.
and neither one is scratched, although the bridge is not
wide enough to have eight tires on it at one time.

"Get the —— outta here; I don't wanna hear any of
that ——!"

"Pardon me, gentlemen, I could not help but over-
hear you, going by, and I just wanted to say that today is
not 'hot as hell.' Hell is a good bit hotter!"

"Pardon me, sir, you mentioned the 'damn money'?
The only time money will damn a man is when it keeps
him from Jesus Christ."

"I don't want the —— tract! I've read dozens of
'em."

"Come quickly, Brother Ruckman, he's dying. He
wants to talk to you."

"Yessir, preacher, prayer and plain talk, 'at's what
does it every time!"

"More power to ya, preacher; here, take this and
buy yo'self a steak!"

Men running the aisles, jumping the benches, swinging off of tree branches; the choir drowned out by the
congregation shouting.

Moonshiners throwing away whiskey bottles and beer
cans on the roof of the church throughout the services.
Rattlesnake in the driveway. Rattlesnake caught in the
church "fan." Mouse runs out under the pulpit and through
the congregation during the invitation.

Five hundred saved, five hundred and fifty saved,
six hundred saved, six hundred and fifty saved, seven
hundred saved, nine hundred saved. Twenty called to
preach, thirty called to preach, forty called to preach.

Going through the Book for the fifty-fifth time, still
finding things I'd missed. Translating Nestle's Greek Testament, one word at a time, looking up all of the variants
in the critical apparatus for every deviation from the text.

Twenty people were killed when an ammunition
barge exploded in New Jersey (May 19, 1950). One hundred and eighty people were killed in plane crashes in
June 1950. A B-29 in California crashed into a trailer

camp, killing seventeen people (August). Fifteen thousand soldiers got killed in Korea in less than eight months. Eighty-four got killed when a commuter train in New Jersey plunged off a track, an explosion in the harbor at Saigon killed fifty-four people (May 1951), and an earthquake in San Salvador blotted out another hundred. By the end of 1951 more than forty thousand men had been killed in Korea.

I lived and breathed. Why? I have no idea.

The sun came up and the sun went down. McCarthy began his crusade to get the Communists out of the American government, although it was impossible. By now the NEWS MEDIA was Communist, the LABOR UNIONS were Communist, and the National Education Association was as "red" as Bertrand Russell. Four Viet Minh battalions had attacked the French in Vietnam, and Dulles and the Kennedy family were about to get with the Pope and bring the Vietnam War to America. George Bernard Shaw kicked the bucket in November 1950, and along with him the old drunkard Sinclair Lewis (*Elmer Gantry* and *Babbitt*) went home to his "just reward," whatever THAT was. The hydrogen bomb was tested on May 12, 1951, and the polls announced that the "average American" (if one included women and children in the poll) made $1,436.00 a year.

It all passed by me like a blanket of fog. I was knee-deep in soul winning, neck deep in the Bible, and over my head in beginning my THIRD college education. (I finished all of the undergraduate Bible stuff by the fall of 1950 and went into graduate school.) My Greek professor, William T. Brunner, recommended that since my grades were so good in Greek, I should skip three years of undergraduate Greek and go right on into graduate Greek grammar, which I did.

The only thing that deteriorated constantly throughout those years was my relationship with Janie. She never forgot, and she really never forgave. The great Bookkeeper was giving me my "springtime" as a new member of His family; however, he had not forgotten the record. True, my sins were under the Blood, they were "remembered no more" (Heb. 8:12), and all of that kind of thing, but a crop had been sown. *A reaping was coming.* You cannot violate a law without paying the consequences of breaking that law, and if you beat the laws of men, and sometimes you do, you will not violate God's laws without paying the penalty. If I had known back in 1951 and 1952 the price I would eventually have to pay for my wayward, wicked ways (1933–49), I would have probably taken my life on the spot. But God, in mercy, kept things back. There is **"a time and a season"** for everything (Ecc. 3:1). I am sure God had not forgotten the slightest detail:

1. The money stolen from my parents.
2. The houses broken into and robbed.
3. The young people corrupted by my influence.
4. The saints grieved by my conduct and conversation.
5. The ruined young men who followed me as a hero.
6. A Japanese girl somewhere (probably in Hell) whom I had deceived.
7. A string of violated virgins and adulteresses whose homes were now gone.
8. Twenty-seven years of accumulating bad habits, bad thoughts, and bad company. The Book said, **"A companion of fools shall be destroyed"** (Prov. 13:20). The Book said, **"He that despiseth the word shall be destroyed"** (Prov. 13:13). The Book said, **"Be sure your sin will find you out"** (Num. 32:23).

The trouble is that "sin doesn't leave any man better than it finds him" (Bob Jones Sr.). True, I was more experienced than the average Christian. True, I would reach spiritual maturity long before many of them did. True also, I would always appreciate salvation more than most of them would, but I had paid a PRICE. Here I was still "taking" everything in the marriage, and Janie "giving" everything, but it had always been that way. True, I was now a **"new creature"** (2 Cor. 5:17), but Janie had married a drinking, cursing artist-musician. She had not wanted a preacher. *She didn't want one now.* She tried continually to "resurrect" the "old man." When she finally resurrected him, both of our "ships" came in: hers for disobeying Ephesians 4:32 and Ephesians 5:24, and mine for disobeying Ephesians 5:25 and Ecclesiastes 12:1.

I had yet to learn what a long memory God has.

I would take her to revival meetings. If I surveyed the crowd, I was at once accused of looking at the women. When I was called forward to deal with converts at the "altar," I was accused of having looked down a woman's dress if I had been asked to pray with her. One time in a revival meeting in Pensacola, Janie mailed my wedding ring back to me. (You can imagine what a "blessing" that was from a **"help meet"** [Gen. 2:18], when you are trying to get people saved and living right.) On it went. The arguing never ceased. When I really got down in the mouth—sometimes the offerings were practically nothing or I was sick through the whole meeting—Janie would go to Dr. Bob Sr. and talk with him, personally. She did this not because she was burdened, but because she sensed that the "comradeship" between me and the "Old Man" (the term is one of respect in the Infantry; it is what you call the Company Commander) was very, very close. She wanted to insert herself between us. She did this with more than one Christian (male or female) that got into the "inner circle." When she got with "Old Man Bob," she sold HERSELF, not her husband.

Time marched on.

Perhaps the greatest thing that ever happened at BJU came about without any design, and it would appear to be of such little consequence that no one would have noticed it. Certainly, at the time it happened, I didn't notice it.

When the time came to choose my "major" in the post-graduate school, my faculty adviser was an ex-post-man, Dr. William T. Brunner, who had been a pupil of Dr. A. T. Robertson of Louisville for eight years. Brunner had not only memorized all five thousand vocabulary words in the New Testament, but he was quite able to critique the most scholarly Greek Grammar ever written—the one by Robertson. I went to him to ask advice about majoring either in Greek or Theology.

It was a cold, grey, winter afternoon. You could see Paris Mountain from his office in the Student Union building. In those days there were no trees taller than nine feet on the campus. Brunner and I were alone. After a few "pleasantries" he said, "Mr. Ruckman, what do you intend to do in the ministry? Do you intend to PREACH or to TEACH?"

SMALL TALK:

"I want to preach; I want to be an evangelist like Billy Graham."

"Well, in that case, Mr. Ruckman, if I were you I would major in Theology and not in Greek grammar."

"But sir, I've had nothing but A's in Greek now for two years."

"Yes, I know, and I am sure you could handle it, but there is something else you should consider."

"What is that?"

Here, Brunner turned his back on me and walked to the window. He did not turn back to look at me until he had finished his soliloquy. It was as though he were preaching to himself instead of advising me. The soliloquy went like this:

"Mr. Ruckman! Years ago, I fell under the spell of that great Greek teacher, Dr. A. T. Robertson of Louisville. I sat under him for eight years; four years of that time I studied alone with him as a private pupil. And, Mr. Ruckman, when I finished my studies, I could find nothing in the Greek New Testament but grammar and syntax. I have tried to win people to Christ, Mr. Ruckman, but somehow I cannot do it. I wanted to be a soul winner, but I never have led a soul to Christ."

(Come to think of that, Ruckman, checking back, realized that he had not heard *ONE TEACHER* ON THE CAMPUS testify as to having led ANYONE to Christ the *entire time* he had been there. Not even Dean Stenholm, who was in charge of the "preacher boys.")

"I was out in a field last week, witnessing to a farmer who did not believe in a literal Hell. I showed him my Greek New Testament, and proved to him from the original Greek that such a place existed. And you know, Mr. Ruckman, he simply looked at me and said, 'You know what yer trouble is, mister?' I said, 'No,' and he replied, 'Yer trouble is, ya know too much!' "

I said, "I'll major in Theology," and I did.

While I finished work, first on a Master's degree and then a Ph.D., the world went its usual course. All hell broke out in Vietnam (October 1952), and the UN General Assembly—the greatest war-making body in history—set the pace for the American public schools in America by having "ONE MINUTE of silence" in which its members could either "pray" or "meditate." The stupid Americans were now being led by pagans. They had discovered a great truth about "progress" and the increase in communications and transportation: THE MORE *PEOPLE* YOU GET TOGETHER, THE LESS *TRUTH* YOU CAN DISCUSS, for you will offend someone every time you move your head. At the League of Nations (1930) they prayed publicly but omitted the name of Jesus Christ; now (1950) they didn't even say "GOD" when they prayed; they did not dare offend the atheists, agnostics, and scientists. These poor deluded dumbbells were all talking about **"peace on earth"** (Luke 2:14), pretending that the first half of that verse was not there. *It was*. It said, **"Glory to God in the highest."** Immediately eighty-five wars broke out, and they continue today (1998).

"Ike" was elected president—the man who turned over twenty thousand eastern Europeans to the Russians (1945) where they were raped, tortured, imprisoned, and killed. A sex operation turned a male into a female (Mr. or Miss Jorgenson, December 15, 1952; who knows which?), and the old, bloody killer "Uncle Joe" (FDR's term for Stalin) "accidentally" had a stroke (March 5, 1953). The war between the Vietnamese and the French escalated, and when I graduated (1953) Elizabeth II was crowned Queen of England (June 2).

I couldn't have cared less.

CONFRONTATION:

Under the scrub oak and pine at night, out behind

the Girls' Dorms on the way to the trailer court.

"Pete, what if I asked you to go overseas for me as a missionary?" (The "Voice" was back in business, at least temporarily.)

"Well, uh, I don't know. Sure, I'll go."

"What if I asked you to go back to Japan? Would you go?"

(Man, that was a mess of water out there!) After a while I said, "All right, if you say so." I started to continue my walk, but it came again.

"Suppose I asked you to go alone? Would you go?"

I got on my knees out in the field in the moonlight. "But Lord, I have a family. I couldn't go alone."

"But what if I asked you to go, would you go *alone*?"

After a while I said, "All right. All right, God, if I have to, all right!" I started to get up off my knees, but the Bookkeeper wasn't through.

"What if I asked you to preach over there and never get any converts?"

"No converts? Why, Lord, I've got to see people saved! They're going to Hell! Look at all the time I've wasted—twenty-seven years! I've got to have some results!"

"But what if I didn't give you any visible results, what then?"

After ten minutes I wiped the tears out of my eyes and started to get up. I was unable to get off my knees.

"Suppose I asked you to die for me over there, Pete. Do you love me enough to die for me?"

"Yes, Lord, but make it *quick*, will you?" I knew all kinds of ways to die, and when I thought about them I almost got physically sick. They can let live rats eat your head off, or begin at your toes and work up. They can bury you in sand and cover your head with honey and call in the army ants till they are crawling in one eye socket and out the other while you are still screaming. The Gestapo would remove the eyes and plant live cockroaches into the sockets, then sew the lids shut. The Russians would . . . .

"Quick, Lord God, *quick*! For God's sake if I have to die, make it *quick*!"

I thought I was through, but I wasn't. I thought because I was true to my wife, paid my bills, sacrificed for my children, prayed, tithed, witnessed, memorized Scripture, passed out tracts, and didn't drink or smoke or curse, or support "Liberals" that I was consecrated. *A lot of sinners on Christian college campuses have made that mistake.*

"What if it is a slow, lingering, and painful death?"

"God," I said, "I don't see how I could take it. I can't take much pain! I would deny You or something. I don't see how I could stand it."

"But for ME, would you go through it for ME?"

Thirty minutes later I got up and went back to the trailer. When I got up I was "broke." I was flat broke; I was "sold out." And I haven't had a "dime in my pocket" since that day. That was forty-seven years ago.

Eleven people died in an earthquake in California (July 21, 1952), twenty-eight more perished in a plane crash in Waco, Texas (August 4), fourteen protesters got killed in Kimberley, South Africa (November), and fifty got killed in Casablanca during riots (December). A storm in Great Britain devastated the eastern coast, killing two hundred people (February 1953), sixty people got killed in a trolley crash in Mexico City (February 21), an earthquake in Turkey killed a thousand more people and left another fifty thousand homeless (March), five were killed in the eruption of a volcano in Japan (April 27), forty more were killed in Calcutta in a jet plane crash (May 2), one hundred and twenty-four were killed in a tornado in Texas (May 12), and another tornado in New England finished off another ninety-two people.

I survived. Why, I have no idea.

They got saved in Memphis, they got saved in Charlotte, they got saved in Asheville, and Byrson City, and Bristol, Tennessee, and Attapulgus, Georgia. A thousand got saved; twelve hundred got saved; fourteen hundred got saved. Another dozen young men got called to preach. In John Rawlings' church I was preaching to two thou-

sand at a time and preaching to three thousand at a time
in Beauchamp Vick's church. In other churches I was
preaching to a "packed house" of forty people. Church
splits, pastors fired, and a deacon sleeping horizontally
on the front bench during "revival."

Business meeting: one member hits another in the
mouth with a Bible. Business meeting: adulteress piano
and organ players "churched" while all of their relatives
cursed the preacher. A mob (literally) waiting outside to
get me and the pastor for "hurting someone's feelings."
Spitting blood out over the pulpit from a hemorrhaged
bone operation after the extraction of a wisdom tooth.
Lying in bed in a hotel for a week (during the meeting)

with Asiatic flu, and going into the pulpit every night hacking and spitting and coughing. Passing out in overheated churches in the winter and kneeling down in the pulpit to crawl out the back end of the church while a brother "led in prayer." I would lie down in the snow until I recovered and then crawl back in through the Sunday school rooms and reappear at the end of the prayer.

Controversies over the *RSV* and the *ASV*. Mountain people shouting and "running the bases," packed out churches, people literally "in the windows." Prayer altars so wet with tears you could mop them. One grown man crawling down the aisle to the altar, refusing help from anyone in getting there. One old drunk taking me by the lapels and saying, "Ah got saved under you here last year, and ah ain't doin' so well with the bottle, but ah want you to know that you are the only preacher ah could ever understand, and ah missed a freight train out of here tonight to hear y'all preach!" They got saved in Mobile and New Orleans and Atlanta, in Jacksonville, Detroit, Cincinnati, and Pensacola. I beat the bushes out in Wing, and Florala, and Andalusia, Greenbriar, and Mulberry, Alabama, and launched out into the "boonies" in Landrum, Inman, Tyron, and Columbus in the Carolinas. "The grace of God upon me, the Bible in my hand! In distant lands I trod, crying, Sinner, come to God! *I'm on the battlefield for my Lord!*"

CHAPTER FOURTEEN

The Permissive Will of God

Between 1949 and 1953 some things had happened to me that I was not aware of. I knew that I had become a Bible-believing street preacher; that was obvious. I knew that the Book I had begun with was still the word of God from cover to cover, and that Fundamental "Christian scholarship" was just Roman Catholicism in another form. I knew that I and my wife were never going to "make a go of it" no matter how many children we had, but the Book had said, **"Art thou bound unto a wife? seek not to be loosed."** (1 Cor. 7:27), so there was nothing to do but stick it out. I knew also that soul winning was the greatest thing in the world, and I still had aspirations to be a second "Billy Sunday," or at least a "Billy Graham." But two things had taken place that did not register till later.

1. The South had "gotten to me." I was picking up a southern accent. I was getting to where I liked chicken and fish better than beef and steak. I was turning more and more to vegetables instead of meat. I was developing an appreciation for southern "culture" that I had not had when I came down to the University of Alabama back in 1942. Months and months of preaching in the hills of Carolina, dealing with drunks on the streets of southern towns, "dinner on the grounds" at country churches, and private invitations into Christian homes all over Alabama, Georgia, Mississippi, and Tennessee were slowly but surely converting me into a "rebel." I liked fried okra. I wanted homemade biscuits with "red-eye" gravy. I put pepper sauce on my black-eyed peas and fried green tomatos.

And that wasn't all. Ever since the days of Fort Benning, the natural creation of God had become more real to me each year. Up until then I had been a "city boy" with the exception of my sojourning at Camp Mishawaka and a few weeks at CMTC. But now I was roaming the Blue Ridge and the Great Smokies. *There were the trees!* And ah, what power they exerted over me now, especially in the fall. What an artist's orgy! The blue mist in the early morning filling the valleys; the snowy tops of Wagon Wheel Gap and Grandfather Mountain and Mt. Mitchell at certain seasons; the deep gorges into the moonshiners' dens where it was so quiet at times you could "hear yourself think." There were huge birch trees and pine trees, towering elms and poplars, and further down in Dixie the live oaks and magnolias. I ate gumbo and crayfish Bisque with the Cajuns in Louisiana, barbecued pork in Georgia, "maters and taters" in the backwoods of Tennessee, and grits with "cracknels" in the Black Belt of Alabama. In my travels I decided that if a man could choose the place of his abode on this earth—and up till now I had never been able—the place would either have to be in the middle of a dense forest in the Smoky Mountains or near a beach by the ocean. Trees and oceans: the rest could be dispensed with.

2. I began to see why Southerners believed in "separate but equal facilities." I learned about the blacks by being where they were and dealing with them. One week in Hale County, Alabama, I dealt with nothing but blacks and led over forty of them to the Lord. I preached in black churches. I found out something: *BLACK* FOLKS ARE NOT LIKE *WHITE* FOLKS. I spent a lot of time studying the Civil War and American history that I had not spent before. Most of my reading now was from Zondervan, Baker, and Eerdmans publishing companies. My fiction reading stopped altogether, and now it was SERMONS by McClendon, Mackintosh, Sunday, Moody, Torrey, Finney, Spurgeon, Wesley, Whitefield, McClaren, Morgan, Sam Jones, Bob Jones, Haldeman, Riley, Norris, Mordecai Ham, Chrysostom, Luther, E. J. Daniels, Jesse Handley, Hyman Appleman, Bud Robinson, etc.

One book a day plus "through the Book" once a month. The commentaries piled up. The books on archaeology and geography piled up, and the books on sermon outlines and sermon illustrations piled up.

3. I had not learned yet how to become a normal human being. My life (erratic, eccentric, and dehumanized up until now) was still sporadic and unnatural and still dehumanized. Although I was beginning to learn things about human nature I had never learned before—all I learned in the infantry was that, "if it don't make sense, there's a buck in it" and, "the tough guy is always the guy who 'has the edge'"—I still lived in the abstract. It was still a *picture world* (and what else could it have been for an artist?) where I was not really aware of the needs of others. I was totally wrapped up in serving God, and although I was keeping Matthew 10:37-39, I was not keeping Ephesians 5:25 or Hebrews 13:3. The pace was too fast. But when I looked at the pace, I saw a SLOW pace even at any speed.

The real trouble was that there was not one point of communion any more with my wife. She kept house, took care of the children, cooked a few meals, and occasionally went with me to a meeting. We argued going and coming and when we got home. Once she threatened to leave if I did not quit the ministry. Another time she threatened suicide if I did not quit the ministry. I had no intention of quitting. I had enlisted for life, and I figured that I probably didn't have ten years more to minister. I wasn't slackening the pace for anyone. My motive was Scriptural and proper in the light of Luke 9:23–24, Galatians 1:10, and Philippians 3:14, but it was also an alibi to spend hours and hours on the road, hours and hours on visitation, and hours and hours in the study, "serving." My wife was left to herself. When I took time out to be with her, it only made matters worse; up would come the terrible "past" in less than an hour.

God was going to have to do TWO things to me—neither of which I would appreciate a bit—before He could get Him a vessel which He considered to be "fit for use."

1. I would have to be HUMANIZED. The dance bands, beer halls, bar rooms, barracks, beaches, bayonet drill fields, and back alleys had done such damage that not even salvation had remedied it. I was not sympathetic, and I was not "kind," nor was I polite or courteous: furthermore, I looked at those virtues as "compromises." And a woman, to me, was still a UTILITY, the best of them "sharper than a briar."

2. I would have to fulfill my calling. *I was not fulfilling it.* I was winning souls, that is true; young men were getting called to preach under me, that was true; I nearly always had some results in evangelistic meetings; and I was able to preach "for a living," as the ministry now furnished "full-time support" without the GI bill. But God did not want me to be an *evangelist*; He wanted me to be a BIBLE TEACHER.

I despised teaching and teachers. If there ever was a blind spot in my vision, it was there. I had sat twenty-two years at school desks (six years of Grade school, three years of Middle school, three years of High school, four years of College, and now six years of post-grad). At the age of forty-four I would have spent HALF OF MY LIFE behind a school desk. I despised teaching. I had never been a "spectator" except at the movies, and even then I tried immediately to put into concrete action whatever I saw there. I never have enjoyed watching football games or baseball games; I have played both. I get nothing out of watching golf or tennis; I have *played* both. The only two sports I could ever watch with interest were boxing and hockey: *they moved.* Watching baseball, to me, was the equivalent of playing checkers, only duller. I wanted action.

To me, a "teacher" was a man on crutches who instructed people on "how to run." Of all the teachers that I studied under from 1926 to 1953, I cannot remember having any respect for more than four of them, and two of those were Army instructors. That was four teachers out of about forty-five. One was Major Bronchorst, the bayonet instructor at Ft. Benning; one was Maude Bishop, an old maid high school teacher in Topeka; one

was Max Schoening, my company commander at Fort
Rucker; and one was Mr. Bruce, my manual arts instructor at Boswell Junior High. The rest of them I looked at
as an assorted bunch of wimps, washouts, ding-a-lings,
and dingbats that failed in life and couldn't do anything
else but teach. I never found ONE teacher at Bob Jones
University that I would follow fifteen feet in broad day-
light. I would rather PLAY hockey than watch it, I would
rather PREACH than watch someone else do it, I would
rather WIN A SOUL than tell someone how to do it, and
I would rather *play* touch football than WATCH tackle
football.

That attitude was going to cost me more grief than I
would care to write about. I could not "see" teaching
with binoculars.

Graduation time approached. Bob Jones Sr.—now a
very close friend of mine—talked to me about staying at
the university and teaching. I told him "nothing doing." I
had meetings all booked up for the whole summer ahead,
and I had been preaching in a church somewhere every
Sunday that year that I was going to school in the winter.

I selected for my Ph.D. thesis: *"A History of Practical Theology in the Light of the Book of Acts."* It was
(naturally) a guided missile. It was aimed at the heart (or
the pocketbook, probably) of the men I had sat under at
BJU since 1949. The thesis was simple: *if a man is not
making an effort to win lost sinners to Christ, he is HET-
ERODOX, no matter what his profession of faith is.* Theo-
logically professing to be an "Evangelical" or "Fundamentalist," who believes in the "plenary, verbal inspiration of the original autographs," doesn't amount to a pile
of gummy bears if the professor is *not ACTIVELY engaged in carrying out what those "autographs" said.* My
thesis hit the graduate faculty of BJU like a cement truck
colliding with a Volkswagen.

First, Dr. Whitte gave me the only "C" I had in six
years of work because he saw the way I was heading.
Secondly, Dr. Brokenshire, who was supposed to examine the thesis, got ill and wound up in the school hospital. (He never recovered completely and died shortly af-

terward.) Thirdly, Dr. Barton Payne (now deceased) began to lay assignments on all the classes that I was in that were so heavy that when the exams came, NO ONE in the class passed but me. Fearing that such a performance would get back to the administration, Payne quickly "upgraded the spread" so at least HALF the class would pass. But in so doing he had to raise my grades from 75 and 80 up to 100; a couple of times he had to give me a grade of 105 in order to get the right percentage of the class up to 70.

All three men were Five-Point, Amillennial Presbyterians who had never led a soul to Christ in a lifetime.

As "D-Day" approached, I had to "counsel" with Dr. Payne about the coming thesis. He was ready to reject it.

DIALOGUE:

"You see, Mr. Ruckman, your thesis does not contain enough original sources. You have not cited enough material from original sources."

"Well, that is partly true, but I did for the last half of the thesis; about from 1700 A.D. on."

"Yes, but you have covered too large an area to do the work satisfactorily. Let me show you."

And here Dr. Barton Payne went to his shelf and picked out HIS thesis, which he had written at the University of Southern California. I examined it. It contained writing in Hebrew, Coptic, Aramaic, Greek, English, Latin, German, and French.

"What," I asked, "is the exact purpose of this thesis?"

"Well, as you can see, it is a thesis to prove that 1 Samuel, as it stands in the Syrian text, is probably from the Hebrew instead of the Greek Septuagint."

"Well," I said, "having proved THAT, what have you proved?"

"Oh, Mr. Ruckman," he said, "a thesis is not a complete work. It only forms a foundation for further works. For example, after finishing a thesis like this, one could take up 2 Samuel."

"Well, suppose you proved conclusively that 1 and

2 Samuel in Syriac came from the Hebrew instead of the Septuagint. What then?"

"I . . . I'm afraid I don't understand."

"Well, Doctor, according to the *founder of this institution*, BJU is interested in two things: not merely academic excellence, but PRACTICAL application. It seems to me that your thesis fails to meet the standards of this school. What is PRACTICAL about your thesis?"

Ah, beloved, that tied the rag on the bush!

As a consequence of these brushes with the faculty, I had an ambush awaiting me when the time of my "defense" came. I couldn't have cared any less. I knew now what "Christian scholarship" was. No one was going to kid me about "godly" scholars any more. At BJU, these were supposed to be the very best in the land—the cream of the crop. They were nothing but BACKSLIDDEN HUMANISTS. They had no final authority but the man who paid their bills. They were not soul winners, they had no burden for lost souls, and every one of them had spent his life following men (either their writings or teachings) instead of God.

When the time for the defense of the thesis came, Brokey went to the infirmary, and Whitte and Payne refused to appear. This drew the attention of Dr. Bob Sr. immediately, and he called both professors in, one at a time, and grilled them. Then he found out what he had on his faculty all along: two baby-sprinkling, Five-Point, Amillennial Calvinists WITHOUT A SPIRITUAL BONE IN THEIR BODIES. (He had three more he didn't know about!) He shipped both of them, but that delayed me from getting my Ph.D., and I did not get it until the next year.

Shortly after dumping Whitte and Payne, Dr. Bob Jones Sr. found Dr. Brokenshire dead in the school hospital. He had died while going to the rest room. Upon returning to the dead man's bed, Dr. Bob found that "Brokey" had been grading student report cards just before his death. The last card he had graded was mine, and on the back of this card Brokey had written, "This man can teach HEBREW." This increased Senior's pressure on me tremendously—the pressure to stay at BJU and teach—but I could not see it. I did not want to be a teacher. *I despised teaching.*

Well, I was held up a year in getting my degree. When I got it, I walked out of Homer Rodeheaver Auditorium on the north side and started down the sidewalk. Then I heard a voice say, "Young man, come here!" It was a high-pitched, raspy voice that I had heard before in a Bible conference. It was the voice of Ernest Reveal, Superintendent of the Evansville Rescue Mission. "Young man, come here!" Reveal was sitting in a car with Fred Afman (a graduate teacher at BJU). I came up to the car, and before I could say a word, "Pappy" Reveal said, "KNEEL!" *"Befehl ist Befehl,"* so I knelt. He reached his arm out of the car window and placed his hand on my head and gave me the only unofficial "ordination" I was ever to receive. He prayed for me for about five minutes. I thanked him, got up, and went on my way, blissfully unaware of the leadership of God in my life at this peculiar "ordination." I had just been ordained wearing a cap and gown and holding a Doctor's degree of philosophy in my hand; thus all three of my degrees had come out as *TEACHER'S* DEGREES (B.A., M.A., and Ph.D.). There wasn't one RELIGIOUS degree in a frame.

It is one of the ironies of Fundamentalism that two dormitories now stand on the campus of BJU which bear the names of a man who recommended me to teach there, and a man who left me his sermon outlines in his "last testament." Brokenshire willed his Kittel's Hebrew Bible to me—which I still have (1998), and Pappy Reveal, who ordained me (see above) sent me three bound notebooks containing his sermon outlines when he died. I still have them. You will find Brokenshire Hall and Reveal Hall at BJU, but Ruckman "hath left his name for a curse." Evidently Bob Jones Jr. and Bob Jones III just USED Reveal and Brokey; they were (and are) not in the least bit like them.

As if to nullify His own leadership, the Holy Spirit visited me with a series of revival services in Bay Minette, Alabama, that you would not believe. Concurrent with

**Typical Bible Conference
Canton Baptist Temple—1960-1970**

graduation, I had a week of meetings in the First Baptist Church of Bay Minette. A city-wide revival broke out that resembled something like the days of Charles G. Finney and Billy Sunday. People got saved right and left: Presbyterians and Episcopalians as well as Baptists. Lawyers got right, construction men got saved, high school students witnessed in the hallways, five young men got called to preach, and so many people were coming forward at the invitations, the Sunday school rooms could not hold them, and they were squalling so loud the church secretary could not get the "cards" filled out. Following this outpouring, ten men in the town got together and bought me a brand new, ten thousand dollar, three-bedroom, two-bathroom home on a half-acre of land. My payments were one hundred and fifty dollars a month with nothing "down." And so, after four years of living in a forty-foot plywood trailer, I moved into a veritable mansion. One of the fruits of that revival was a man named Dickman, who got interested in a sign ministry and wound up putting Scripture signs in nearly every State in the Union and even in Germany.

From this time until 1959, I was an "evangelist," like I had wanted to be. I barnstormed the country, preaching from Los Angeles to Nova Scotia and from Key West to Chicago. Every summer I preached at the combined "Youth Camps" for the BBF in Michigan, Ohio, and Indiana, and I discovered that by 1964 one hundred and thirty-five young men had been called to preach in these meetings. I preached all over Alabama, Florida, Mississippi, and Georgia and then began to preach "up north" in Ohio, Michigan, Pennsylvania, and Indiana. John Rawlings and Beauchamp Vick were the gentlemen who opened the doors for me in these early days; I met them at Aubrey Mitchell's church (Wilson Avenue Baptist) in Mobile, Alabama. Hugh Pyle also recommended me for meetings, and for a very brief while I was in the good favor of John R. Rice, who published the results of my meetings in his column, "With the Evangelists." God gave me another beautiful, healthy child (John Michael, September 3, 1956), and all my bills for my new house

Priscilla, Pete Jr., Janie, Diana, Peter, Mike, David
(1960)

Pete Jr., Mike, David
(1999)

were paid on time.

But now our domestic troubles reached their peak. Janie cared nothing about the new house. She threatened to desert me if I did not get out of the ministry. The arguments only increased in intensity. She didn't like my friends in Bay Minette. Finally, she raised such a fuss about the house and the payments that we sold it and bought twelve acres of land out on the south side of town, with a Jim Walter home on the front lot. It had two bedrooms and one bathroom. On I went down the road: Kansas, Mississippi, Arkansas, Kentucky, Delaware, Maryland, Oklahoma, etc. One thousand got saved, twelve hundred, sixteen hundred, two thousand. On and on. By 1959 I had been through the Book about sixty-five times. I had finished translating every word of every verse in Nestle's Greek New Testament from Matthew to 2 Peter. I had found perhaps FIVE things in that Greek text that "shed light" on my English text. In the same period of time, I had found an average of FORTY things EACH READING that I had made from the English text. I saw quickly that the power and blessing of God was not on "the Greek." It was on the English. Koine Greek was a dead language, and only a dead-head would use it.

I continued to preach on the streets, in the churches, in the jails and penitentiaries. I had one meeting in Atlanta, with an interdenominational church, where I thought only two people had been saved, but I was told by a member there (thirty-five years later!) that immediately after that meeting the whole church had gotten saved (about twenty adult members) and confessed Christ openly and had been rebaptized. Fourteen prisoners in the Federal penitentiary at Atlanta openly confessed Christ for the first time in response to my public invitation.

Janie threatened suicide if I didn't show her more attention; one time she made a half-hearted attempt at it by slashing her wrists. On another occasion she tried to throw herself out the door of the car while we were traveling down the highway at fifty m.p.h. in the middle of the night. I went on with the ministry.

While I was going "down the road," French para-

troopers landed at Dien Bien Phu (November 1953), the
hunt for "Reds" continued under McCarthy (February
1954) till Edward R. Murrow—a dyed-in-the-wool FDR
international Socialist—finished off Mac over the radio
with the backing of President Eisenhower. On May 17,
1954, the Supreme Court took the first step for utter
demolition of the public school system (May 17, 1954):
they ordered enforced race-mixing by Federal compul-
sion. Two hundred and fifty thousand Vietnamese—most
of them Roman Catholic—fled to South Vietnam as Ho
Chi Minh took over Hanoi (October 10, 1954), Einstein
kicked the bucket (April 18, 1955), the Communists set
up the Warsaw Pact (May 14, 1955), and Russia set off
its first hydrogen bomb (November 26, 1955).

Following the Supreme Court's disastrous decision—
done by a violation of States' rights—Rosa Parks decided she would sit in the front of a bus in Montgomery,
Alabama. Following her, "riders" took turns until the
white people QUIT RIDING THE BUSES: *they bought
cars.* Autherine Lucy entered the University of Alabama
(February 1956), and Ike sent troops with bayonets into
Little Rock, Arkansas (September 25, 1957) to let the
states know that they were now FEDERAL PROPERTY
(Fourteenth Ammendment) and BELONGED TO WASH-
INGTON, D.C. ("Join the Army and see the high
schools"). With the influx of the Africans came the first
real BLACK-WHITE MAN: Elvis Presley (September
1956). He brought to American teenagers African music,
African morals, and an African drug culture for "soul
brothers." He lived off of five prescription drugs plus
liquor. He was a Charismatic Church of God "Christian"
from Mississippi. The head of Sun Recording Company
said that he filled the bill for a "white man who could
sing like a nigger." The time for Africa had arrived.
America was ready for the jungle.

In preparation for the Antichrist's ten federated kingdom (Daniel 2), the European Common Market was set
up in ROME (March 25, 1957). John XXIII replaced
Pius XII (Adolph Hitler's old buddy) and became the
first Red Pope in the Vatican. He began to center all of

Rome's "theology" around standard MARXIST themes: social justice, oppressed minorities, unequal distribution of wealth, the right to self-determination, and human rights. These reached their apex in the ministries of Paul VI and John Paul II, who cooperated with Communism in all of its outreaches, especially in its opposition to Israel and the capitalistic system in America. In 1959, Castro conquered Cuba after finding out that Stalin was a traitor. Stalin had been denounced by Khrushchev (June 5, 1956) because of "bad press" over the way he conducted himself in office. In August 1959, Hawaii became the fiftieth state in the Union. Alaska had been admitted the previous January.

By this time, the Ruckman family was "in crisis." In 1958, a television ministry opened for me, and for the first time I could take my natural God-given artistic ability and put it to use NATIONWIDE. I had the only truly VISUAL medium in the U.S.A. for the Gospel, having drawn more than two thousand Biblical chalk talks. But as this ministry opened, the family feuding reached the place of near-violence. (I had slapped Janie several times back in the old days, but being a Christian I did not feel that I could do such a thing again. It was strange to me. When I drank and smoked and cursed and abused her, she had wanted to stay, but now that I was behaving myself and not abusing her, she wanted to leave.)

Our years of grieving the Holy Spirit had taken its toll on me. I was not exempt from **"a weariness of the flesh."** Little by little I was slipping back toward Egypt, although it was still just in the "heart" stages. But it is the **"backslider in heart"** that Solomon warns about (Prov. 14:14). I was myself on the brink of stepping out on her again, and there were plenty of "prospects." I was thirty-six years old, but my time in the Book had brought my countenance back to the visage of a twenty-five year old. I looked younger in 1958 than I had looked in 1948.

On September 31, 1959, my fifth child was born. Finally, I had consented to call one of the boys a "Junior," my reasoning, all along, being that one "Peter S. Ruckman" in this world was certainly enough to last till the Advent. But this was Peter S. Ruckman Junior, born in Pensacola, Florida. (We drove back and forth to Pensacola for hospitalization, but it was nothing much to do as I had to drive there almost three times every month to catch planes for the meetings. We very rarely used the airport in Mobile.) While carrying this third boy, Janie became even more neurotic and emotionally upset than ever before. There were constant threats of divorce or suicide, which continued after Peter Jr. was born. Finally she faked a "paralysis" and pretended she could not walk or stand. In order to take care of her, I cancelled half a dozen meetings and returned to Bay Minette. The idea was that "I wouldn't be away so long if I really loved her, etc.," so I dropped the evangelism and tried to pastor a small church there that my converts had started in a funeral parlor following the great revival. They were now meeting in a Seventh-day Adventist church and preparing to build. This pastoring went on for several months (August to October of 1960).

In the meantime, Castro—after claiming that he was not a Communist—declared that he *was* and promptly nationalized all American property in Cuba (August 7). The press went crazy over some Negroes winning events in the Rome Olympics (September), and quickly a South African Communist (Albert John Luthuli) was given the Nobel "Peace" Prize for inciting riots in South Africa (December 10). Later M. L. King Jr. was given the same prize for the same performance. In keeping with the back-to-the-jungle movement, Louis B. Leakey, a British evolutionist, decided that Adam and Eve were BLACK. He claimed the oldest human ancestors were Africans (February 24, 1961).

America's first Roman Catholic president took office (November 1960), and not only escalated the war in Vietnam and tried to attack Cuba (Bay of Pigs), but passed an "under the table" bill which gave him the right to confiscate all railroads, airports, ports of embarkation, private property, household goods, and bank accounts, and would further allow him to remove families from their domiciles and ship them anywhere. This "emergency" act still stands on the books. Roman Catholics have a dictator complex: Catholicism is the Fascist form of professing Christianity. Castro, Batiste, Sandino, Sandinista, Ortega, Trudeau, Mussolini, Hitler, Allende, Trujillo, and Peron were all members of the same church: *the church that spawned Napoleon, Charlemagne, and Hitler.*

On April 26, 1961, Kennedy and the CIA "invaded" the Bay of Pigs and destroyed the lives of nearly a thousand American Cubans. All of them were killed or captured but a handful that floated back on small boats. At the last minute, the loyal "son of the church" refused to back up his own church members with ships or planes, and they were slaughtered.

Some more things happened. The Berlin Wall went up (August 1961). Hemmingway, one of "old" Ruckman's favorite authors, blew his brains out (July 2). He had been hanging out with sodomites at "Sloppy Joes" in Key West. And as Janie prepared to desert her evangelist husband, Kennedy, the Roman Catholic president, "upped" his "advisors" in Vietnam from seven hundred to sixteen thousand, thus, for all practical purposes, declaring war on the North Vietnamese. No one raised an eyebrow. By this time the press controlled the MINDS of the American people, *and JFK was a "god" to the American press.*

While Janie was in her wheelchair, she made some plans. This time everything was laid out in great detail. She planned to desert and take all five children with her and leave a trail behind her that would guarantee my destruction one way or another.

1. She had been seeing a doctor regularly, and when she left she would phone him and tell him that she had been BEATEN. To prove this, she would have to show some bruises; so she got a violent argument going where I grabbed her by the wrists (without hitting her) and shoved her up against a table (without hitting her) and a sink (without hitting her). She showed these bruises to a doctor. Her skin was always ultra-sensitive after the birth of our third child, and it didn't take much more than a

touch to leave a mark.

2. She then contacted my mother and father "long distance," and warned them that I was turning out like Johnny. I had become a raving "religious fanatic" and needed to see a shrink.

3. She contacted the man that led me to Christ (Hugh Pyle) and told him that I was threatening her life and the lives of our children.

Having set this scenery, she "flew the coop" one morning, stealing the car and taking all five children with her. Back she went to "mama" on the farm—Hale County, Alabama—and left me without transportation in the Jim Walter home.

All phone calls to Sawyerville were cut off; all mail was returned.

I came back to an empty house and found a note on the door with this pious inscription: "This time give it all to God." *I had done that years ago.* But Janie had never given me to God. This time she had been forced to, but it came in the form of "voluntary abandonment," not surrender to the will of God.

Now some dark days came. By agreement with her brother, Janie had the car brought back to Grove Hill, where I picked it up. This left me with a used car, an empty house, a one hundred and ten pound German shepherd named "Chief," and another ninety pound German shepherd named "Duchess."

Two days after she left, John Rawlings phoned me up and asked me if I was going to fulfill an evangelistic obligation I had made with him a year before. I told him, "No." He wanted to know why, so I told him my wife was sick, and I couldn't come.

He said, "Your wife has deserted you, hasn't she?" (I learned then how fast "bad news" travels. All the brethren had "alerted" each other all the way down the line. I evidently was more of an issue than John R. Rice and Bob Jones Jr. had pretended that I was.)

I still objected. I said, "Listen, brother, I can't go on with this mess the way it is. I'm getting out."

Rawlings said, "Did God call you to preach?"

"Yes," I answered.

"Did he call your wife to preach?"

"No."

"Well, then, you can't quit just because SHE quit, can you?"

He had me. But still I planned to quit. I told him I would take the meeting with him and one other meeting I had scheduled up in Memphis, but after that I was "getting out."

There followed some lonely days and nights. You have no idea what it is like to come back daily to an empty house where FIVE children had been playing incessantly. I didn't miss Janie, but I missed my children. Christmas was just around the corner. My mother and father were seeking to have me committed. My ministerial friends had lost faith in me. My meetings were cancelled, and I had two dogs to do something with and didn't know what to do with them.

But time and tide wait for no man. The bills would still come in: car payments, house payments, utility bills, etc. A man has to have an income. What could I do for a living? Well, I really couldn't do anything. I was thirty-nine years old and had never been hunting, and had only been on three or four fishing trips. I had never worked as a carpenter or bricklayer; I could not weld or do masonry. I had never written out a check, because Janie had handled all of the finances. I knew nothing about book-keeping or storekeeping; I had never held a job anywhere except as a disk jockey or a lifeguard or a dance band drummer, and all of those occupations were "out." I wasn't a good enough electrician to do much of anything, and I had no experience in construction work.

I could drive a truck. That was it! I would pick up enough money to pay my bills by driving a truck. I phoned up my good friend Clyde Reynolds of the Mobile Rescue Mission and told him my situation. Would he pay me fifty dollars a week to drive a truck for the mission? Sure, he would.

"Come on over," he said, "and we'll put you to work tomorrow." So I went over to Mobile.

A typical shot of a 49-year ministry.

FEEDBACK:

"Well, here I am. Where's the truck?"

"Oh, outside in the alley. We don't have any pick-ups for about an hour."

"Well, maybe I'd better take it for a spin and get used to the gears and the steering, you know."

"Well, you won't have to do that, Pete."

"Why not?"

"We always have plenty of guys who can handle the truck."

"But I thought you said you would give me a job."

"I did. We have a good job for you, and I will pay you fifty dollars a week to do it."

"Good," I said, "what is it?"

"Well, Pete, we have a dozen or so Christians here who meet twice a day for Bible study: about two hours each time, and they want you *to teach them the Bible*."

It is amazing sometimes to see how slow some people are to "get the message": I still didn't get it, but I took the job. It went on for about eight weeks.

In the meantime, my friends (and I had some real friends left) were trying everything they could to get some kind of communication going between Janie and me. My German friends from Elberta, Alabama, (a German settlement) came up and had a long talk with me. It surfaced that they had been keeping an eye on Janie for several years, especially in my absence when I was gone on meetings. Their opinion was that I was fortunate to have gotten rid of her. My other friends contacted Bob Jones Sr. and tried to get him to "arbitrate," but when they got his mail and saw the prospects, they advised me against going to him. The gist of his correspondence was that he would protect the University at any cost in such a "scandal." My friends were more interested in Janie and me than they were his school. Finally, they got Janie to write and say that she would come back *if* I would see a psychiatrist (the idea being to get me a psychiatric record that my parents would use to get me committed). I went to THREE of them (one in Ft. Benning, Georgia, one in Holland, Michigan, and one in Tuscaloosa, Alabama); all three of them gave me a clear slate. Janie then said that she would come back *if* I resigned the church and went back into evangelism. I did this, but she did not come back. The last "offer"—of course, it was all nonsense—was that *if* I had a vasectomy she would come back. This was taken care of in 1962. She did not come back. She had no intention of coming back. My friends thought that I was obligated to do all this, going the second and third miles, etc., to make things right, so I went the "whole distance." But by the time the fourth compromise arrived, I was absolutely against it.

The winter of 1961 was the worst one I had in my life since my conversion. Small meetings, small income, had to get rid of the German shepherds, etc. Empty house; very few plane rides, for there was no one to take me to the plane or pick me up. I took the car and a small eight by ten trailer with me. I slept in the trailer in the snow and ice in December, January, and February, while taking meetings, and then returned to my empty house in the springtime. Several times I thought quite seriously of taking my life, and one time even got the gun out, loaded, and made some "passing gestures." But it is amazing how BIG the muzzle of a pistol looks when you have it pointed right at your eyes!

On I went down the road. I had preached in Jackson and New Buffalo, Michigan; Hagerstown, Maryland; Hamilton, Lebanon, Franklin, Columbus, Canton, Cincinnati, and Cleveland, Ohio; Kansas City, Kansas; Kansas City, Missouri; Middletown and Dayton, Ohio; Butler, Alquippa, and Ambridge, Pennsylvania; Foley, Elberta, and Gateswood, Alabama; Ridley, Dyersburg, and Covington, Tennessee; and Guthrie, Knoxville, Louisville, and Bowling Green, Kentucky. By 1962 I had covered Atlanta, Savannah, Macon, Athens, Valdosta, Attapulgus, Summerville, Augusta, and Waycross, Georgia, plus Landrum, Inman, Travelers Rest, Spartanburg, Columbia, Greenville, Sumter, Timmonsville, Darlington, Greer, Fountain Inn, Laurens, Woodruff, Pickens, Clemson, and Liberty, South Carolina, plus Gastonia, Concord, Cherryville, Morgantown, Kannapolis,

Hendersonville, Gastonia, High Point, Jacksonville, Fayetteville, Charlotte, and Greensboro, North Carolina. Men and women got saved; they got saved and got baptized and joined Baptist churches.

By spring, with a trial coming up (they *tried* divorce cases in those days, if you contested the charges), I had made up my mind to get out of the ministry. I wrote for my transcripts from Bob Jones, the University of Alabama, and Kansas State College, and prepared to go back into secular education, as a "teacher." But at this time, I suddenly got a call from the Brent Baptist Church in Pensacola (the church that Hugh Pyle had pastored when he led me to Christ). The pastor there—a certain Dolphus Price (graduate of Tennessee Temple)—had resigned and started another work a few miles away, and the place had been left in a shambles. Brent had started a Christian school, which was now bankrupt. It was over three hundred thousand dollars in debt and had a bond program that wasn't registered properly, plus two hundred thousand dollars worth of bonds that would have to be paid for after a split that had decimated the congregation. They had gone from over one thousand to two hundred overnight. There were eight deacons running this remnant, and every month when they showed the "tab" to the church it consisted of five pages of sixteen inch paper, single-spaced, with bills on them: everything from piano tuners and flower shops to roofing companies and office supplies. It was this group that asked me to "supply" for them till they could get a pastor. I consented, with the agreement that when they got one I would resign immediately, as I intended to go into education. I moved my little trailer to Pensacola and parked it on the church lot and drove back and forth between there and Bay Minette while the trial was "shaping up." They gave me forty-five dollars a week.

My "supply" was to last one and a half years and it terminated in my being called to pastor the church: the church I was saved in.

The trial came off in 1962 as John Glenn orbited the earth (February 26), Kennedy committed the Army to permanent war in Vietnam (February 28), and the press built "Jackie" into a goddess. She was called "THE QUEEN" of the White House to reinforce the standard Roman Catholic, Fascist position. *This would make Kennedy a "KING."* (The press did the same thing with Dukakis later by claiming that the *"Duke"* might become the "King": *Time* and *Newsweek*, 1988.) Jackie was immediately connected with Gandhi, the Indian Communist (March 12), so the "circle" (M. L. King, Gandhi, the Pope, and the Kennedys) would not be broken. As the trial finished, our Catholic president sent American troops into Thailand (May 29).

The results of the trial (two sessions) were:

1. Janie had no grounds for divorce, whatsoever, but had simply deserted her husband.

2. The laws of Alabama stated that if a woman (or man) deserted the "other party" and did not become reconciled in one year, the divorce was automatically given to the party that was deserted.

3. Split custody gave the children to me in the summertime and to her in the wintertime, with me having "Christmas privileges" for one week. We would both drive to Bay Minette for "pick-ups and deliveries." No alimony, only "care and maintenance" for the children: two hundred and fifty dollars a month.

Janie had tried to use the oldest girl, Diana, in the trial to prove her points, but the thing backfired, and she was caught in "collusion" in her testimony, and her whole case fell apart. Having some political contacts in Montgomery, Alabama, through her father (Pop May), she got the case up to the Supreme Court of Alabama, but it did no good. "Judge Hall's decision" stood as given.

Before the bench we were both asked one question: "Are you willing to take your part of the blame for this failure in the marriage?" I said, "I will take all the blame she wants to put on me," and Janie said, "Absolutely NOT!"

And that was the end of the marriage from my unsaved days.

The next summer I took my children out to California in the car. In the face of a Welfare charge that I was not a "fit father" to take care of little children, I took all four of them (Diana stayed at home with her mother) more than four thousand miles in a car that had no air conditioning—in the middle of the summer—and "fathered" them through El Paso, Texas; Denning, New Mexico; Needles, California; the Grand Canyon; and the redwood forest in Sequoia National Park. Disposable diapers out the window the whole way, burned-out brake repairs, exploding radiator, dumping water on each other in the car, revival services, dealing with constipation and diarrhea: the whole works. When I got back with them, all of them "fit as a fiddle," the "Welfare" had to shut its mouth.

I preached at Lake Hume north of LA while in California, and there one night at a table full of preachers and their wives, I was asked the question of all questions, a question which probably interests self-righteous Pharisees more than any question in the Bible. A sort of lull ("before the storm") descended over the table at a certain place, and in this vacuum a preacher sitting across from me suddenly said, "Do you think a divorced preacher is qualified for the ministry?"

I sensed that thirty pairs of eyes and ears were turned onto the same channel. I quickly sent up a Nehemiah prayer (Neh. 2:4) and asked, "What did you say?" (This gives the Lord time to give you the answer; I had often used this stratagem in "Open Bible Forums" when a particularly hard question was asked.)

FEEDBACK:

"I said, Do you think a divorced preacher is qualified for the ministry?"

"Well, look at it this way," I said, "suppose you and your wife are having trouble and not getting along."

Wham! On target. Fire for effect! His wife was sitting right next to him, and she suddenly turned beet red. He shifted nervously in his chair (Brokenshire and Father Sullivan all over again) and cleared his throat.

"So, one day she ups and quits and leaves you. Are you going to quit the ministry because she quits?"

"Well, I don't know exactly what I would do."

"Well, did God call you to preach?"

"Yeah, he sure did."

"Did he call your wife to preach?"

"No."

"Well, then, how can you quit just because she quits?"

Finally he said flatly, "Well, I never thought about it that way before." I said, "Well, think about it. Please pass the salt."

The years 1961 and 1988 are the only two years in my life as a child of God that I would never want to live over again. In both cases a professing Christian woman had just deserted and abandoned the ministry; in both cases my children were caught in the middle of a bust-up; in both cases neither woman had *scriptural grounds* for leaving; in both cases my adversaries thought that I had been "wiped out." In both cases I had friends that stuck with me to the end; in both cases the women left in winter; in both cases the length of the marriage was sixteen years; and in both cases the women left just when *a national television ministry had started*. The events were so similar that up in 1990, looking back, I could come to only one conclusion: *a man has to reap what he sows*. I had thought when my family busted up in 1961 that all of the installments had been paid. They had not been paid. For sixteen years I had been the "taker" and Janie had been the "giver." True, I had been faithful to her ever since my conversion, and true again, I had supplied all her material needs (a maid two times a week, a new car every two years, etc.) and tried to supply her spiritual needs, but in vain. The wounds had been made too deep; the scars too permanent. There were none of those things in a marriage that women look for from their husbands in the way of little endearments, compliments, special gifts, personal intimacies, etc. The marriage had started wrong; it had to end wrong, and it did.

Years later (after an eleven year "grace period") God was going to give me a chance to see what it was like to be in Janie's shoes: in the shoes of a married

Christian whose partner did all the TAKING and GAVE NOTHING. And when it came, it would be the same length of time (*within one month*) of the time I had spent with Janie. I was destined, way back in 1961, to run another sixteen years of married life where I remembered all of the birthdays, anniversaries, and remembered to say all of the intimate little things in the right way at the right time, lavished thousands of dollars on gifts and "dates," and set a young woman up as a queen in my home, as well as the church. In exchange for it, I received a Florida "incompatibility" notice in August of 1988.

The Bookkeeper had a long memory.

But back in 1962 I entered upon a period of my life that was so relaxed and comfortable that the only way it could be described, Scripturally, would be "to be in a backslidden condition." I got all my children in the summer. In less than three years Diana, the oldest girl (whom the mother had tried to use in the trial,) came to me and confessed her sins and delivered Pete and Michael to me permanently. Janie had wound up in an apartment with no food or older person to take care of them. I got all my kids back "full-time" in 1968 and put Pete and Mike in school at Pensacola (Brent Elementary).

In the meantime, Brent had called two pastors (Sheehan from Georgia and Pete McGuire from Texas), but both of them had backed off when they saw the bills. So there I was, still there, now living in a small white house (25 St. Johns St.) that had been a nursery for the Sunday school. Brent sold their school building to Arlin and Becky Horton and continued slowly but surely to pay off their monstrous debts. I told them I would pastor until they were out of the "red," and I kept my word.

Henniger, Rawlings, Bob Gray, and Vick did not back off from me: neither did Mullens or Modlish (Rochester). I still preached every summer at the large youth camps in Chatauqua, and now my income was back up again where I could take meetings. For two years I had subsisted on forty-five dollars a week from the church by driving weekly to Mobile and Panama City (or Fort Walton Beach) and teaching small Bible classes. These extra "services" netted another forty dollars a week. In 1962, we started Bible classes in the "cafetorium" behind the church on Friday and Saturday nights, and this drew another forty dollars a week. Things were picking up, but they were picking up through TEACHING THE BIBLE.

I despised teaching.

On June 25, 1962, the Supreme Court (after destroying the public schools) decided that they didn't need prayer any more, so they outlawed prayer in a school system that had begun with Bible reading and prayer daily (1700–1900). As prayer went out, the Africans came in: Ole Miss got its first Negro through Federal court order, backed up with rifles and bayonets (September 30, 1962), while George Wallace (April 25, 1963) took the first open, public, Conservative stand against enforced race-mixing. (Later he was shot in an attempted assassination.) The Catholic President Kennedy ordered the Armed Forces to Birmingham, Alabama, and then appeared himself at the Berlin Wall in his "god" role to tell the Germans that he was a BERLINER ("Ich bin ein Berliner")—which was not only a bald-faced lie, but as hypocritical a piece of political bunko as ever bunked with a politician. There were TWO BERLINS: he didn't say *which one* he was "for."

The Jews hung Adolph Eichmann for doing what Eisenhower did at the end of World War II (May 31, 1962), and Marilyn Monroe committed a very suspicious "suicide" after intimating that she would tell the press what had gone on between her and the Kennedy brothers (Bobbie and Jack). Mrs. FDR died (November 10, 1962), and Vatican II opened (October 11) to present the greatest display of horsefeathers since the Council of Trent. John XXIII, with the backing of the Kennedys, *Newsweek*, *Time*, CBS, NBC, and ABC, let the world know that even though the Catholic church "never changes," it NOW had "changed." No more crown on the Pope, no more prohibitions against meat on Friday, bingo and wine were still Christian practices, but so were Bible study and "dialogue" with "Fundamentalists." Inwardly, nothing changed: the Pope was still the head of all professing Christians (Baptists, Methodists, and Anglicans included), forgiveness for sins was still only through an ordained Roman Catholic priest, and ALL of the articles of the Tridentine Confession were still binding upon all priests, nuns, bishops, archbishops, and the Pope himself. *This confession approves of the one hundred and twenty-five curses placed on Protestants, Jews, Moslems, and Buddhists by the Council of Trent* (1546–1564). They are still binding and in effect. The bloody creed was tactfully covered up by announcing that "Mass" could now be said "in the ver-nacular." The old, bloody killers were still bloody killers, but now they had "good press."

Johnny 23 bit the dust in June 1963, and was followed by a radical Communist, Paul VI, who finished the council by encouraging priests in Central and South America to engage in REVOLUTION against "capitalistic imperialism." On June 13, 1963, Kennedy's two Catholic buddies—the president of Vietnam and the head of the secret police in Vietnam—were horrified to find a Buddhist monk had burned himself to death in Saigon, protesting ROMAN CATHOLIC INTOLERANCE of the Buddhist religion. The Catholic archbishop of Saigon was another one of Diem's brothers.

Following the enthronement of a Communist pope, America's greatest fornicating Communist (Michael Luther King Jr.) "had a dream." He dreamed of a gray America with a mongrel population (August 28, 1963). This was a prelude to the greatest Communist legislation ever passed anywhere, including Cuba and Russia: The Civil Rights Acts of 1964, which destroyed not only the public schools and private businesses in America but eventually placed the HEW in charge of CHURCHES and FAMILIES. King, a religious Liberal (who professed to be "Baptist"), was an habitual fornicator and "the most notorious liar" in the U.S.A., according to the FBI. He is the only American "hero" whose life records cannot bear examination, *or even be looked at*. Years later, when

Pen and Ink Sketches—1980

Abernathy confirmed the FBI record with a personal, eye-witness testimony, the news media (who had made a god out of him like the Kennedy brothers), drummed up nationwide groups to claim that Abernathy was a liar or a psychotic. *But still, no one looked at King's record.*

At the time, I wasn't concerned with these matters. I had been (temporarily, at least) given a new lease on life. With the deacons running the church, I had little responsibility. With the children gone in the winter (the first two years) I had time on my hands. I began to write. Up until that time, I had only written two books: one on *The Mark of the Beast*, and one on *The Bible Babel*. A Christian woman in town (Mrs. Rood) set up the first press for these books but was not able to continue publishing them, so they were transferred to some Christians in Palatka, Florida. I now sat down and wrote *The Kingdom of God versus The Kingdom of Heaven*, and *Rome—The Great Private Interpreter*. I wrote them on a mechanical, stationary Underwood typewriter and set three of them, myself, on a portable linotype machine called a "Varityper."

And now, for the first time, I really got acquainted with hunting and fishing. I had experienced nothing in regard to these when I was growing up. Now I got into it up to my neck: hunting wild turkeys, hunting deer, kicking up quail coveys, going to dove shoots, picking off squirrels with a .22 (seventy-four in three years), and so forth. Up till 1960, the only thing I ever aimed a gun at was a man or a silhouette of a man.

Then came the fishing, and my, what fishing! A professional fisherman named Bill Sharpe from Tupelo, Mississippi, "broke me in" with bass fishing, using homemade "buck tail streamers." He showed me how to fish the hydroelectric dams (Sardis, Grenada, Pickwick, Jim Woodruff, etc.) as well as the ponds and streams. Soon I was fly-rod fishing in the backwaters of the Tensaw and Mobile Rivers. Then came top water plugs, shallow runners, deep runners, "yellow-tailed Sallys," pork rind on the "weedless hook," homemade "Baby Dalton Spinners," and then the greatest adventure of all: hour after hour on the hot white beaches of Florida, fishing for bluefish with top water plugs—homemade out of broomstick handles.

A veteran fisherman named Noble Boyett (an Army veteran as well, wounded in the ETO in WWII) showed me how to use the mullet cast net ("throw net"). So there were more splendid hours out in the starlight, out in the moonlight, out on the "dark nights," wading in the bayous, the canal, the bays, the ocean, and the inlets: mullet, redfish, spots, croaker, pompano, trout, sheephead, spadefish, and sometimes even shrimp. Ah, what a life! Ten thousand dead in Vietnam, hundreds dead and injured in riots in Cairo, Haiti, Syria, and Saigon, and here I was drawing my breakfast in with a net under the summer stars over Florida! There is nothing on this earth like fresh mullet fried within twelve hours after it is caught. Black pepper and garlic salt in the corn meal, and brother, you have a feast that would put a red snapper or a king mackerel off the table!

On June 17, the Soviet Communist Supreme Court of the U.S.A. did just what Stalin and Lenin had done in Russia: *they banned THE BIBLE from every classroom in the United States*. No sooner done, than someone (no one knows who to this day) blew out Kennedy's brains (Nov. 22, 1963). The alleged killer (Oswald) was immediately killed by Jack Ruby, who immediately "died." The Roman Catholic Diem (Vietnam) also accidentally "died." The CIA was through with them.

Since **"all things work together for good to them that love God,"** the year 1961 marks the beginning of my "humanization," and 1962 began (literally) a new life for me. Certainly I had spiritual life in Christ as a **"new creature,"** but from the human standpoint I had not yet gotten off on the right foot in this physical life. Janie was a "holdover" from the old life. To keep fights and discord to a minimum, I had immersed myself in the Bible and the ministry (1949–1961), but in so doing, I had aggravated two things in my character that were already at fault.

1. It made me more "bookish" than ever, and God knows I was bookish enough when Christ found me.

2. It had put me in a place where I was always in the limelight as "the evangelist" and thereby only "brushed" the lives of the people I preached to: there was no *involvement*. I was still seeing the Christian ministry "afar off." Now it came in upon me and engulfed me. I was now a "pastor." I was a pastor, supposedly without one qualification for the **"office,"** but I was in the office (and I wound up being "senior pastor" in the city of Pensacola, having pastored in the city for more than thirty-seven years).

During 1962 to 1964 I preached in Tallahassee, Florida; Taccoa, Georgia; Chattanooga, Tennessee; Fernadina Beach, Jacksonville, Tampa, St. Pete, Lake City, Panama City, Pensacola, Cantonment, St. Augustine, and Orlando, Florida; Dacoma, Oklahoma; Benton and Blythesville, Arkansas; Johnson City, Elizabethton, and Bristol, Tennessee; Columbus, Tryon, and Winston-Salem, North Carolina; and in Weumpka and Mobile, Alabama. I had already preached in Gadsen, Grove Hill, Linden, Demopolis, Greensboro, Selma, Montgomery, Florala, Wing, Andalusia, Robertsdale, and Birmingham, Alabama, before this.

At Brent, I had to deal with everyone directly. My friends were devoted; my enemies were vicious. I was "down in the ranks with the troops," so to speak. Once again, I was on the "company level" with the "rank and file."

Every time it looked like I had drunken the dregs of a cup, the Lord would refill it—or keep on filling one that hadn't been drained, I don't know which. Looking backwards from 1964 I saw an amazing thing: a young man, setting out in life at breakneck speed, being stopped dead in his tracks five times and forced to start over. I had begun with aspirations as a military man but had wound up training to be a radio announcer. The war blew this to pieces, and I found myself in the infantry determined again to be a "thirty year man." The incidents in Japan had finished that off, so I had to start all over again at twenty-six years old after completing a college education. Just when the new start in radio (WABB and WEAR) was getting me somewhere, I had gotten saved and run off to school to go clear through college AGAIN; this time training to be an evangelist. Now at forty years old I found that I was a PASTOR. I felt like I was running in a circle. (What I was doing was getting "experience"!)

And there was one more item: the Book said, **"pastors and teachers"** (Eph. 4:11), with no comma between the two callings. Pastors had to be **"apt to teach"** (1 Tim. 3:2). I was actually teaching Bible four hours a week in addition to the regular Wednesday and Sunday services. That isn't all; young men began to get called to preach right and left in my ministry, and I had to ordain eight of them while I "supplied" at Brent. Immediately they wanted to know where to go to school. I sent them to BJU. One year, every president of every society at BJU was from Pensacola. I still had faith in Old Man Bob, so I sent them to him. I didn't realize that now (1961–64) "Junior" was in charge of things, and the whole operation was gradually being melted into a smooth, cultured, slick, pious bunch of sissies who would do nothing but brag about the past.

Every student I sent to BJU came out rejecting the *Authorized Version* as the Holy Scriptures. Not one survived if he finished the courses. Luther was out; Melanchthon was in. Every time one of my young men "bombed out," the Lord would get hold of me and say, "Aren't you kind of stupid? You get those young men saved and called to preach, and then you send them off to learn how to deny the Book that got them saved and called to preach. Why don't you teach them yourself? Why don't *you* start your own school?"

I didn't want to start a school. I didn't want to be a teacher. *I despised teaching.* I liked to preach on the street (and still do), but "teaching"? Like Brokenshire? Whitte? Payne? Afman? Panosian? Wisdom? Martin? Price? Custer? Zodhiates? Robertson? Brunner? Machen? No, thank you.

STATIC:

At the Cleaners, after having a mix-up over some "glad rags."

"Oh, I am so sorry, Mr. Ruckman, for the mix-up. I am new here and didn't get the ticket right."

"Well, it's straightened out now."

"You see, I'm only fifteen years old and I've just been substituting for my mother, cause she's been real sick."

"Don't worry about it—no sweat. Just give me the suits."

She looks at the ticket.

"Oh, I see you are a doctor!"

"Well, kinda. That is what you call a Ph.D.—a Post Hole Digger. I am actually the pastor of the Brent Baptist Church."

"Oh, you are? You are a *preacher*?"

"Yes, that's right."

She laughs. "Oh, well, good. I thought you looked more like a TEACHER!"

("Never mind, Lord, that is enough for one day!") It's strange how He goes about it, isn't it? One young convert of mine came down from Ohio (seventeen years old) and slept in my front yard because he didn't want to wake me up. In the morning when I let him in and fixed breakfast for him, I asked what he was doing down in "this neck of the woods."

He said, "Well, I heard you had started a school, and I wanted to come down." ("Never mind, Lord, never mind.")

But the humanizing process was the biggest thing.

Sick babies. A mother carrying a baby that had Hodgkin's Disease. The baby is crying for momma to stop the pain.

She can't stop it.

A little girl in an oxygen tent; a little girl only twelve years old, dying of cancer, pawing at the tent and saying, "Daddy, what is this for? Do I have to have this?"

Crying couples trying to get their lives straightened out.

A single woman trying to raise three children by working in a plant, and the gas and lights being shut off every winter because there is no money to pay their bills.

A young man going off to Vietnam and coming back all crippled up after someone rolled a grenade into his hole.

A father out of work and going back to drink to drown his problems. A drunken daddy in jail, with his little girls (eleven and fourteen) trying to sell peanuts on the street to take care of "momma."

A deacon threatening to burn my house down or starve me out of the pulpit.

Business meetings with women screaming and pounding their fists on the table.

Little caskets two feet long going down into the ground. Weeping mothers and fathers at funerals, testifying to the grace of God over the caskets of their children.

A deacon threatening to beat me up or sue me in a court of law.

Fixing cuts and scratches of little children who came to DVBS.

Marrying the young couples.

Eating out three times a week, as the members fix three hot meals for me and my boys (Peter and Mike).

NIGHT SCENE:

I go to a woman's house at 2 a.m. to tell her that her forty-year-old son has just been killed in a gun fight with his ex-wife's lover.

"I have some bad news for you, Mrs. Charles." (I do not say this to her until she is up and dressed and sitting with me and a deacon at a small coffee table in her kitchen.)

"Well, preacher, ah been expectin' some for some time now."

"It's about your boy, Edwin."

She blinks, takes a sip of coffee, and folds her hands in her lap.

"I hate to tell you this, Mrs. Charles, but he is dead. He was killed about two hours ago."

She sits quietly and doesn't flinch. (I am reminded of the man who came to my door with the announcement:

**Stringer of fish—1968
(With my oldest son, David)**

he was blubbering so badly I could hardly make out his words. He was one of Edwin's friends.)

"How did it happen?" the sixty-year-old woman asks blankly.

"Gunfight," I say. "They both had guns. They've arrested the man who shot him."

"Over his former wife, ah suppose," the mother says.

"Yes," I say, "that was it."

She drops her head for a moment, then lifts it, takes another sip of coffee, and then says softly, "Ah mighta knowed it was goin' to happen. Had to happen, sooner or later."

"Can we make any funeral arrangements for you, or contact anyone?"

"No, preacher, ah can handle it."

"If there is anything we can do . . . ."

"If there is, I'll contact you. You know, preacher, you already done the best you could do for me."

"How's that?"

"Well, one of your *students* (there it is again!) led Eddie to the Lord just three weeks ago. He come to me hisself and told me that he had gotten saved, and ah think he really meant it."

"Well, thank God for that, Mrs. Charles; thank God for that."

And on it went: on and on. After three years of hunting and fishing and even golf (!), and three years of counselling, soul winning, teaching, marrying, and burying people, I began to assume the form and shape of a PERSON instead of a machine. I was becoming a "human being," just like the rest of the human race. It would actually mean an entirely new life—the *fourth one* that I had been given since leaving Topeka, Kansas. Yet with this new life would come the frailties and handicaps that one gets from joining the human race. I would be subject to humanistic pressures, humanistic feelings, and humanistic emotions in a way that I had not been before, and therein lay the danger.

CHAPTER FIFTEEN

The General's Grandson As Teacher

The pressure to start a school mounted. Among the Bible students on Friday and Saturday nights were always some young men who wanted to learn Greek. Then letters began to come in from youth workers, in churches "up north," asking me where they could send their young people to learn the Bible. I knew they would never learn it at BJU. At BJU they would learn some things, and they would learn them in a clean environment, but everything BJU knew about the Bible had been in print before 1929. Furthermore, no one at BJU had the guts to tell any student the Biblical truths about the Millennium, the Judgment Seat of Christ, the Rapture, the eternal security of the believer, the local Baptist church, or the right mode of water baptism. (Some of this changed slightly after 1970, but this was due to the total collapse of the Methodist, Lutheran, Presbyterian, Anglican, and Charismatic groups in the U.S.A.)

Finally, a woman in the church (Mrs. Rood) offered to give me a four acre piece of land if I would set up a small school. If that were not enough incentive, five other Christians offered to pay for the first "building." It would be a Jim Walters five thousand dollar "house." I tried to add things up.

1. Teaching every night during the week would cut my bluefishing and mullet fishing down 80 percent. The blues are best at sundown and sunup; mullet at night.

2. I would have to teach a minimum of twelve subjects the first year, including Greek, and the third year it would still be twelve, plus Hebrew.

3. There was already friction in the church between

the young men who had come down from up north and our deacon board, which up till now had run the church from top to bottom. The young men all preached on the street, and this was "ruining the testimony of the church" in town. (The deacons and their supporters wanted a "classy" church—a sort of isolated "social group" that would be looked up to by people in town.) They had already forgotten that three years ago when I came to them, the people in town laughed them to scorn, and not for their *public witness*: it had been for their BUM CREDIT.

4. Couldn't I just get by with the tapes? Ever since I showed up at Brent, people were "taping" me. In those days all of the machines were reel to reel. The first "cassette" showed up about 1964; it had a WIRE in it instead of a tape. But every time I opened my mouth, someone was taping me. By 1968, there was a regular battery of recorders in a room at the back of the church, recording ten copies of every sermon and every Bible study. Couldn't I just let these do my "teaching" for me? My "fans" had taped every word of every verse in Genesis, Exodus, Daniel, Ecclesiastes, Isaiah, John, Matthew, Acts, Romans, 1 and 2 Corinthians, 1 and 2 Timothy, Hebrews, James, and Revelation.

5. Setting up a school would double my load. I was already pastoring about two hundred people and taking Bible conferences every other weekend all over the country. In addition to this I was thinking more and more about writing. I had jammed so much information into my head it seemed like it would split if I didn't let it out, because in the interim (1960–62) when I was trying to recover my balance and "get on my feet" I had gone back to reading history and particularly military history. Gradually, the little wood house across from the Brent Baptist Church was filling up with German books and German military music. I had discovered a great historical truth: that a nation smaller than Texas had taken on Russia, the U.S.A., Britain, Canada, and France (and even Italy in the First World War) and kept them at bay for six years, and having lost *two World Wars in succession*, they had

First Bible Classes (Brent Baptist Church) 1960

Graduating class of 42 students—1978

a higher MORALE, in 1965, than the U.S.A. had after *winning two*. The thunderous tones of "Parademarsch der Langen Kerls," "Frei Weg," "Der Hohen Friederberger," "Wenn Wir Fahren Gegen England," and "Wenn Wir Fahren auf den Mehr Hinaus," came out through the walls several times a day. My old friend Roy Clipper (Kleipper) from Elberta was a great help in these times—his grandmother was from die alte Heimat—and the German influence got stronger and stronger. The more I studied the German military on an individual level (I had studied only their battle tactics—German General staff, Prussia, up till then), the more I became determined to *stay in the ministry*. If I got into teaching it would be teaching THE BOOK. If the unsaved German "Schuetzen" in the Wehrmacht could go through what they went through for a demoniac Catholic demagogue, what did the Lord expect from ME?

I set up a school.

It would be called "The Pensacola Bible Institute."

Its purpose would be primarily to train young men for the ministry, but because that, in itself, covered such a vast field, I decided to concentrate on two things and two things *only*: learning THE BOOK and learning how to PREACH it. Otherwise, the school was simply a Bible Institute, not a College, not a Seminary, not a University. We would not be in competition with Pensacola Christian Schools, Bob Jones University, Tennessee Temple, Baptist Bible College, or Liberty University; we would simply be a THREAT to them if they tried to teach young men the same things WHILE, AT THE SAME TIME, DESTROYING *THEIR FAITH IN THE BOOK.*

The curriculum was three years of night schooling—this was done so the students could make a living at regular jobs. We had no campus, no dorms, no fences, no parking lot, no hall monitors, no "demerit" system, and no rules or regulations beyond the bare minimum: no smoking or drinking, no drugs, no theater attendance, hair not touching the collar, and dresses for the female students. All married young men could bring their wives to class free; we would not charge them tuition. First year courses were Preparation and Delivery of Sermons, Evangelistic Song Leading, Old and New Testament Survey, Beginner's Greek, Church History I, Basic Theology, Genesis, John, Romans, Matthew, and 1 and 2 Corinthians. Second year courses were Church History II, Prep. and Delivery II, Life of Christ, Biblical Archaeology and Geography, Baptist Missions, Local Church, and Greek II, plus Galatians through Colossians, Exodus, Acts, and 1 Timothy to Titus. Third year courses were Advanced Greek, Basic Hebrew, Advanced Theology, Problem Texts, Manuscript Evidence, Prep. and Delivery III, Exodus, Daniel, Hebrews, and Revelation.

This made twenty-nine different courses (actually thirty-two, for the Greek and Church History courses) with twenty-nine grade books, twenty-nine roll calls, and nine textbooks—not counting the Bible for the Bible classes. (I wound up writing five textbooks for use in my own classes: *Church History, Science and Philosophy, Problem Texts, Local Church*, and *Manuscript Evidence*.)

Classes were six to ten p.m., Monday, Tuesday, and Thursday, with a ten minute break between classes: prayer meeting on Wednesday night. Sometimes there would be classes on Friday night with the load going seven to ten on Monday and Tuesday nights. Later, after I left Brent and set up the Bible Baptist Church (I did not do this until I gave the folks at Brent TWO YEARS to get back on their feet, but they never did: they sold the church to the Hortons), we would go to classes Wednesday night from six to seven, take an hour out for prayer meeting, and then go on from eight to ten.

We began with twelve students. No parking lot. At first, no indoor bathrooms. At first, no real heating (a small gas heater) and one window-sill air-conditioner. Bobbie Scumner (who always majored in sticking his nose into everyone else's business) told a Rice-ite (or a Jones-ite, I don't remember which) that believing the Book was a "heresy" started by Ruckman, who headed up a "cult" in Florida which had "a very small school." It was, but in the next twenty-four years it turned out more Bible-believing, street-preaching soul winners than PCC and BJU could turn out COMBINED. What they did graduate they did not produce, create, or "turn out." They had a hand-picked, ready-made clientele; they *didn't* produce anything. Our young men were not preachers' sons and were not raised in churches. Most of them came off the streets, or out of the military camps, or out of the bushes, and the vast majority of them had only been saved one or two years. Thirty percent of them were converted Catholics. Occasionally, we would have a bright young man, raised in an independent Baptist church, who had already gotten a "call" of some kind, but of forty-two young men we now have on the foreign field, only eight of them had their calling before they came. BJU and PCC could produce nothing like it; not with student bodies of two to four thousand.

Our second year had twenty-two students; the third year about thirty, and up to about two hundred in 1996.

In August of 1964, Johnson sidetracked nine hundred and forty-five million dollars of the taxpayer's money to pay all the blacks who had lost jobs when the Civil Rights Act went through. Brezhnev replaced Khrushchev (October 17), and the greatest fornicating Communist in America (Michael King Jr.) was given the Nobel Peace Prize for two years of riots, law breaking, and destruction of property (December 10). On March 28, dressed in a North Korean Communist hat, King led a group of Catholic priests, Communists, Liberal preachers, and assorted bums to Selma. They left a string of condoms, beer cans, and cigarette butts on the way, plus some circulars advertising nightly *burlesque* shows; they were invitations for "white girls" to come out and "loosen up." Jungle time had come. America was now "in the brush": Presley's music, welfare handouts, drug culture progressing, black Communists disguised as "civil rights workers," and white Communists disguised as "political activists." McCarthy was dead, and LBJ was alive. Patton was dead, and Bobby Kennedy was alive. MacArthur had been canned, and Jesse Jackson had been promoted.

LBJ sent another fifty thousand troops into Vietnam (July 28, 1965), and then another hundred thousand, and then signed two more bills to load up the taxpayers to take care of the jungle culture (Medicare, July 30; voting rights, August 6). Watts was promptly burned to the ground, and Chicago, New York, and Cleveland erupted into Communist riots by blacks who had been encouraged by Johnson and King. Four people were killed, and more than a hundred and fifty injured, but it was considered to be proper. However, every time anyone was caught who killed even one black "civil rights worker" they were arrested and imprisoned. The pattern became clearer. A black could kill a black or kill a white, *but a white could not kill a black*. This Supreme Court "ruling" was instituted in the 1970's on a national scale and carried out to the letter. Murder was judged on a *color basis*, and capital punishment (and punishment of police officers) was determined by the COLOR involved in the incident. In 1989, this reached a peak, where members of the Detroit Symphony Orchestra had to be hired according to their COLOR instead of their *musical ability*. The Civil Rights Acts (1964) had completely bankrupted the American economy, because it insisted that every employer in America had to hire people *who might destroy his business or at least be a detriment to it*. The Japanese, Chinese, and Saudi Arabians stepped into the gap that King, Kennedy, and Johnson had created.

In the meantime, I had reached (by a miracle) the ripe old age of forty-five, which I had never expected to see. I was still playing golf and tennis, fishing, and hunting, and I was also taking Karate and Judo classes. The Bookkeeper, whatever His plans were in the future (and He had plans!) was giving me an interim, an interlude, a fresh start; a parenthesis before the next series of tests, rewards, and chastisements. I looked behind me and suddenly realized that my boyhood idols and the heroes of my young manhood were falling. They were falling right and left; when would the reaper visit *me*?

Gertrude Stein had died in July 1946. H. G. Wells went the very next month (August 13). W. C. Fields left this earth at Christmastime, 1946: he lived and died an unsaved drunkard. Henry Ford died at eighty-three (1947).

Bill Robinson had died in November 1949, and George Bernard Shaw died in 1950. Somewhere behind me now lay a dead John Dewey (the forerunner of the modern jungle high school), a dead Eva Peron (July 1952), a dead Santayana (1952), a dead Prokofiev (1953), a dead Eugene O'Neil (November 1953), a dead Matisse (1954), a dead Thomas Mann (1955), a dead Oliver (Laurel and Hardy), and a dead Mike Todd (Liz Taylor's husband, 1958). This string of corpses stretched out behind me through the years; the people who had influenced me when I was growing up: General Marshall, Ethel Barrymore, Clark Gable, Emily Post, Gary Cooper, Ty Cobb, James Thurber, William Faulkner, Georges Braque, Gracie Allen, Harpo Marx, Herbert Hoover, and then Winston Churchill. The passing parade was passing. **"It is appointed unto men once to DIE, but after this the judgment."**

You cannot imagine how it feels to write down these names, one by one—the people that MOLDED you—and realize that you yourself, the chiefest of sinners (1 Tim. 1:15), are still "alive and kicking." I would live to see not only the deaths of Dillinger, Capone, Bonnie and Clyde, Homer Van Meter, Lucky Luciano, Machine Gun Kelly, Ma Barker, General Patton, General MacArthur, Bertrand Russell, and my own mother and father, but the deaths of Joan Crawford, Bette Davis, Myrna Loy, Bing Crosby, William Powell, John Wayne, Abbott and Costello, Artie Shaw, Rocky Marciano, Benny Goodman, Tommy and Jimmy Dorsey, "Bear" Bryant, Judy Garland, Ho Chi Minh, Fred Astaire, Edward G. Robinson, James Cagney, Joe Louis, Duke Ellington, Louis Armstrong, Ingrid Bergman, Arthur Fiedler, and *nine presidents*.

Some folks live a charmed life. Khrushchev didn't bury me. I watched them bury him. Something was sustaining me; I knew what it was. It was A BOOK. *Just one Book*: just "ink printed on paper." I knew Someone was sustaining me. *Just One*: just one crucified, buried, and risen JEWISH MESSIAH (Christos) who some day would be coming again to "receive me" to Himself.

From 1964 to 1972, I lived as a single man and raised my two boys (Pete and Mike). David was at Livingstone College on a basketball scholarship, and Priscilla was at my old alma mater (Alabama)—a Phi Beta Kappa. Diana had married (Mrs. Walker, now) and lived in Tuscaloosa for a while, and then in North Carolina, and then back in Greensboro, Alabama. I had a lot of help surviving the lonely years. As a matter of fact, even with my Germanic morale boosters I never would have made it without the prayer and support of some close friends who got me "over the hump" (the Mitchells, the Clippers, the Gilleys, et al.). I didn't dare trust a remarriage after the mess I had been through, and I was as "gun shy" as a Jew in the Warsaw Ghetto. I continued to pray for Janie to "get right," but as the years passed I saw that these hopes were in vain. She actually picked up the old life that I had left in Alabama (1949) and consorted with a number of male "friends" on numerous occasions. The children told me about all of this later.

As America moved deeper into the jungle, with the anti-Vietnam riots, massive drugging of Vietnam troops through black "soul brothers," the advent of the Beatles—all of whom were dopeheads—and enforced race mixing at every level, the VD rate doubled, the assault and battery rate tripled, the rape rate quadrupled, and the murder rate went out of sight: better than ten a day in ONE city.

I did what I had done for fifteen years; I traveled coast to coast preaching the Book, but now I was pinned down to Pensacola at least four nights a week TEACHING the Book. In all fairness and honesty, I must confess that I did not even take this calling as seriously as I should have taken it until about 1980. *I despised teaching.* To make up for it, I took my students bluefishing, dove shooting, and mullet fishing. I taught them what I had been taught. My library shelf picked up about five books a week, or about two hundred and fifty a year. In the meantime, I was reading books from all of the pastors' libraries where I was having meetings; the rate of "a book a day" continued. (It was a miracle that I was not stone blind by the time I was forty.)

A gift from a graduating class—1969.

The original Board of Trustees

Skinner, L'Wright, Mitchell, Gillet, Packman, McCaughey

One by one, the Lord began to produce Bible-believing pastors and teachers, evangelists, and missionaries from the work. Every year He would turn out two or three real gems and a half a dozen more "average" types, but every graduating class believed THE BOOK. True, we had some ding-a-lings and "wimps" in every graduating class, but never more than two at the most. I would say that in a graduating class of twenty-four students, four of them would be Bob Jones or Hyles Anderson material (except they all preached on the street and had three years of Greek, in addition to believing the Book), six more would be the average run-of-the-mill ministerial student (not too bright or sharp, but good, solid, substantial, well-balanced young men). The rest would be just normal, Bible-believing young people who might or might not do something for the Lord when they got out. Not all of them, of course, were young. We had men in their fifties and sixties attending. One student was seventy-two years old. No matter who claimed to have "the most unusual university in the world," we could put them off the map when it came to the "unsual." In the same class our youngest pupils were fifteen or sixteen, our oldest in the sixties. In one classroom, taking the same subject, were college graduates and men who had flunked out of Middle School. In the same classroom were retired Army and Navy men and converted High school junkies who had never had a uniform on. Some of the students had been saved more than ten years, but most of them less than four.

I taught them the Book. I taught them the Book was the "final authority in ALL matters of faith and practice," and that since it was **"quick, and powerful, and sharper than any two-edged sword"** they could use it to critique any scholar at any time. I taught them that no professor, no scholar, no school, no seminary, no linguist, no university was EQUAL to the Book, let alone superior to it, and that Bob Jones, Lee Roberson, Jack Hyles, Billy Graham, Jerry Falwell, Arlin Horton, Dr. DeHaan, Theodore Epp, John Rice, and all of their friends and associates *wouldn't have a JOB if it were not for that Book.*

I taught that when a country loses *the Book* they are through, and I taught them that a country never loses the Book till it loses confidence in the Book, and *confidence* in the Book is always destroyed slowly and subtly in Christian colleges and seminaries THAT *PROFESS* THE "FUNDAMENTALS OF THE FAITH." I made no apology in 1964 for that teaching; I make none for it now, thirty-four years later. I taught them they could USE any book as long as they believed *THE* BOOK, and I taught them that if a man makes his living USING a Book he does *not* believe, while deceiving his supporters into thinking he believes it, he is an APOSTATE FUNDAMENTALIST: in short, a liar, a fraud, and a *hypocrite.* I made no apology in 1964 for teaching them this; I make none now, thirty-four years later.

I taught them that any preacher who is afraid to do what every preacher and prophet in both Testaments did—publicly proclaim the truth in a *public place* to a hostile audience—is not worthy of his calling or profession. "Any preacher" included every major Christian pastor, evangelist, Bible teacher, university professor, dean, and chancellor on the continent. I taught them further that the most important thing in their lives was *their personal relationship to Jesus Christ,* and this was to take precedence over their jobs, their families, their relatives, their "church work," their ministries, and their "goals." I made no apologies for it then, nor any now.

I laid a heavy missionary burden on them, and there was a heavy local church emphasis given to every student who showed up. I pointed out the errors of Stamism (Bullingerism: Hyper-Dispensationalism), and Calvinism (the Five-Point TULIP system), and the Charismatics (Gorman, Copeland, Swaggert, Hinn, Hagin, Roberts, et al.) and briefly showed them the errors of the Jehovah's Witnesses, Seventh-day Adventists, and so forth. In Church History I, emphasized that history is *anti-Catholic,* and that therefore if a man is not an anti-Catholic (in the sense of opposing the hierarchy and its teachings), he is FALSE in his approach to *history*. By virtue of his ignorance, he is not capable of TEACHING HISTORY or COMMENTING on it. I presented all the Popes as bloody killers, worthy of Martin Luther's description of them as "Your Hellishness" and "Most Hellish Father." *Foxe's Book of Martyrs* and *The Bloody Theatre* were part of the curriculum as well as the works of Avro Manhattan, O. C. Lambert, and Paul Blanshard. My students were better informed on world affairs than the editors of *Life* and *Time* magazines.

I taught my students *Nestle's Greek New Testament* with the critical apparatus and showed them how to use the apparatus to prove that the faculty and staff of BJU and Dallas Theological Seminary were some of the most accomplished *liars* that ever conned a sucker out of his tuition money. I let my students use *thirty-two* versions of the English Bible to confirm them in three great truths:

1. Only the *King James Bible* contains ALL the truth (see 2 Cor. 2:17 or 2 Tim. 2:15 in ANY other version, for example).

2. Every English Bible printed since 1880 is a Roman Catholic edition of the *Jesuit Rheims Version* of 1582 (*NKJV* partially excepted).

3. The fact that you can "lead people to Christ" with them, or find all the "fundamentals of the faith" in them, is no more significant than leading someone to Christ with a Wordless Book (which can be done) or finding a gold ring in a sewer (which has been done).

I taught my students that there is one absolute authority for TIME on this earth, and it is located in England. The one absolute authority for LOCATION on this earth is in the same place, and so is the British Thermal Unit for measuring TEMPERATURES in China, Borneo, Mongolia, Greece, Siam, Haiti, Honolulu, and Fairbanks, Alaska. I taught my students that God's breath, as well as His "hand," was on the Book they HAD ON THEIR DESK, and that when they left this school they would carry their final authority *in their pockets*. Final authority was never to be invested in seven things:

1. The Roman Catholic Pope or his church.

2. The UN or any lawmaking body connected with it.

3. A Greek or Hebrew lexicon.

4. An English dictionary.

5. Any copies of copies of Greek or Hebrew manuscripts.

6. Any rotten piece of junk like an *ASV, NASV, NIV,* or *RSV.*

7. Any scholar's opinion or "preference" about anything, no matter how "godly" or "scholarly" he was.

At the Pensacola Bible Institute you graduated following a BOOK, *not* a man. Your faith was in a BOOK, *not* a man, and you stood up for a BOOK, *not* a man. No one left here thinking that the Pensacola Bible Institute had been "raised up by God" as a "Bastion of Orthodoxy" to boldly stand for "the fundamentals of the faith" with a "militant stand" in a "World Congress of," etc. I had better sense than to believe that kind of crap before I was saved (except before I was saved, we called it something else). Students left our school knowing they had a sure foundation that they could carry on their persons. They were "rooted and grounded" in THE WORD OF GOD, not some collection of fundamentals or principles extracted from copies of something that WAS the word of God before it got lost. I put the Book on my students like God had put it on me. I had called it "the word of God" in the record room of the radio station at Gregory and Palafox (WEAR) in 1949, and I did not move from that position ONE TIME in the next forty-nine years. I didn't "call" it that because I "could" call it that, or "for all practical purposes, could call it that." I called it that *because that is what it WAS*, and that is what it IS, and that is what it *SHALL BE* till you hit the Judgment.

If the reader would like to know exactly what was taught at PBI from 1964 to 1990, all he has to do is obtain The Bible Believer's Commentary Series on *Genesis, Exodus, Matthew, Acts, Hebrews*, etc., *The History of the Christian Church* (two vols.), *The Christian's Handbooks to Biblical Scholarship* and *Science and Philosophy, Problem Texts, The Local Church, The Mark of the*

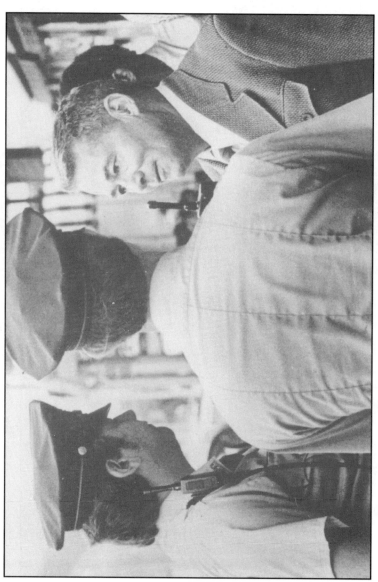

Encounter with the "Fuzz" (street preaching) —1965

Pitcher for church's softball team—1975

Beast, and *The Sure Word of Prophecy*. These books will give the reader about eighty percent of the material that was taught. In addition to this, English courses were installed (Miss Meacham) after about six years of operation, and all throughout the operation the ministerial students were required to do personal work and preach on the street. Our textbooks for the preacher's classes was Gibbs, *The Preacher and His Preaching*. Our basic theology book was Evans, *Great Doctrines of the Bible*. We used no single textbook for missions but gave the student all of the material on how about five different missions boards conducted their business, material from five different histories of missions, biographical material on the lives of thirty different individual missionaries, and then exposed the student to a minimum of twelve missionary speakers a year.

The student's grades were constructed on a 33 percent basis: a third of his grade was his grade average on quizzes, a third was the grade he received on his final examination, and a third was his ATTITUDE while attending school and church. I count "attitude" to be of such importance that it makes up a third of a student's grading. With me, EFFORT is the outstanding expression of *attitude* in the Christian life, and EFFORT (whether in trying to master the Bible, getting along with your wife, passing tests, staying in fellowship with God, preaching, teaching, paying one's bills, finding a job, keeping a job, or in trying to overcome sin) to *me*, is worth more than brains, talent, money, education, sweetness, sincerity, cooperation, piety, or cleanliness.

This is an idiosyncrasy with me which must have taken hold of me very early in life, and I never "shook free" of it. My conversion never changed that fixed opinion. I could forgive a man nearly ANYTHING if he had thrown himself into the battle heart and soul, but I would hardly forgive a man for *coughing* if he didn't do his best. Bob Jones Sr. said, "It is a sin to do less than your best."

I quickly learned that the main reason people WORRY is because they always fear in the hour of crisis that they had *not* done their "best." To me, Mark Spitz (the Olympic seven-gold-medal winner) and Mark Gastineau (the linebacker) were SLOBS. One could have improved his time in the water by a quarter of a second to maybe two seconds by a simple expedient: cutting his hair. The other would dance around like an Indian, congratulating himself after sacking a quarterback—doing *what he was supposed to do*. Some of the hotdoggers on the "gridiron" need to read Luke 17:10. The author of those words was the One who *created* swimmers and football players.

My teaching system was unique because my circumstances and goals were unique in the realm of Christian education. I had no pressure on me to pay any bills or build any buildings. I had no need to "matriculate" a given number of students at a given time. I had no Alumni Association to hassle for funds. I had no bond program, no big savings account, no real staff (McGaughey and three other teachers helped me out through the last thirty years of operation); no dorms, no cafeteria, no Association or Convention, and (above all) no necessity to appear to be "scholarly" or put on a show to convince anyone we were "spiritual" or had "high academic standards." This made my position completely unique, and no one who knew the education business could say otherwise without lying. I didn't even know where any of my students were after ten p.m. They might have been drunk down at "The Happening" or "Trader John's" or "Rosie O'Grady's." I gave adult privileges to my students because they had adult *responsibilities*. PBI was in a class by itself with no near competitor. It still is.

My method was simply to IMPART KNOWLEDGE. I had no intention of trying to trick the student, or trap him to see how brilliant he was, or how much knowledge he could absorb. My goal was to *impart to him what I knew*, however little or much that might be. To do this I used the simplest, plainest language possible (downright crude and vicious at times) in the "street Koine" of the late twentieth century. *The students were given all the questions on each test before the test was given*. They were to learn the answers to these questions. I was not interested in trying to catch them to see what they hadn't studied or hadn't learned. I had but one design: *I wanted them to GET THE MATERIAL.* They got it, and in so doing they became the targets for a thousand apostate Christian teachers in Colleges and ten thousand Christian graduates from those Colleges, plus the friends and supporters from those colleges. At PBI, any dumb-bell could get information from the Holy Bible that the graduate Seminary professors, or the world's greatest Greek scholars didn't even know was in the Book, and buddy boy (let me tell you!) they knew it by INSTINCT whenever one of our grads crossed their path.

To protect the apostate faculty members at BJU, Bob Jones Jr. invented the terms "Ruckmanite" and "Ruckmanism" (1970), which soon became universal symbols of identification in Japan, Spain, Australia, Germany, Italy, and the Philippines as well as the U.S.A. His son, Jones III, coined the phrase "King James Onlyism" to mark out the new "heresy" (an "ism") which everyone should "beware" of. Both expedients were *to cover up the infidelity and lack of courage of Bob Jones University.* They were to protect its TEACHERS: Ruckman was a TEACHER.

CHAPTER SIXTEEN

Disaster
In the Directive Will

There are three "wills of God" mentioned in Romans 12. One is good but is not *acceptable*; one is acceptable but not *perfect*, and one is perfectly good and perfectly acceptable and *perfect*. (Don't look for it in the "original Greek," because it is not there.) I was now in the directive will of God as far as my *calling* was concerned. That isn't all. I was now a human being as well as a "saved sinner." Further, I was now fully equipped to write. Beginning again to write, around 1968, I put out sixty-nine publications in the next twenty-one years; at least ten of these ran more than four hundred pages, and several more ran over two hundred pages; three ran over eight hundred pages. A man named Moore, at Brent, took over the printing until I left there, and finally I was able to set up my own bookstore out by the school. Littlejohn and Neidlinger ran this entire operation from about 1976 to 1988; Neidlinger having operated it from 1988 to 1996.

Down at Brent, things came to a head around 1968. The deacons, who had been losing their hold over business matters for years, went to work and split the offering up into separate funds so their own bunch would have a "nest egg" stashed away to work with if they had to leave; they then sued me and two other deacons and took us to court in Pensacola (Judge Mason presiding). The judge threw their case out of court. The next Sunday seventeen familites were missing from a total of about sixty families. (They all showed up two miles down the road at the Burgess Road Baptist Church, where their new pastor, Bobby Tidwell—a son of one of the women who went with them—was given the boot in less than four years and started a church downtown.)

I stayed at the guns. Bob Jones Jr. had been putting pressure on me to resign since two of his favorite graduates, Arlin and Becky, needed the Brent Baptist Church as a part of their "Ponderosa" for an imitation BJU—another interdenominational sissy school: a billion dollar launching pad for "lady fingers." I stayed "put" and fired away. The church was getting "out of the red." By 1968, its credit was good anywhere in town. Souls were getting saved, adults were baptized, young men were called to preach. Time marched on.

Mao launched his "Cultural Revolution" in China (1966). Richard Speck murdered eight nurses (July 19), and Charles Whitman shot twelve people from the top of a tower in Austin, Texas (August). Reagan was elected as governor of California (November 8), and "The Greatest" (unlike his predecessor, Joe Louis) chickened out of the Army, changed his name, and claimed that he was a conscientious objector. He got away with it: *he was the right color*. Cassius Clay had made another neverending and monotonous series of "firsts." From now on the newspapers and magazines were so intent on proving racial equality that they felt compelled to print every "first Negro" to do this or that, who showed up. Of course, all they proved was that *some race was so far behind that it was NEWS when ONE of them caught up*.

Since no Negro had been connected with the forming of the Constitution, the Declaration of Independence, the Bill of Rights, the Bible, or the invention of the radio, telegraph, airplane, rocket, sewing machine, washing machine, automobile, steam engine, combustion engine, television, rifle, pistol, sulfa drugs, tractor, telephone, electric range, plastics, computer, laser, chloroform, vaccines, penicillin, or the motorboat, he had to be "in" on SOMETHING. So, 1964 to 1996 was just one endless, repetitive series of "the first black mayor," "the first black general," "the first black coach," "the first black person to win an Academy Award," or a prize in literature, or a prize for medicine, or a prize for music, or a prize for art. In the 1980's it got funny: "the first black" to serve on a board of directors of a branch of advertisers connected with Exxon, or "the first black" to be principal of a grade school where half the children were white, etc. Black women judges began to show up on television with white men calling them "your honor," and in 1968, when we competed in the Olympics, the entire news media (CBS, NBC, ABC, the Hearst and Gannett papers, plus *Time*, *Life*, *Newsweek*, etc.) renamed the official salute of the Communist Party "THE BLACK POWER SALUTE." They did this with four dozen *photographs of the Communists in Spain giving the same salute*, without a black man in the picture, and *another four dozen photographs of Cubans under Castro giving the same salute*. The clenched fist is THE official salute of the Communist Party, and has been since 1921.

Israel, thanks to German teaching and German military tactics, went through the Arabs in six days like a wildcat going through a paper bag (June 1967). Paratroopers had to be called out to stop the Communist riots in Detroit which did away with one hundred and fifty million dollars worth of property. Police were ordered just to stand by and watch the stores being looted by blacks. They did. I have the photographs. The thieves were the *right color*, otherwise they would have been arrested on the spot. Thurgood Marshall became the first halfbreed to get on the Supreme Court. He was appointed to appease the rioters. Blackmail. BLACK mail. Black male. Rapp Brown and Stokely Carmichael, two of King's buddies, called for armed revolution and a violent overthrow of government. They got away with it: they were not *white. Oliver North was the wrong color.*

The Tet offensive smashed through South Vietnam and finished off several thousand more Americans (January 31, 1967). Frisco became "Fruit City" for faggots (in 1967) after the rock concerts, and Haight-Asbury became the capitol of sex perversion. On April 5, James Earl Ray assassinated (supposedly) the greatest fornicating Communist America ever produced. Michael (not Martin) was shot outside his room in the Lorraine Hotel in downtown

Memphis. Blacks promptly rioted in four cities (Chicago, Baltimore, Washington, and Cincinnati, April 9), stealing more than five hundred thousand dollars worth of goods and destroying more than fifty million dollars worth of property. They got away with it.

After the "dissenting minority" left Brent, I stayed till the bills were paid. Our offerings picked up, and our attendance picked up. However, my condition was not "picking up." Living alone, without a help-meet now for nearly nine years, had not been pleasant. The devil had worked me over good on more than one occasion. I saw that I could not continue the way I was going. I needed a permanent help-meet, and if I messed around much longer I would get involved with a married woman somewhere and then "the brethren" would have a field day. But a second marriage would also give them one. *Second marriages are "verboten" in the Sanhedrin.* All Pharisees teach Roman Catholicism at this point: no remarriages as long as a former wife or husband is alive ANYWHERE, although they may have remarried ten years ago and be engaged in raising another family. (All of these matters are covered in our work on *Marriage, Divorce, and Remarriage,* so there is no need to discuss the theology of it.) I could take a chance and maybe lose my shirt, or I could go on the way I was going and take another chance on losing my shirt.

After months of praying, I decided to remarry. The problem was, who? And I quickly learned that my people were not so much set against me getting married, as marrying someone *they* didn't like. From my standpoint, I didn't think things through as coldly as I would have in the old days, at least not between 1943 and 1949. I knew that she would have to be a young woman, because no woman over forty could keep the pace that I kept no matter how lively she was; I also figured on a "soul winner." But I did not figure on a pastor's wife. I intended to *resign* when the bills at Brent were paid off, and then it would just be teaching and evangelism. That way, the fanatics who were so concerned about the "bishop" in 1 Timothy 3 would have to shut their mouths.

Of course, they *wouldn't*, but that would only magnify their hypocrisy in the first place.

The girl I picked turned out to be young. She was young, and she was pretty. She was scripturally divorced, and she was a soul winner (or at least, so I *thought*). I had known her family for several years, and in her own situation she had scriptural grounds for divorce and had taken them. Her former husband had taken a few classes at the Institute before the family broke up.

A brief meeting (for the first time in ten years!) with my former wife, Janie, convinced me that all hope of re-establishing that family was gone. She came down to Pensacola for two days to see the children, and in the hour or so that I talked with her, she did nothing but talk about my unfaithfulness from 1944 to 1949. *She had never fogotten any of it.* I had her accusations memorized, I had heard them so many times at BJU. She left, and I never saw her again.

In 1972, I married Sherry Ruben, the daughter of Mr. and Mrs. Littlejohn. Littlejohn was to run the bookstore at a later date. We had not been married two months when she informed me that she did not want to be a preacher's wife, and we had not been married two years before she tried to take her life with sleeping pills. I found myself in the nightmare, again, that I had just *left*. But this time, two things were different. I had not loved the girl I had married in my unsaved life; I loved this one. Furthermore, I loved her family, and this included not only her two little girls (Laura and Rachel), but her mother and father and her sister and brother. They were all regular church attenders and interested in the Bible. The second thing was, I saw (or I *thought* I saw) the absolute necessity of making this marriage work "or else." (Three strikes, and you're out!) I had to keep this one together at any cost; *it was the "any cost" that nearly destroyed me.* The Bookkeeper was getting ready to close the books, but Ruckman's book was not going to close until he knew what it was like to give everything in a marriage and receive nothing back but rebellion or indifference in return. The time had come to pay the piper for

Rachel and Laura

a bill run up between *1944 and 1961*. I paid it to the year, and nearly to the MONTH.

Bobby Kennedy got the life knocked out of him (June 8, 1968). Blacks marched on Washington, D.C., to demand that the taxpayers hand over their money "or else" (June 25), there was a riot at the Democratic convention in Chicago (August 29), and the "first black woman" was elected as a Representative. She was a black Communist who had Communistic affiliations all her adult life. She represented the twelfth Congressional District in Brooklyn, NY: 95 percent *black*.

The first astronauts to orbit the moon returned safely (December 27), and as the new year came in, violence in Ulster broke out (January 4, 1969), where the terrorist IRA, in conjunction with the Pope, was still trying to eradicate the free state of Ulster and force it into an "anschluss" with Eire: Hitler, all over again.

By April 1969, more than thirty-four thousand Americans had been killed in Vietnam in a no-win war where the leaders had no intention of doing anything but killing time—and men.

Armstrong, after memorizing a Darwinian piece of propaganda written on a slip of paper, spoke on the moon. It cost us twenty-five billion dollars to get him there, and when he returned he didn't bring back ONE answer to ONE problem that he was sent up there to look into. It was the Darwinian monkey men who had hoped that the "secrets" of creation would be opened if they got to the moon. They bombed out. And they bombed out to the tune of another ten billion dollars on Jupiter, Venus, Saturn, and Mercury. Ted Kennedy was "wanted for President" and *murder* (July 30, 1969) but got out of it: right relatives, good press, right political party.

The jungle shot up its tropical forest another three thousand feet at the Woodstock Festival (in New York, August 17), where rock, drugs, fornication, dope, liquor, nakedness, demonism, and African dances mixed beautifully. Many of the teenagers painted real witch doctors' masks on their faces. (Benny Goodman and Gene Krupa had finally "cashed in" with the help of Presley and the Beatles.)

Lt. Calley made a "goof" at My Lai after two hundred and fifty thousand protestors marched on Washington, DC (November). Charles Manson got himself a good reservation in an air-conditioned cell (plus television and three meals a day), for life, for organizing the murder of seven people. He wore a black cross in the middle of his forehead and professed to be "the angel of the bottomless pit" (Rev. 9:11).

The Kent State disciplinary action took place (called a "massacre"), and thousands of sex perverts began to come out of the woodwork (June 28). They pleaded Michael Luther King's plea: *discrimination*. Janis Joplin, Angela Davis, Daniel Berrigan, and Idi Amin took the headlines in 1970 and 1971. Idi Amin killed more blacks in *eight months* (more than twenty thousand of them) than the whites in South Africa killed in *TWENTY YEARS*. The press backed him up and let him get away with it: *he was the right color*. The Catholic terrorists in Ulster doubled their killing rate, and the press backed them up; so did CBS, NBC, and ABC (August 25, 1971).

I let my people at Brent give me a "closed ballot" vote on the marriage, after an afternoon in prayer. The vote was two hundred *for* it and one hundred *against* it. I resigned under those conditions. In the first place, I wouldn't think of staying and fighting a third of my congregation (although I could do it without missing any sleep!), and secondly, Brent was now, after fourteen years, "out of the red." Their bills were paid. Whoever I left the church to would not have to pay a dime more than "operating expenses": we had cleared two hundred thousand dollars worth of bonds and three hundred thousand dollars worth of church bills. I resigned and gave the people I left two years to get the work on its feet. They went from three hundred, to two hundred and fifty, to two hundred, to one hundred and fifty, to one hundred (with two different pastors called in), and then as they began to argue among themselves they went from one hundred to seventy, to fifty, to thirty. The last deacon that left said,

The Lord's "Junkyard Dog"—1970

Preachers' Fellowship—1980

"You'll never get this thing going. Your trouble is you are all too full of pride. The truth of the matter is, you wouldn't really be satisfied with any pastor but Ruckman, and you're too proud to let him know it!"

I founded *The Bible Baptist Church* in 1974 with seventeen members. We were running over one hundred in less than two years. During that time we built two more buildings for the school and a bookstore. Then after that, another building with two classrooms and a gym. All of it was completely paid for before 1989. Brother Mitchell, a retired Marine officer, handled our finances.

And here began a dual life. I had to placate an implacable wife who would not come to peacable terms of agreement on ANYTHING. She wanted to be a nurse, but when I gave her permission she dropped it; and then complained about me preventing her from becoming one. I couldn't discipline either of the girls after they got to be eleven and thirteen years old, and there was something just short of a fistfight everytime I disciplined them BEFORE that.

Out in public, it was the "happy Ruckman family" with "Ruckman's new wife," but inside the house it was "there's a towel on the floor, there's paper wrappings on the floor, the trash is not taken out, the backyard looks like 'nigger city,' the windows shouldn't be shut, the blinds should be pulled, the clothes have to be changed daily [especially suits], the bedroom wasn't right, the kitchen wasn't right, your driving wasn't right, the church wasn't right, you don't know how to counsel people, your maid Evelyn [who had already been with me for ten years] didn't know what she was doing, none of your children were any good, you don't know how to take care of your dog," etc.

I bought the flowers, the candy, and extra diamond rings, took the lady out for meals, and if that weren't enough, took her on three honeymoons (just her and me) to Germany, and then to a Christian camp every summer where the girls could swim, play ball, and ride horses. Nothing availed. Fights going to the airport, fights returning, fights on the way to church, fights (or deadly silence) all the way back. It began within *two months* after our marriage and increased with time. Eventually, articles for the *Bulletin* were being torn out of my typewriter while I was typing, paintings were being knocked off easels while I was painting, and glass was slung around the house. ("What a fellowship, what a joy divine . . . !")

Every one of her needs was supplied, and she had the privilege of being in one of the most evangelistic and Biblical works in the United States; she could pick her friends from that group. She had only *two* close friends in a congregation of about five hundred (at the start one close friend in a congregation of one to three hundred). Almost every married woman she got near got a DIVORCE. *I counted FOUR of them in TEN years.* Her real comforter, guide, counsellor, and partner the whole time was not God; it was her sister, who had married one of my students (James McGaughey). I found out quickly that my spouse had no prayer life at all, and she didn't read the Bible through one time in a year; but I loved her, so I "covered up" for her, and I loved God, so I tried to make it work. It worked like "Liz and Dick."

In the meantime, the ministry accelerated. The congregation picked up, the school picked up, the Bible conferences picked up (although Bob Gray and Harold Henniger dropped me), and the soul winning went right on. They got saved in Benton, Arkansas; Tulsa, Oklahoma; Green Bay, Wisconsin; Frederica, Delaware; Flint, Michigan; Lansing, Michigan; Cincinnati, Ohio; Comfort, Texas; San Antonio, Texas; Los Angeles, California; San Diego, California; Seattle, Washington; Las Vegas, Nevada; and Rochester, New York: now it was twenty-six hundred, twenty-seven hundred, twenty-eight hundred, twenty-nine hundred, three thousand. The tab went up: about three thousand saved between 1960 and 1980, perhaps more. The bookstore began to put out Bible study tapes and sermon tapes to the ends of the earth. There followed gospel tracts in four different languages (English, Chinese, German, and Spanish), radio programs, and television chalk talks. The "battle for the Bible" opened up now in full blast, and the apostates at BJU, PCC, and other places had to *pretend* that they were Bible believers. When this didn't work, they tried a number of things.

1. Banning students from reading my books or listening to my tapes.

2. Banning students from hearing WMEZ, where I broadcasted.

3. Banning books by Edward Hills (or David Otis Fuller) on their campuses.

4. Labeling ALL Bible believers as "Ruckmanites," even the ones who had never read my books or even knew my name.

5. Branding all Bible believers as members of a "CULT" because they would not correct the *Authorized Version* with the guesswork of its "godly critics."

The years from 1972 to 1980 were years of training young ministers. I held Bible conferences as usual—about every other week in the summer and once a month in the winter. In the meantime, I wrote. Domestic matters did not come to a "showdown" until Laura and Rachel hit their teens (thirteen and fifteen), and then the "chickens came home to roost." During this time, I wrote several book-length commentaries on books in the Bible, a series of books on the *NASV*, the *New KJV*, and booklets containing chalk talk sermons. I had already painted a score of paintings for the Christian Hall of Fame in Canton, Ohio, but now felt compelled to start on the book of Revelation. By 1988 I had completed one hundred and forty-four large acrylic and oil illustrations of this book.

I had a twenty-two foot "cruiser" I took the kids fishing in, but Laura and Rachel never got the "hang of it," as there was no way to teach them anything without their mother interfering. To give my wife and I something we could "do together," I taught her how to play raquetball and tried to teach her how to play golf. But she found something to fight about every time we got on the racquetball court, and ONE lesson in golf finished her; she would not be instructed on how to hold the club, how to look at the ball, how to swing, what club to use, *or anything else.* (She then complained about my not "spending time with her." Where had I heard THAT ONE before?!)

On I went. General Blucher's drummer boy (about 1810–1815) didn't know how to beat a "retreat" on the drums. "Old Vorwaerts" (that's what they called Blucher) rode into battle on the "lead" charger when he was over seventy years old. I had reached the impossible age of fifty-nine in 1980, and yet still the Lord was putting up with me. Ah, the grace of God!

One hundred and forty-seven had been killed in a train wreck in Mexico (October 6, 1972), another hundred and seventy went to meet their Maker from a jet crash in Moscow (October 14), and ten thousand went out into eternity in one day in an earthquake in Nicaragua (December 25). I wasn't in the train, or the jet, or in Managua. In Nigeria, one hundred and eighty were killed in a plane crash (January 22, 1973), an airplane did away with a hundred and twenty-two more in Paris (July 11), one hundred civilians got bombed out of their lives in Damascus (October 9), and eighteen hundred more got killed in Tel Aviv (November 6). **"For what is your life? It is even a vapour, that appeareth for a little time, and then vanisheth away."** (James 4:14).

Terrorists killed thirty-one people on a U.S. jetliner going from Rome to Athens (December 17), and down in Sao Paulo, one hundred and seventy-five died in a blazing office building (February 1, 1974). Seventy were dead after Iraqi and Iranian troops clashed (February 10). In Bali, a Pan Am jetliner crashed, killing a hundred and seven aboard (April 1974), and at that date the Catholic terrorists in Ireland rang up a total of one thousand Protestants murdered in Protestant Ulster. The news media continued to back the Catholics up and does so today. (The Pope said nothing but, "What a shame!").

Six people were killed by a bomb in a garbage can in Brescia, Italy (May 28, 1974), ten thousand people went out to the Judgment in India due to smallpox (June 5), and to match them, the Lord wiped out another ten thousand in Honduras with a cyclone (September 20). **"A**

thousand shall fall at thy side, and ten thousand at thy right hand . . . ." Ruckman was still alive. The Christians wanted him dead. (By 1987, his wife wanted him dead.) The Catholics wanted him dead, and the Christian scholars in Christian colleges and universities would have given two years' salary to attend his funeral. *I lived.*

An earthquake in Pakistan (December 20, 1974) "wasted" eighty-seven hundred people, the Catholic terrorists killed seventeen more in England (November 1), twenty-three more in Dublin (May 17), and then one hundred Vietnamese orphans got killed in a plane crash (April 4, 1975). I had been married less than three years before an Eastern jet crashed in New York, killing one hundred and nine people (June 1975), one hundred and eighty-eight Moroccans got killed in another jet crash in Agadi, and the Catholic terrorists murdered another twelve Protestants in Belfast (October 2). I had been traveling an average of sixty thousand miles a year by jets and turbo-props since 1951 (over one hundred and forty-four thousand miles). **". . . he kept him as the apple of his eye."** (Deut. 32:10). How a rotten apple like me survived these massive killings I will never know till I get home to glory.

Eighty-two died when a Lebanese jet crashed in Saudi Arabia (January 1, 1976). Another earthquake in Guatemala snuffed out *fourteen thousand* lives (February 1976), one in New Guinea took *nine thousand* lives (July 8), *eighteen* Ethiopians were executed for trying to overthrow the government, a flash flood in Colorado killed a *hundred and thirty-nine* people (August 1976), *three hundred* Rhodesians were killed in Mozambique in the same month, and also in the same month *eighty-one* people were executed in the Sudan for attempting to over-throw the government. Two planes slapped into each other in Yugoslavia (September 10), killing one hundred and seventy-six people, *one hundred and two* more were killed in a U.S. 707 crash in Bolivia (October 13), and an earthquake in Turkey took off another *three thousand* people.

One hundred Moslems returning from a "pilgrimage" were drowned in the Red Sea (December 23), Cairo rang in the new year (January 1977) with *forty-four* killed and six hundred injured, and an earthquake in Rumania in March killed *seven hundred and fifty*.

A hotel fire in Brussels killed *three hundred and two* (May 23), and a fire in a nightclub in Kentucky burned another *hundred and sixty* to death (same month). I have been in a minimum of *seven hundred motels* since 1949, and I was in a minimum of *forty nightclubs* before I was saved. **"God be merciful to me a sinner."**

While they were "dying like flies" (and drowned rats, and flaming moths, and crushed ants), I was still "on the field." Fifty-six years old now, supposedly within four years of "retirement." If I had stayed in the service as a "thirty-year man" I would have retired three years ago (1974). I was to go *twenty-seven years past retirement age* for any man who had been at work for thirty years in the same place. I preached through Texas (Graham, Dallas, Fort Worth, Arlington, Comfort, San Antonio, and Monahan). I preached for Carter in Haines City, Florida, for Brother Monroe in Florence, South Carolina, for Lavonne Lowe in St. Pete, Florida, for Brother Ware in Orlando, Florida, Batema in Pomona, California, Kuchens in Dade City, Florida, Pack in Tulsa, Oklahoma, Bonam in San Antonio, French in Baton Rouge, Dinant in Flint, Bobby Clark in St. Pete, Culberson in St. Pete, for Sears in Middletown, Ohio, Brother Clinton Hale in Indianapolis, Gregg Dixon in Indianapolis, Brother Garmon in Tampa, and Scotty Drake in Tampa. I was up in King George, Virginia, and Wadsworth, Ohio, with Harley Keck in Green Bay, Wisconsin, and Mullins and Modlish in Rochester, New York, Tom Duff in Troy, Ohio, and Bob Grey and Lester Roloff in Jacksonville, and with Oswald Smith and Harvey Springer in Texas. I preached for Brother Peace in Knoxville and Brother Mangus in Louisville, Brother MacPherson in New Orleans, and God knows where else.

They got saved; they got saved right and left. They were not saved while "sharing God's love" or "letting Christ come into your life," or "making your decision for Christ," or "letting God solve your problems." They were

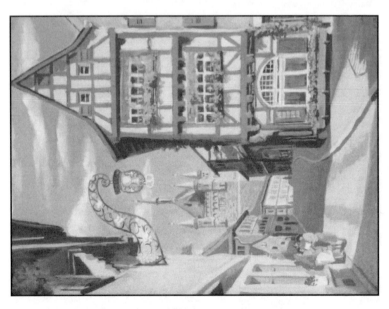

saved under old-fashioned, Bible-thumping, Hellfire and damnation, North Carolina, hide-tearing, skin-ripping, bark-peeling PREACHING.

The cup of life for millions was being dashed all around me. It had been that way for nearly half a century. My turn would have to come, but "oh, the riches of his goodness and his grace!" Oh, the mercies of the One **"whose mercy endureth forever!"** My cup ran over while thousands, more worthy than I, were broken like light bulbs thrown on the pavement.

A cyclone in India eliminated *ten thousand* in one day (November 20, 1977), *two hundred and twenty* got killed in riots in Ecuador, an airline crash in Singapore killed a hundred (December 1), and then over *one hundred and ninety* more disappeared in collapsing scaffolds (April 7, 1978); rallies for Khomeini, gun battles in Palestine, fighting between Syrian and "Christian" troops, and strikes. A Charismatic preacher from Frisco—who preached racial integration, women's lib, homosexuality, welfare, food stamps, affirmative action, tongues, healing, and Socialism—put the "topping on the cake" in Guyana. He laced grape Kool-Aid with cyanide and finished off nine hundred and nine suckers who had believed the news media and television. Jim Jones stood for (and promoted) every project being promoted by the news media at the time of this writing. He had every OSHA and HEW license available, and he was a Charismatic, exactly like the Bakkers and Swaggert (and Gorman, Hinn, Roberts, Hagin, and Kilpatrick).

The years rolled by. You have no idea what it is like to see the men and women who "raised" you going off to Hell one by one. I was "raised" in the *theater*, in the *library*, in the *Army*, and in the *classroom*. The people that died may have been "nobodies" to the reader, but they were my peers, mentors, guides, counselors, and TEACHERS "comin' up." Spencer Tracy died, Eddie Cantor died, Errol Flynn died, and then Jack Benny, and Walt Disney, and Boris Karloff, and Bela Lugosi, Jane Russell, James Cagney, Charles Laughton, and Wallace Beery. Harry Truman died December 26, 1972. Edward

G. Robinson (Little Caesar) died January 26, 1973. Eddie Rickenbacker died July 24. Pablo Cassals, the cello player, died October 22. Gene Krupa (my idol from 1939), cashed in October 16, 1977, and was followed by Ben Gurion (December 1), Chet Huntley (March 20, 1974), Dizzy Dean (July 11), Charles Lindbergh (August 26), and Jack Benny (December 21). I had seen their movies, I had read their books, I had listened to their music, I had heard their jokes, I had watched them play ball, and I read of them in the newspapers for years. They were dead. **"The wages of sin is death"** (Rom. 6:23).

I outlived Susan Hayward (deceased, March 17, 1975), Chiang Kai-shek (April 5), Casey Stengel (September 29), and Haile Selaisse (August 27). I preached and taught *the Book* while Francisco Franco expired (November 20), Paul Robeson died (January 23, 1976), Lily Pons died (February 13, 1976), General Montgomery died (March 24), Paul Getty and Johnny Mercer ("That Old Black Magic") died, and Mao Tse-tung died. They were followed by James Jones, Joan Crawford, Werner Von Braun, Groucho Marx, Guy Lombardo, and Bing Crosby. **"Death is come up into our windows"** (Jer. 9:21).

I taught the Book. In 1978, someone invited me to conduct a tour of the Holy Land, and I jokingly told them, "I'll go with you, but dump me off at Frankfurt and pick me up on the way back." They bought me a round trip ticket to Frankfurt, and I went. I stayed two weeks in Germany, preaching in Sembach, and Zweibrucken, and then I went down to Berchtesgaden and up to the Eagle's Nest. To get some contact with the old Wehrmacht, I whistled "Erica" and "Lil' Marleen" and made contact. I put out German tracts all over the country and even got some into East Germany. I took my wife through Ludwig's castles in Neuschwanstein, Fuessen, and Cheimsee, and strolled through Dachau. We left a string of tracts in Catholic cathedrals from Oberammergau and Mittenwald to Munich and Frankfurt.

I made another trip two years later, but on that trip the Lord got hold of me in a way that I would never forget. This time I went to Hitler's birthplace (Branau on the Inn River) and passed out tracts, and then up into the speaker's rostrum at the Nuremberg Sportspalast. I stood where Adolph had stood and gazed at the empty field in front of me. It could hold FOUR Astrodomes with room left over. I thought about what the old water color artist must have seen from there. The thought struck me that the dictator had been a *speaker* and an *artist* and an *infantryman*. Satan had gotten him when he was a little boy. What if someone had been in Branau, where I had just been, and had given him a gospel tract, like I had just given a dozen schoolboys in Branau who were coming home from school? Where was the next dictator being born or being raised?

I took my wife to the opera house in Vienna and feasted her on some roast pheasant before we went. Walking through the Wien rose gardens on the way to the opera, I was almost in tears. I was seeing, occasionally, that stiff walk, those cold blue eyes, that military bearing as certain individuals passed us. I could see the elderly people (all well-dressed) sitting in the parks, many of them doing absolutely nothing; not even reading a newspaper. Austria had the second highest rate of suicide in the world. This was the home of Freud, Strauss, Jung, and Frankl. **"Professing themselves to be wise, they became fools"** (Rom. 1:22).

Gradually I picked up the language, but never well enough to really engage in a lengthy conversation, and this became a burden to me. I was in Vienna. I was in Muenchen. I was in Berchtesgaden. I could pass out tracts, and I could ask a man if he were saved or "redeemed," and sometimes (if he knew a little broken English) go a little further, but I could not get down to "brass tacks" in regards to the man's individual past and his need for Christ. I enjoyed the scenery less and less, though God knows it was "Ausgezeichnet," but I wanted to deal with the ex-infantrymen; *the old blood was still there.*

One night in a Brauhaus, I was stopped by a man coming out of the rest room. He was about my age. He was a little drunk. When he stopped me he began to talk. He cried as he talked. He actually talked for ten minutes

Tracts for some Bavarian "Blass" Musicians

before finding out I could not understand all he was saying. To this day I don't know what the man said to me, but he cried the whole time, and he was not *begging* for anything. There wasn't a "bitte" or "geben" or "beten" or "lienen" in the whole conversation. No "geschenk," "geld," or "gabe" in the carload. I wish I could have led him to Christ.

In a hotel, in downtown Wien, I lay on the bed waiting for my wife to get dressed. We were going to a ballet.

AN OLD ACQUAINTANCE:

"What is wrong with this country, Pete?"

"They're lost. They're lost. They are going to Hell. I can see it in their eyes."

"People are going to Hell everywhere."

"I know, but these people—I can't stand it. When I think of someone like Elvis or the Beatles going to Hell, it doesn't upset me, but these people . . . They have good manners, they are disciplined, they are clean, they are obedient, they are brave. I can't stand it."

"There is no difference: For all have sinned, and come short of the glory of God;" (Rom. 3:22–23).

"I know, I know, but it still gets to me. Rommel—is he in Hell with Hitler? Pips Priller! Is he in Hell with Himmler? God, *you* know! *You know!*"

"Well, what is the matter with this country?"

"They don't know anything about Your Book, Lord. They know EVERYTHING except Your Book."

"Why is that?"

"Well, I guess it is because they don't have any Bible—" I almost said it. Then I bit my tongue and looked straight up at the ceiling.

"No Bible *what*, Pete?"

I whispered it out loud, but quietly, oh, so quietly! *I didn't want to hear it myself.* "Bible teachers. They don't have anyone to teach them the Bible."

"And what did I call YOU to do?"

My teaching was never the same after 1980. I returned home thinking that a call to teach THE BOOK was the highest calling on the face of this earth, and the next seven years I really WORKED at teaching. I redid all the courses, wrote syllabuses for three of them, wrote textbooks for four of them, and didn't go up into the classroom anymore without reviewing the lesson. Up till then, I had just picked up my notebooks and gone in and "winged it."

I had not been home three months when God got hold of me again, up in North Carolina, in an old-fashioned, Bible-thumping, base-running, shouting, King James "Jubilee" and put me down on my knees for thirty minutes crying out for Deutschland. I told God I would give the church and school to my associate and go now (at the age of fifty-nine) if He wanted me to. He said, "No." I rolled on the wooden floor of the old country church (behind the platform, where no one could see me).

"Send somebody!" I called, "Send somebody! Anybody! They are going to Hell. They have been through Hell here, and they are going out into Hell there! Do something! Send someone!"

"Pray ye therefore the Lord of the harvest, that he will send forth labourers into his harvest." (Matt. 9:38).

If I never got a prayer answered on this earth, I got that one answered. Getto and Gilley went to Germany; Trosclair and Forte went to Germany; Sindram and Attwenger went to Austria; Ballard went to Austria; Sherousse and others went, and by the grace of God we were able to print Luther again, in regular print, with several of Erasmus's readings altered to match Beza's readings in the *King James Bible.*

Hubert Humphrey died (January 3, 1978), Paul VI died (August 1978), and his unfortunate successor, John Paul I, who was a little too anti-Communist, kicked the bucket before he had been "reigning" two months. The circumstances attending his "heart attack" were above credibility (not "suspicion'), and *Murder in the Vatican* (Avro Manhattan) pretty well tells the story. Pope John Paul I was succeeded by a professional Polish actor who was to make a world record as the greatest international

Illustration (Isa. 11) for the Book of Revelation (Acrylic)

**Freight train destroyed paint truck
driven by Dr. Ruckman—1977**

politician the world had ever seen.

Thirty were killed in Guatemala (October 1978), *two hundred and seventy-three* were killed in the worst plane disaster America ever had (May 29, 1979), Golda Meir died (December 8, 1978), *seventy-one* people burned to death in a hotel fire in Spain (July 12, 1979), and "the first black woman to remain in a cabinet" stayed; she was a mulatto named Patricia Harris. Half-breed Thurgood Marshall "swore her in," so he was "the first half-breed to swear in a half-black." M. L. King was the "first black to get shot with a rifle at a motel in Memphis," and Jesse Jackson was "the first black to lie about how it took place." (A lot of "firsts" get missed by the press.)

Hurricane David killed *four hundred* people in the Dominican Republic (September 1979), and who cares LESS about it today, not twenty years later? **"There is no end of all the people,"** (Eccl. 4:16). *Two hundred and seventy-five* died as a plane crashed in Antarctica (November 28), Al Capp (Lil' Abner) died (November 5), Richard Rogers (Oklahoma) died, Jimmy Durante died, Jesse Owens died, and Alfred Hitchcock died. The following celebrities followed them to the graveyard: Peter Sellers, John Lennon (Beatles), Mae West, Joe Louis, Bill Haley (Comets), Albert Speer, Natalie Wood, Admiral Rickover, Hoagy Carmichael (Stardust), Henry Fonda, John Belushi, and Ingrid Bergman (1980–1982).

By now, I was beginning to gather some friends "on that beautiful shore." When I was first saved I could not look forward to seeing any "loved ones" in heaven, for I had no saved "loved ones." But now (1980), I was beginning to understand the lyrics which said, "Oh, the friends that now are waiting in the cloudless realms of day! Who are calling me to follow where their steps have led the way. They have laid aside their armour and their earthly work is done! They have kept the faith with patience, and their crown of life have won!"

Glenn Schunk, the man who got me preaching on the street; gone home. Clay Hadley, my fellow graduate from BJU; gone home. Big Bob Perssons, my song leader; gone home. Dr. Bob Senior, my hero and "role model";

gone home. Alex Dunlap, the great anti-Catholic; gone home. Jimmy Stroud, my Rescue Mission buddy; gone home. Dr. DeHaan; gone. Charles Fuller; gone. Bob Ingle; gone.

Norman, my Episcopalian doctor; gone home. (My mother and father and sister had all died in 1966, within three months of each other. But not one of them professed saving faith in Jesus Christ; they lived and died as sprinkled, "confirmed" Deists.) Sgt. Biggers, saved in Wing, Alabama; gone home. Big Jim Quigley of Ft. Walton Beach, gone home.

Dear old Mom May from Sawyerville, Alabama, the woman who gave me my first Bible; soon to be **"absent from the body, and to be present with the Lord,"** (2 Cor. 5:8). Her sister (Aunt Rosa); gone with her. Pappy Reveal, who "ordained" me; gone. Oliver Green; gone. My ex-infantry buddy Russell Fell (Elberta, Alabama); gone. Lester Roloff; soon to go in a plane crash. Lee Larson (Panama City) dead, Francis Gilley (one of my board members) gone, Jim McKay gone, Brother Hedricks gone. Nevada Steve Homoki, who taught me to snap a twenty-two foot bull whip, gone home to glory, and dear old "Homer" soon to go. Homer was our church "mascot," an old bachelor who had been a bum for years. He was converted but had "one oar in the water" most of his life. He was one of the greatest blessings our church ever had. They were piling up. Soon Dallas Billington, Fighting Bob Shuler, and B. R. Lakin would leave the "vale of tears" and go home to sit down at the King's table and **"eat bread in the kingdom of God"** (Luke 14:15).

"Oh, think of the home over there! By the side of the river so fair! I am going to a country where the roses never fade! Meet me there, meet me there, where the tree of life is blooming, meet me there!"

Some day I would go "home." I knew *now* where "home" was. I often was homesick, but never again was I in the condition I was in the night that I stumbled unshaven, half-drunk, crazy with sin, and half-dead with fatigue into that deserted Methodist church and cried, "Oh, God, take me back! I want to *come home*!" I didn't know where "home" was then, but I know where it is *now*. I can point to it: straight at it from any place in the northern hemisphere. "Walking along life's road one day I heard a voice so sweetly say, 'They're building a mansion in heaven for thee. 'Tis a beautiful, beautiful home!'"

They got saved: thirty-five hundred, thirty-eight hundred, four thousand. By 1985, over six thousand sinners had professed to have found Christ in my meetings. It would be over seven thousand by 1990.

They came from the four corners of America. I had preached for Brother Rawlings (Cincinnati), Beauchamp Vick (Detroit), Robert Taylor (Tallahassee), Brother Rogers (Canton, Ohio), Art Martin (Canton, Ohio), Jimmy Stroud (Memphis), Aubrey Mitchell (Mobile), Adkins (Knoxville, Tennessee), Pierce (Dothan, Alabama), Fleming (Dayton, Ohio), Powell (Knoxville), Loturco (Hobart, Indiana), Ken Blue (Seattle, Washington), Weido (Arlington, Texas), and the usual meetings with Dinant, Rawlings, Bonam, et al., scheduled every year. On it went: Lawson in Knoxville; Ingram in Frederica, Delaware; Schmuck in Red Lion, Pennsylvania; Gipp in Auburn, New York; Lackey in Mt. Airy, North Carolina; Herbert Noe in Livonia, Michigan; Bobbie Ellis in Ft. Myers, Florida; Don Green in Lansing, Michigan; and I have lost track of the rest of them.

CHAPTER SEVENTEEN

Harvest Time

Four months after my fifty-ninth birthday I put on ice skates for the first time and went out on an outdoor rink to play ice hockey.

Very often when I would get injured (1972–1980) playing racquetball or "blood ball" (a very "militant" form of water polo, played in three feet of water), my wife would say, "What are you going to be when you grow up?" I would always reply, "I'm going to be a hockey goalie." It was the only game I could see that looked like an infantry attack and a bayonet assault *combined*. At fifty-nine, I sported two teeth knocked clear out of my head by elbows and fists in games played AFTER I was forty years old, stitches on the feet and face from games played after I was fifty years old, and later I would nearly have my eye knocked out of its socket by a hockey puck; but that was after *sixty*. I was, you might say, "a fugitive from the law of averages." A train wreck in a paint truck, filled with turpentine and gasoline, put me off the racquetball courts for a while, but not long.

I could hardly stand up on the skates, and once I got moving I couldn't stop. But playing "goalie" didn't require a whole lot of skating, and at first the players were all just "church kids," and they didn't "lift the puck." After two winters of this they began to "lift the puck." In the meantime, I had installed street hockey as part of the curriculum at PBI, and when the new gym went up, the first thing we did was pad the sides, put a board railing around both ends, a net above it (after Pam got her nose broken from a slap shot off the "point"), and built two heavy-duty goals. Between 1980 and 1990 (sixty to sixty-nine years old) I "tended the net" (the old gatekeeper) about two hours on roller skates, fourteen hours on ice skates, and four hundred hours on my feet. "Goalie" is where the ACTION is. You don't relax in front of "the pipes." You can't even relax when the puck is at the other end of the rink. The sweat streams at twenty degrees (in OUTDOOR rinks), the blood pounds, and the adrenaline runs. I have had two-hundred-pound men go over my shoulders into the net—one blade on each side of my shoulder—at twenty miles an hour, and drive the posts clear back to the wall. Several times "semi-pros" and "league players" got on the teams, and I had to field pucks (you feel like dodging them instead!) that came at you in a blur. After a near disaster, I learned to wear a helmet and mask every time, plus steel-tipped shoes (as well as the standard equipment).

While Custer and Kutilek, Hymers and Hudson, Hutson and Hobbs, Horton and Hindson (amazing how many h's get in there!), Sumner, Panosian, Afman, Melton, Duncan, Walker, Jennings, Combs, MacRae, Farstad, and Price raved and ranted about the "errors in the *King James Bible*" and anathematized Bible believers all over America as "Ruckmanites," I was wearing the "blocker and catcher" and concentrating so hard on the "pass" (or going out to "cut down the angle") I couldn't have given one of them the time of day if he had asked for it. And by now (1984) I was playing blood ball with the GRAND-CHILDREN of the men I had played it with in the 1950's.

"But they that wait upon the LORD shall renew their strength; they shall mount up with wings as eagles;" (Isa. 40:31). Whatever sacrifices I had made in family matters before then (or after then), whatever troubles I had gone through trying to reach people for Christ before then (or after then), and wherever I may have failed my friends or family in my zeal to get the word out (before or after then), had been worth it. My "harvest" was going to be not only another busted up domicile, but it was going to contain the latter half of Galatians 6:8 as well the first half.

Overseas, a bomb in a car blasted *fourteen* people into eternity (January 1983), Iran invaded Iraq (Febru-

Pen and Ink Sketches—1993

Pen and Ink Sketches—1996

ary), and Hindus killed *six hundred* Moslems in raids in India (February). *Seven* got killed in Lisbon in a gun fight (July 1983), *sixty-four* were killed in a coal mine blast in South Africa (December 12), and the Russians shot down an American Airliner in Korea, killing all *two hundred and sixty-nine* aboard. Nothing was ever done about it.

Another first was "the first black Miss America" (Vanessa Williams, a lesbian half-breed). The press did not mention "the first black mayor to bankrupt a city," although there was one, or "the first black mayor to sell and use crack and cocaine," although there was one. "The first black athlete that died of drug abuse" was buried somewhere, and "the first black to rape more than ten women" was jailed somewhere, plus "the first black to be released by Syria" (January 1983). No one found out who "the first black was in Vietnam to introduce drugs to the U.S. Army" (*Heroes and Heroin*, Westin and Shaffer, Pocket Books, New York, 1972), creating a drug problem so great the *Federal government could not handle it*, so the Army became one third BLACK. That way the "soul brothers" could get their dope without being "warred on."

Two hundred and sixteen Marines got killed in a bombing in Beirut (October 25), but the press (with the Pope) continued to back up the PLO. God was emasculated to a neuter "person" (October 14, 1983) in the NCCC, to make Him fit company for the growing mob of lesbians and faggots that were entering the churches. On November 2, 1983, Reagan signed a "National Do-Nothing Day" (M. L. King's birthday) into an American law, thus making Michael King "the first black to become a national hero who had a life history that could not bear examination even by his FRIENDS" (a truly unique "first black" if you ever saw it!).

Catholic terrorists killed *five* people in London with a bomb (December 17, 1983), and another *twenty thousand* people lost their lives in fighting in Iraq, Iran, Cambodia, Laos, New Guinea, Afghanistan, Jerusalem, New Delhi, Angola, South Africa, Poland, and various places.

Concurrent with its return to the jungle, America picked up another good old African jungle disease—AIDS (April 23, 1984), sporting over four thousand known cases. It was brought here by a sex pervert who served as a "steward PERSON" (not a stewardess) on an airliner.

Jesse Jackson went down and had a nice, chatty talk with his buddy Fidel Castro (June 26), and the price of the average American home went clean out of sight for any black who thought he was going to get "advancement" from the NAACP. As the blacks moved in, the whites moved out, so the "average home price" for an American in 1983 became one hundred thousand dollars (June 29, 1984). My three bedroom, two bathroom brick home on a acre of land was a little below average. It cost *twelve thousand dollars*.

Well, in the next few years (1984–1987) Marcos went out (Philippines), and Cardinal Sin took over his government, using Mrs. Aquino; Richard Burton and Indira Gandhi went the way of all flesh, Goetz got tried FIVE times for the same offence, and the greatest black Communist in Africa got M. L. King's NOBEL PEACE PRIZE (Bishop Tutu, December 10, 1984) for inciting riots that killed more than *five hundred* people. Michael Jackson, another "person," and Madonna, a Catholic belly dancer, took America deeper into the jungle, and since rock and drugs have always been good bedfellows, the drug traffic became THE INDUSTRY in America, putting General Motors and US Steel to shame.

To help out the Communists in Africa, all of the rockers and rollers and "heavy metallers" and "acids" put on a concert (July 13, 1985). The money went to the Communist leaders in Ethiopia and central Africa under the guise of "helping little children who were starving." *The parties in power knew who to feed and who to starve.*

In 1985 America went bankrupt, and for the first time since 1914, became a DEBTOR nation (September 16). As she had moved into Communism and integration (1933–1980) with the reckless abandon of a raving maniac, eastern Europe had decided that BOTH OPERATIONS were a *failure*, so when the Berlin Wall finally collapsed (1989), America found herself caught with Karl Marx back in 1850 and "Liberty, Equality, and Fraternity" (from 1783). *She was one hundred years behind the times due to believing her news media.* Japan and Saudi Arabia mopped up on the suckers.

I preached and taught the BOOK. Long before my wife deserted me and got a "dissolution" on the grounds of "incompatibility" (so she could marry a policeman), my returns from "sowing the word" were coming in. It surprised even me. Of course I had believed the Book, but I had no idea that God could do through me what He had done when the sheet was "tallied up." I had not expected to live to see forty, and I traveled *thirty years* beyond that. I had not wanted to do anything but be an evangelist, and when that work stopped I figured I would never do much of anything but "stay afloat." But when God enables you to find out what He wants you to do, and then gives you the health and strength to do it, the results are remarkable.

Here before me were young men that I had personally trained. They had not been turned over to a faculty while I "headed up" the school. I was not a Dean, or Chancellor, or "Emeritus." I was the classroom teacher of these young men. Many of them I had hunted and fished with, and I had been in many of their homes with their families. These were not a "student body," they were my sons (and some of them daughters) in Christ that **"whom God hath given me in this place"** (Gen. 48:9). And what Sturmtruppen they had turned out to be!

Dear old *Nathan Bemis*! He flunked the second grade and the fifth grade and never finished middle school. When he came to us from the Navy he spelled Bible "Bibul." He flunked Greek twice, but he finally passed it, won souls, and witnessed the whole time he was here, and prayed the fake healer Ewing out of town. Then he went up to Kalispell, Montana, in the middle of winter and pastored a church of ten people in a Quonset hut in thirty degrees below zero. He has been up there preaching on the street and winning souls to Christ for nearly twenty years.

Then there was *Art Martin*, a building contractor from Canton, Ohio, who came down and took a sixty percent cut in income to attend school. I have seen him so tired in class after laying bricks for nine hours that he couldn't keep his eyes open. He went back to Canton and began a church in the basement of his house and after faithfully preaching to a handful of people (sometimes just his own family), God gave him one of the prettiest buildings and best locations in the state of Ohio.

Then there was *Floyd Elmore*, who never made lower than a ninety-four on any test and usually made over ninety-eight. He had turned down a scholarship to Harvard to come to PBI. When he graduated he went on to Dallas and earned graduate degrees.

One of our boys wound up as a lawyer (*Dave Rimmer*), and another one as a medical doctor (*Keith Perrine*). Another one (*Jonathan Richmond*) became a pilot and set up an independent mission board that took on the support of over forty missionaries.

There was *Wayne Mund*, who went out as an evangelist to commercial fishermen, having been one himself before coming to PBI. He set up radio broadcasts all over the world to preach the Book in fishing areas.

Then there was old *John Paisley*, who packed up when he graduated and took off, **"not knowing whither he went"** (Heb. 11:8). Going blindly by faith (with less than two hundred dollars in his pocket), he wound up in Oregon and became the associate pastor of a church running over one thousand in Sunday school.

Bill Haag became a missionary to the Caribbean, Russia, Cuba, and Central America and led over two thousand people to Christ in personal work.

Bruce McDowell said God had called him to preach on the street (ditto *Gerald Sutek* and *Bill Eubanks*), so he went out on the streets of America for fifteen years and never missed a meal or a time payment.

Weldon Jones, a boy from Germantown, Ohio, wound up in Guadalajara and set up THREE Mexican churches after learning to speak the language like a native.

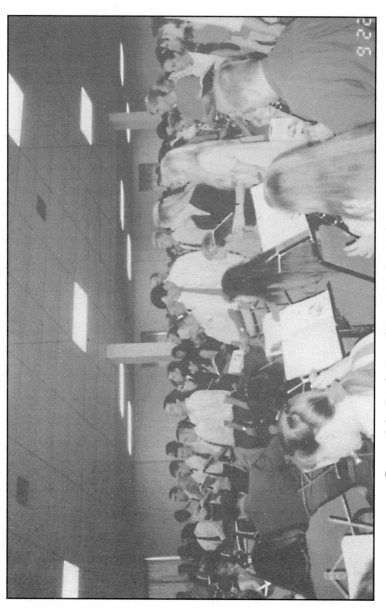

One-third of the Church Orchestra—1993

Street Hockey Players—1988

Oh, my God, what a privilege! *Oh, my God, what a luxury!* Oh, my God, what unmerited kindness and goodness to Lt. Peter S. Ruckman, 0927153, DI in hand-to-hand! I taught these boys Greek and Hebrew and taught them Church History and Biblical Archaeology. I taught them Theology, Problem Texts, Manuscript Evidence, and every verse in Genesis, Exodus, Daniel, Matthew, Acts, Romans, 1 Corinthians, Hebrews, James, 1 and 2 Peter, 1 and 2 Timothy, Titus, Revelation, Galatians, John, Ephesians, Philippians, and Colossians. Me! Old Peter S. of the back alleys, the barrooms, the nightclubs, the dance bands, the drill fields, The Cape Mendecino, The General Grant, The Sigma Nu fraternity, and the radio stations. I was getting a chance to redeem my wasted life. It was "harvest time," and the harvest was as white as a snow field.

Max Gortney got him a country church in North Carolina, *David McPherson* began "from scratch" in New Orleans and set up a fine Baptist congregation. *Eric Brazelton* pastored in Ohio in the same church more than fifteen years and witnessed to every family within five miles of him in any direction. *Mike Napier* pastored three small churches after he graduated. *Tom Woodward* went back to his hometown in Milton, Florida, and pastored for years, winning people to Christ, building a new plant and setting up a world-wide printing ministry. *Sam Gipp* pastored and then went out as a full-time evangelist, taking his family with him on the road. He wrote three excellent books.

Roger Randall wound up pastoring a Bible-believing, missionary-minded church in Harrison, Ohio, and was a great supporter of missionaries in Mexico. *Karl Baker* began "from scratch," just outside Paris Island in South Carolina, and got people saved and trained young preachers for the ministry. *Jack Patterson* wound up with a "Ranch" for delinquent young men after working with Jack Hyles for years and serving a great apprenticeship with Lester Roloff. *Rick Sowell* wound up with one of the finest evangelistic churches in America in Toledo, Ohio: King James from parking lot to baptistry, no apologies to anyone living or dead. *Tom Bard* pastored in New England, so did brother *Kehoe*. *Herman Fountain* set up the largest children's home in America (next to Roloff's) in Lucedale, Mississippi, and fought the Soviet judges for years. *Ronnie Bonds* pastored in Tallahassee and *Matt Burchard* in Iowa. *Rick DeMichele* wound up with the largest Biblical work in the state of Idaho (at Boise) and never had to alter one word in the *AV* from 1975, when he came to us, to the time of this writing.

God had let me in on all of this, if you can believe it. I was getting a chance to form and shape the ministries of young men who could do more in their places of service than I could do in a lifetime. The poor, benighted heathen at BJU, who were using a Book they didn't *believe*, were turning out NOTHING during this time but Bible-correcting girl scouts. PCS during this time did not produce ONE Bible-believing, street-preaching, soul-winning pastor or evangelist. The Lord gave them to me right and left every year.

And what more can I say without being wearisome? You did not know these young men. *I did.* I taught them how to preach on the street, and *went out* with them and *preached* with them. I taught them how to knock on doors, how to pass out tracts, how to deal with Catholics, and Campbellites, and Charismatics, and I taught them that the highest authority on this earth was THE BOOK they carried on their persons. I taught them that there didn't live on the face of this earth one man smart enough to correct ONE WORD of it.

Bill Bailey went overseas to Greece as a missionary, so did *Larry Theros*. *Ben Gilley* went over to Germany as a missionary, so did *David Trosclair*. *Brother Wheat* went to Australia, so did brother *Stroud* and *Mike Gilbert*. The *Haas* brothers went separate ways: one to Canada and the other to Mexico. *Mazaferri* wound up in Italy, and *Miller* in Scotland. God enabled me to spread myself around the globe. *Christopherson* and *Linton Smith* took Taiwan for "home," and *Robert Chancey* and *Billy Delaney* wound up in Ulster. *Greg Rhinehart* got a fine Baptist church going near Panama City, Florida; *Chris*

Huff and *Brother Heaton* got them going north of Detroit; and *Dan Gilbert, Tony Murga,* and *Steve Andrus* set
up Bible-believing, Baptist churches in "the land of fruit
and nuts." I trained *Biggs, Coonfield, Hatfield, Kipp,
Lince,* and *Ryman.* They all wound up pastoring independent, Bible-believing, Baptist churches. So did *Matthew
Welch, Robert Hays, Mike Roberts,* and *Mike Napier.*
And time would fail me to tell of the work of our men
who went out into prison work and work with delin-
quents (*Jhant, Pierce, Saucier,* et al.). *Sturmtruppen.* Not
a Bible corrector in ranks. *Not one "man follower" in the
whole army.* Everyone of them believing the Book and
following the One who gave it to them. *Bryce Stevens,
Lamar Chennault, Steve Cooper, Waddle, Danny Zorn,
David Cagle, Sam Cupa, Mike Roberts, Scott Strobel*
(New York), *Kyle Stevens* (Minneapolis), *Ron Sykes*
(South Africa), *Burris* (Virginia), et al.

By the time my wife deserted me and took all of her
relatives out of church with her (her sister had married
my associate of twenty-two years, James McGaughey),
the harvest was in full-swing, and the reapers were throwing the golden grain into the "loft."

In the meantime, Grace Kelly (Monaco) had been
killed in a car wreck (September 10, 1982), and Tennes-
see Williams kicked the bucket (February 25, 1983).
Coach Bear Bryant of Alabama was dead (January 26,
1983), Arthur Godfrey was dead (March 16), Jack
Dempsey hung up the gloves (May 31), Johnny
Weismuller (Tarzan) was dead (January 20, 1984), and
General Mark Clark (Rome) died (April 16). I had man-
aged by the grace of God to outlive Count Basie, James
Mason, Truman Capote, Mark Chagall (artist), Josef
Mengele (Auschwitz), Rock Hudson, Orson Wells, Yul
Brenner, James Cagney, Broderick Crawford, Benny
Goodman, Teddy Wilson (Goodman's piano player),
Carey Grant, Andy Warhol, Liberace, Danny Kaye, Rita
Hayworth, Erskine Caldwell (writer), Andres Segovia
(guitarist), Rudolph Hoess (Hitler's deputy), and Jascha
Heifez (violinist).

I had been living on "borrowed time" since 1960.

How God had put up with me for the years since then (twenty-eight up to my wife's desertion), I know not. And He had gone far beyond just "putting up" with me. My cup had run over. It was the cup I had picked up in 1949 when I threw away the world's cup: **"I will take the cup of salvation, and call upon the name of the LORD . . . O taste and see that the LORD is good;"** (Ps. 116:13, 34:8).

This time, instead of panicking or getting bitter, I sat down and **"consulted with myself,"** as the Scriptures say (Neh. 5:7). This time it was going to have to be clear and analytical, at least after the first flush of depression and anger. This time, in many ways, it was worse than before, for now the enemies of the Book had been given something they could use (till they hit the Judgment Seat of Christ) as an alibi to destroy the faith of young men and women in the Book. "Ruckman's life" was now in perfect condition to throw into the face of every "incoming class" of young people in every Alexandrian hellhole in America. They would not miss the opportunity, you can be sure. This time my *friends* suffered more than I did. My biggest disappointment was that God had not intervened at the last minute and prevented the woman from forcing a non-Scriptural divorce on me which I did not want. As a matter of fact, *I do not believe in divorces even where there are scriptural grounds for them.* I have never recommended divorce to anyone and do not recommend it now. I have always believed (since the fourteenth day of March, 1949) that forgiveness and restoration are the solution, *even where the grounds are Scriptural.*

But here I was, single again. There was no question about what my "ex" had been doing since she left. The reports were ample, and it was common talk. The problem for me was, "what now?"

1. I was alone in a three-bedroom, two-bathroom house on an acre of land with three cars in the driveway. Who but a fool would think that was equipment for a single man? My friends in Texas paid off the woman's "equity" on the house, so I didn't have to sell it. The

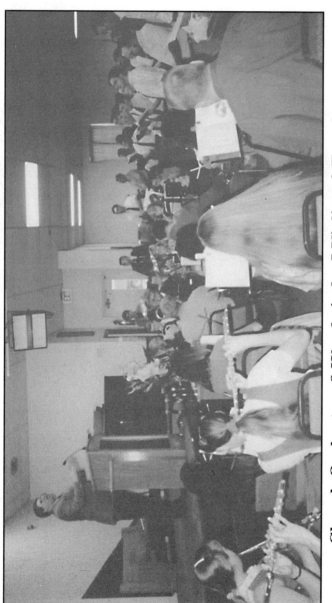

Church Orchestra: 8 Woodwinds, 5 Violins, 2 Trombones, Baratone and Bass Tubas, 4 Trumpets, Cello, Saxophone, Guitar, and Drums.

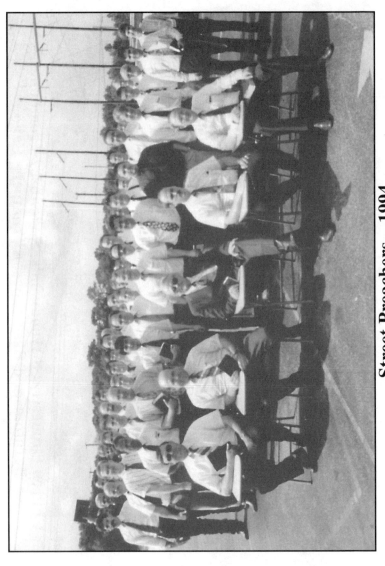

Street Preachers—1994

divorce proceedings cost nothing at all because the "care and maintenance payments" (until she married, which was less than a year) were less than the house allowance from the church. I didn't lose a penny. When Janie left I had lost everything: the house and the land.

2. I could stay single, as I had done before, and take a chance on "staying clean." This would still be extremely difficult even at sixty-six years old for, believe it or not, there were still "prospects" everywhere, and in the last two years before my wife left I was nearly in as backslidden a condition as she had been the whole time. I had gotten "near the precipice" several times after 1985. The only conditions that my former wife gave me for coming back was that I give the church to her brother-in-law and give the bookstore to her father. I remembered something from 1961. "I'll come back to you if you quit the church and go into evangelism," "I'll come back to you if you have an operation," "I'll come back to you if you see a psychiatrist," "No, I meant I'll come back if you see MY psychiatrist," etc. The woman had lied. *She had no intention of coming back.* I remembered also my "ex" saying, in the presence of her father, "I haven't thought about leaving you. What makes you accuse me of that?" and her father confirming it: "You are just imagining things." Pretty good imagination.

3. If I was going to "try, try again" after two debacles like I'd been through, it would take one of two things: lack of brains or excess of guts. This time I didn't waste nine years waiting for anyone. This time I said, "Old buddy, God must be about through with you. Just make sure when He takes you home that the house and land are in good hands. God gave them to you. There is on this earth somewhere a real Christian woman who loves God and puts *Him* first in her life. Where is she?" I began to look. I looked where I knew the faces and people best: in my own congregation. I had looked in three or four directions when I remembered something. There was a single woman in the church who was raising three boys by herself. My former wife had sent me to pick up these three boys to take them to DVBS in the

summer, but I had not met their mother. Now I saw her. She was there every Sunday. I inquired of the people who sat next to her if she had always been there every Sunday: she had been since about 1986. Furthermore, she was working a forty hour week while sending these boys to Pensacola Christian Schools. This time I didn't do as much *praying* as I did *checking*. ("No mistakes this time, Peter S., Enough is enough.") What I was looking for was a PASTOR'S WIFE. This time I would put that consideration above EVERYTHING.

The woman I "checked out" was Pamela Irene Huggins, the daughter of a Mr. and Mrs. Merritt. Pam's grandmother was from the alte Heimat. Long before I actually "dated" Pam I checked with her closest friends (the Charons), who had known her all of her life. I watched how Pam reacted when her father died of lung cancer. I checked the place where she worked to see if she had been witnessing: *she had*. There were other "possibilities" showing up throughout all of this, but none impressed me like Pam. I decided I would invite myself to her house to eat with her boys so I could see how she conducted herself at home. For three months I ate with her and her boys, once a week. I watched her discipline them; I watched her "overlook" them at times. I saw her house and how she kept it, and during the "stakeout" I would drive by the house to see if any "men friends" were there. Not only that, I phoned at various odd hours to see if I could pick up a male voice. I was as suspicious and gun-shy now about women as a boy would be about a doctor picking up a needle. Pam "panned out." The woman had a prayer life. She studied the Bible on her own. She was practically raised in a Baptist church. She loved church, and she loved *church people*. She lived in a tiny, run-down, two-bedroom house with practically no yard and no luxuries of any kind. What began with pity and sympathy gradually turned into real love.

I will make a long story short: my school secretary (Mrs. Mitchell), who had been with me for twenty-four years, counselled me to have a public wedding in church, which to me seemed like the biggest mistake I could

Dr. and Mrs. Ruckman in Germany

Street preaching with Bro. Trosclair

!!! Germany !!!

make. Both previous marriages had had only two witnesses. But "girding up my loins" and taking a mighty
leap of faith—and let me tell you, THIS leap was the
biggest leap I ever leapt in my life!—we got married in a
regular Sunday night service after the offering was taken
up: bridesmaids, wedding cake, rice, shaving cream on
the car, the whole works. Standing room only.

I was flaunting my faith in the face of the apostate
Fundamentalists who were going to "cash in" on my
marriage. But it worked. The woman turned out to be a
gem. She was the woman of Proverbs 31 that I had
preached about and heard talked about all my life but had
never *met*. There was no disappointment after that marriage, and there has been none since. I have my ten children now (I always did say I wanted at least *ten*), and my
house once more is filled with boyish laughter, games,
playing, fighting, scoldings, hot meals, fellowships, German shepherds, German music, and fun. **"Come . . . in
full age, like as a shock of corn"** (Job 5:26).

If I were to die tonight, I know my house and goods
are in the hand of a godly woman who loves God and
loves me, and three little boys now have a fine home they
probably never would have had. *God had saved the "des-
sert" for the end of the meal.*

The women in the church took to Pam immediately,
and she made friends right and left. At 5420 Rawson
Lane even the peach tree had edible peaches on it, the
commodes weren't stuck any more, no one punctured
tires driving out the rock driveway, no one complained
about the toys or the fishing net left in the yard, no one
complains about the heat or the cold: it is "another ball
game." To this day (July 1990) I am not used to it, and I
fear I am getting MELLOW: soft and *fat*.

Back we went to Germany on our honeymoon. Back
to Berchtesgaden and the "Eagle's Nest," but this time
"alles in Ordnung"—everything was in order. In the first
place, it was First Class over and back, in the front of the
DC-10. In the second place, all of our activities were
spiritual. In the third place, the trip this time was made
with the right woman. I preached a four-day meeting for

Brother Trosclair in Nürenberg, took Pam to see Ludwig's castle on the Cheimsee, and then we "saw the scenery" while running down relatives of Pips Priller in Ingolstadt and the sister of a German here in Pensacola. We were unable to make personal contact but left tracts in German in both places, and a note on the door of one of Priller's children (or grandchildren) in Ingolstadt.

I took Pam back up to the speaker's rostrum in the Sportspalast, through the Deutsche Museum in the old city of Nuremberg, and through the medieval town of Rottenberg; we went to a concert in Salzburg. We left a string of tracts as we went. I turned Pam loose on the Autobahn in an Audi that had some kind of turbo set-up that re-used fuel as the car went. She had the thrill of driving seventy m.p.h. in the "slow lane" and then "gunning it" to pass at eighty. Neither of us tried the third lane: there were cars in that lane going from one hundred to one hundred and thirty miles an hour with ten feet between the bumpers.

Sitting up at the "Kehlstein" we could see Italy, Austria, and Germany at one time. God lifted the clouds long enough to see the whole panorama for nearly an hour. German Alps in front and to the left, Italian Alps to the left rear, and the Austrian Alps on our right and right rear. "Oh Lord my God, when I in awesome wonder consider all the worlds thy hands have made!" Pam actually cried when we left Germany, for no apparent reason. It was "in the blood." Her grandmother and grandfather (Wagner) had come from this homeland. It was the first time she had ever seen it. **"Thou hast kept the good wine until now,"** (John 2:10).

CHAPTER EIGHTEEN

The Full Cup

Instead of destroying the ministry, the remarriage accelerated it. I had been through this thing now three times. I had resigned Bethel Baptist Church in Bay Minette when Janie had left (1960), I had resigned Brent Baptist Church in 1972 when I remarried, and I had resigned Bible Baptist Church in 1985 when Laura and Rachel got completely out of hand and their mother had backed them up. The brethren were always hollering, "He doesn't qualify. He doesn't qualify!" One of the most backslidden apostates in the country (the head of the Bible department at BJU) wrote that "Ruckman should not be given a preaching opportunity in any church" because of "the revealed will of God," and so forth. So I took the brethren at their word: *I resigned.* To make sure "the revealed will of God" was done, *I resigned THREE TIMES.* I often wonder what would have happened to some of my good, godly, dedicated, "once-married" brethren if they had resigned ONCE. I think they all should try it just to make sure they are in "the revealed will of God." Who knows? *They may ALL be out of "the revealed will of God!"*

The first time I resigned, God began a tape ministry that went literally to the ends of the earth—and is still going, only the volume had quadrupled. The second time I resigned, the Lord opened up a book and tract ministry which went literally to the ends of the earth. The third time I resigned, the Lord opened up a television and videotape ministry that stretched from Fairbanks, Alaska, to Haiti, and from Athens, Greece, to Honolulu. To aggravate the "good, godly," once-married brethren to the point of hysteria, the Lord threw in a tract ministry in four languages, a cassette ministry (running over eight hundred hours of material), a prison ministry (correspond-ing and sending material to "jail birds" in three dozen "slammers"), and a ministry to 300 native Filipino and Nigerian pastors. This was THROWN IN "extra" on top of the one hundred young men who entered the full-time ministry themselves. **"Now unto him that is able to do exceeding abundantly above all that we ask or think,"** (Eph. 3:20).

The Lord evidently has some very peculiar ideas about His "revealed will" that Custer, Bob Jones III, Sumner, Combs, Jennings, Hymers, Hudson, Waite, and company know NOTHING ABOUT. Perhaps they should spend a little time "searching the SCRIPTURE" (instead of "the original Greek") to find out what the revealed will of God IS. I sometimes suspect that it is their "godli-ness" that makes them so *stupid*.

It is now 1992. How now, brown cow? I have no idea. I am expecting the Rapture at any minute, if not sooner. If the Lord tarries, I know the future for all of us: hospital beds and graves. If the Lord tarries even one more year, all "hell" is going to break loose nationally and internationally. I have no illusions whatsoever about man's attempts to "bring in the kingdom" without the King. I know man. I know men. I have spent all of my life with grown men, beginning before I was fifteen years old. Christ said **"beware of men"** (Matt. 10:17). I know what will happen to the humanists who are engaged in "ending man's inhumanity to man" when Christ returns (Matt. 22:41). The Bible is quite clear on these matters. We may all wind up in jail before it is over, but if we don't, we will wind up at the undertaker's.

But it has been one FEAST, I'll tell you!

Here, one year short of the allotted **"threescore and ten,"** all I can say is: *"It has been some banquet!"* I was given a full cup both sides of Calvary. I cannot ask for a refill. I can't hold any more. Every ambition I ever had in life has been fulfilled to the letter, even those carnal, fleshy, and ungodly desires of the **"mind"** (Eph. 2:3) as well as the spiritual, Christian things of the New Testa-ment. I know the bite of the serpent and the adder's sting

Dr. and Mrs. Peter S. Ruckman

in the "bottom of the cup" (Prov.). I know what it is to have to reap the ravages of a dissolute youth. I have had to unload the ships that I sent out, and I have had to do it alone, down on the pier, with no one to help me: dead cats, dead shrimp, eggshells, coffee grounds, rotten fish, dried vomit—the whole load. Only the grace of God sustained me through the ghastly mess. Now, near the end, it is only sunlight, illuminating the whole landscape clear to the Celestial City.

When my "ex" left, Brother Neidlinger took charge of the bookstore and in a "trice" a wealthy converted Jew decided to invest in the work. Neidlinger put out an illustrated pamphlet called *Millions Disappear: Fact or Fiction?* This amazing pamphlet (in less than a year) received more than five hundred signed decision slips (with names and addresses) of men and women who received Jesus Christ. We don't know to this day how many people got saved that we know nothing about. The Fundamentalists, as usual (especially the post-Tribulationists), had another fit. Our aim was a million copies, and the presses are rolling right now.

By a Nielson rating, I was now (1992) preaching to twenty-three thousand people every week in the Pensacola-Mobile area alone. The chalk talks were now on thirty-seven television stations, so the potential weekly audience was well over four million.

I remember the Southern Baptist's fair-haired evangelist, Eddie Martin, (back in 1953), saying to me: "Pete, you will never 'reach the masses' as long as you carry the torch for Bob Jones Sr." Guess again, Eddie.

I remember the advice of a Southern Baptist pastor in Alabama way back in 1952 who said, "Ruckman, if you go on preaching like that, you will have nowhere to preach but brush arbors." I went out and bought myself an axe.

Oh, how I could hear the old deacon's wife at Brent! Mrs. McCleod, waving her Bible in the air and screaming at the end of a Sunday morning service: "You're through! God is all through with you! God has taken your wife and your children, and YOU ARE ON THE

SHELF!" That was in 1966. Some folks really have a "talent" for prophecy, don't they?

Then there was the Major who had pulled out a loaded .45 on me back in 1956, after I had hurt his feelings in a message. He didn't pull the trigger.

Then there was a dope-headed medical doctor in Milton who threatened to cut off my head and put it in a garbage can (1967). He lost his knife.

Then there was the upset young man outside of Birmingham who didn't like me passing him on the highway, so he placed his .38 on the window sill and ordered me over to the curb. I shook my head at him and went on down the road. That was in 1968.

They weren't through with me in 1987. One of my trustees said, "I can shut down this whole operation with one phone call." I had no doubt that he could, and I have no doubt now. *When he does, we won't have to guess who made the call.* So far we are "open," and the damage done to modern "Christian" educators (the apostate Fundamentalist kind) has been so great that they will never recover from it completely. If God "folded" my ministry *tonight*, the books and tapes and videotapes would go right on up to and PAST the Rapture.

I feel now (1992) that I am nearing the end, but of course I felt that way several times before: once in *1949* when I was ready to blow my brains out, another time in *1961* when I lost a wife and five children in twenty-four hours, and another time in *1987* when I thought God was surely through with me once and for all. But who knows? I cannot read the tea leaves or the crystal ball. When I was saved in 1949 I could have sworn on my mother's grave that I would never live to be forty years old, and that was in 1961. I passed the sixties, the seventies, and the eighties, and now found myself confronting 1993.

"Through many dangers, toils, and snares I have already come. 'Twas grace that brought me safe thus far, and grace will lead me home!"

"Hey, grandpa! Did you bring Jeremy?" "Give me some gummy bears, Grandpa!" "Grandpa, what does this mean in this picture?" "We going to the Fiji, Grandpa?"

"Are you coming to eat with us Grandpa?" "HEY, GRANDPA!"

Is that ME? Are they talking to *me*? Are they talking to that baby born on Franklin Avenue in 1921 when Harding was president? Are they talking to that smoking, drinking, lying, swearing, stealing, cheating, fornicating brawler who came out of the dance bands and bar rooms and barracks from the streets of Topeka, Kansas? How can it be? "Amazing grace, how sweet the sound that saved a wretch like me! I once was lost but now am found, was blind but now I see!"

The souls are still getting saved: we had seventeen of them two weeks ago (January 1990). The adults are still getting baptized: we baptized two grown converted Roman Catholics three weeks ago. The prisoners are still getting saved in the jails: *more than fifty since 1989.* The souls are still getting saved on the streets: more than two hundred since 1989. I have had at least one soul saved in every Bible conference I have held since New Years of 1988; sometimes as many as seven. *"The revealed will of God" is evidently an UNKNOWN THING in the major Christian Colleges and Universities in America.*

The thing that put the "icing on the cake" for me concerning "the revealed will of God" now happened, but it did not happen till just before my sixty-eighth birthday. (Eight days before, to be exact.) On November 11 (formerly called Armistice Day, but ditched because the Armistice turned out to be a joke: it is now called "Veteran's Day") we "marched"—literally MARCHED. I had dreamed about it for years but never thought it would come to pass, but now we had a twenty-five piece band in the church and a drum section that "wouldn't quit": three converted rock drummers. I dusted off my old German tuba (1887) and got in ranks. We wore the German colors: red, white, and black (the old German empire), and put our girls in white blouses with black skirts; the marching men wore black trousers, white shirts, and red ties. Down the street we went with scripture signs (two feet square) raised nine feet in the air: **"The wages of sin is death"; "Be sure your sin will find you**

Filipino pastors from Angeles, Luzon,
where I trained Filipino scouts in 1945–1947

Illustration for the Book of Revelation (Revelation 21-22)

out"; "He that hath the Son hath life"; "Come unto
me, all ye that labour"; "He that believeth not shall
be damned"; "In such an hour as ye think not, the
Son of man cometh"; "There is a way that seemeth
right unto a man, but . . . ."; "It is appointed unto
men once to die, but after this the judgment"; "Him
that cometh unto me I will in no wise cast out." Down
Palafox we went with the British military swagger (I
wanted to teach them the Goose Step, but their legs
weren't up to it) and thundering drums: "Onward, Christian Soldiers" and "Hold the Fort." Bible extended straight
out on, "Wave the answer, back to heaven, by Thy grace,
we will!"

The thing had never been seen anywhere in America:
before or since. I told them to look straight ahead, dress
right, and keep rank and file straight. No smiling or laughing. Son, let me tell you, we "put it on 'em!" The reviewing stand said that our ranks were better "dressed" than
the National Guard units, the ROTC units, and the Naval
Air Station personnel. (Ah, if they only had known WHY!)

But that wasn't the big thing. The "big thing" was
something that no one in the parade would notice but one
man. Not a man on the street, or in the march, would
have caught it, for lo and behold, when the units were
formed up and given the route of the march, we marched
(it's still hard to believe!) *right up the street where I had
run in March 1949, turned the corner exactly where I
turned it in the rain running down to the Methodist church
(chapter eleven), and so help me Pope John Paul II, we
went right past the rectory of ST. MICHAEL'S, where I
had my last encounter with the Jesuit from Loyola!*

The Bookkeeper had a long memory.

So, right by Father Sullivan's playhouse, FORTY
YEARS LATER, went his "Catholic convert" blowing a
tuba and waving a *King James Bible* right in his face.
Twenty Bible signs went right by the steps of the
"Father's" front porch. A photographer snapped a picture
at random, and it came out with large scripture signs
completely covering the porch at St. Michael's. One sign
was unmistakable. It said, **"There is a way which**

seemeth right unto a man, but the end thereof are the ways of death."

The Bookkeeper had laid *that* one back for forty years.

I cannot see through the crystal ball. My children and grandchildren are all saved and in good health. Peter Jr. has not yet married. I kid him about it. I tell him it is because he just doesn't have any guts. But then again, I wouldn't really expect him to. I don't really expect *anyone* to try out my "life style." You would never make it. I could no more copy J. Frank Norris in his actual life than I could copy Bob Jones Sr. or John Wesley. The Lord makes no two exactly alike; *there are no duplicates*. I don't know of anyone who follows me in everything, or believes everything I believe, or even could be called a "Ruckmanite." My own children have never taken all of my advice or counsel. The only reason that apostates like Bob Jones III, Jennings, Combs, Hutson, Hudson, Hymers, Duncan, Waite, Walker, MacRae, Custer, Panosian, Price, Martin, Wisdom, et al., like to talk about "Ruckmanites" in a "cult" is to cover up their own *powerless, fruitless, barren lives* which have nothing to show but some pretty buildings and some young people conned into paying money to learn everything *except THE BOOK*.

No matter how many more "breaks" I get in life, the sands of time will run out sometime. No man can stay alive forever on this earth if the Lord tarries. Sooner or later, death will get us all; and "time and tide" wait for no man. Paul *finished* his course. If I have not finished mine yet, it certainly cannot run much longer; the old Adamic body will simply not hold out. But when I look at my life and my "times" (that is why I documented them in this work), I feel nothing but a wave of gratitude and thanksgiving to God for pouring out to me the cup He poured out.

How terrible to live and die like Elvis Presley or John Belushi! What a horror to live and die like John Lennon or Marilyn Monroe! What a pitiful parade of human beings surrounded me as I made the journey from President Harding to President Bush. How sad it is that

God was not as gracious to *them* as He was to me. Getty and Hughes, failures: miserable, miserly, unhappy men. FDR and Truman: frustrated, deceived politicians who accomplished nothing in a lifetime that would benefit one human being on this earth after he was dead. Kennedy and Michael King Jr.: shot down in their youth after serving the interests of unsaved popes and unsaved Marxists. Clark Gable and James Stewart, Carey Grant and Gary Cooper, John Wayne and Spencer Tracy: living their whole lives in fantasy, pretending to be men they never were nor ever could be, and then dying and hitting the Judgment with nothing to show but the filthy rags of their own self-righteousness. What miserable failures!

And what about those Rolling Stones and Heavy Metal, the Comets and the Imperials, Jackson and Madonna, Springsteen, Prince, and Elton John? Poor, frustrated, miserable, lonely people who had to live off liquor or dope (or both), or stuff their bank accounts with money earned by promoting African sex music. Nothing for them but money, food, clothes, cars, fornication, and sex perversion. Solomon had more sex and more wine, and more food and more money, and more houses and more property, and more attention and more talent, and more power THAN ALL OF THEM *COMBINED*, and he couldn't even take a cheerful outlook on life! What a tragedy.

How terrible it would have been to live and die like Alfred Hitchcock, or Frank Sinatra, or Mother Teresa, or Judy Garland, or any other Roman Catholic who placed his "hope" in the "pope" instead of the Lord Jesus. What a fate to give your life to your country as George Patton and Douglas MacArthur gave it and then have your country blackball you and get rid of you because you didn't "fit" their great, ecumenical "new world" of international Socialism. How fortunate I had been not to have been placed in the shoes of Salk, or Einstein, or Von Braun or some moonwalker—some other worldly worldling trying to make "the world a better place to live in." I saw them come and go, and at the end realized that if I had ever envied ONE of them (Artie Shaw, Bernard Shaw, Eu-

gene O'Neill, Norman Rockwell, Glenn Miller, Audie
Murphy, Dillinger, or Mario Lanza) a day in my life, I
had done something so stupid that heaven and earth must
have laughed me to scorn. What ghastly, miserable lives
these musicians, artists, movie stars, war heroes, millionaires, scientists, educators, and politicians had lived when
compared with mine. The whole crew (Joe Namath, President Carter, Jimmy Conners, President Johnson, Tip
O'Neil, Bernadette Devlin, the Shah, Stalin, Lenin, Timothy O'Leary, Westmoreland, Johnny Carson, Dean Martin, Stewart Custer, Bob Jones Jr., Kenneth Wuest, Cardinal Spellman, Fulton Sheen, Afman, Farstad, Martin,
Price, Doug Kutilek, Wilt the Stilt, Bobby Hull, Bobby
Orr, Homer Duncan, Ronald Walker, Babe Ruth, Lou
Gehrig, Arnold Palmer, et al.)—the whole crew living
and dying without leaving one mark on this earth for God
or God's Book.

Some of these characters were Christians who taught
a Book they did not *believe*; they had *used* it to make a
living with while telling people that THEY were the final
authority over the Book. All they marked this earth with
was more proud, stupid, self-righteous young men who
followed them instead of the Book. *They wasted their
lives producing Christian INFIDELS.*

The end is near: whether the undertaker or the
Uppertaker gets me, I know not, but one thing I know,
**"This poor man cried, and the LORD heard him, and
saved him out of all his troubles,"** (Psa. 34:6). If I were
buried this week, I now would have left behind forty-
three years of service in the *right Army* with the *right
Commander*; I would not have been a "thirty year man,"
but a "forty-three year man."

God was so good to me that it would take an eternity to praise Him for it. While the world's **"mighty,"**
"wise," and **"noble"** (1 Cor. 1) got the headlines, God
gave me the *souls of men*. While the world extolled its
"chosen" and raved on them, God sent me down the back
alleys and through the highways and byways to gather a
cluster of fruit (John 15:1–5) that will last millenniums
after this earth is burned to a crisp (2 Pet. 3).

True, I was like a little thirty-watt bulb in a palace containing chandeliers with hundreds of bulbs, each putting out three hundred watts of power, but then again, I received great compensations. I had wanted physical strength: *God gave it to me.* I had wanted intellectual wisdom: *God gave it to me.* I had desired to be a hockey goalie (when I "grew up"), and sure enough I wound up "keeping the gate." The only country I ever really wanted to see outside of the U.S.A. was Germany: *the Lord gave me five trips there.* I always wanted to have at my fingertips the world's great music (Beethoven, Brahms, Bach, Handel, Mozart, Haydn, Schubert, Strauss, Mussorgsky, et al.); I have it: four hundred hours of it coming through eight speakers. I wanted to write: I wrote, and the works are on the market. I wanted to be an artist: I rendered so many works in pencil, chalk, and pen and ink I can't even remember them, and the works in water color, oil, pastel, charcoal, and acrylics go into the hundreds. I had wanted to be a musician, and the Lord gave me first a harmonica, then a set of drums, then a guitar, and then finally a tuba. I had wanted to live by the ocean; that is where I have lived now for more than *thirty years.*

My small acre of land has poplars, magnolias, dogwoods, japonicas, oaks, pecans, and pine trees on it. *I always did like the forest.* Fifty trees are on this acre. I love children: I always wanted to have a big family. The Lord gave me ten children and eleven grandchildren. I have always loved dogs. There has been a German shepherd in my house since 1959. I coveted good health, and the Lord allowed me to play racquetball, touch football, volleyball, soccer, and hockey up into my sixties.

And what else more could any sinner want on this earth? I have a wife that loves me, and I love her. Pam is the woman of Proverbs 31. *All my children are saved.* I can still jog three miles a day and am still teaching ten hours a week and traveling fifty thousand miles a year by Jet.

"And God granted him that which he requested," (1 Chron. 4:10).

One night several years back—I think it was Thanksgiving of the year 1984—I was being driven back to the Holiday Inn from the Twin Cities Baptist Temple in Flint, Michigan. My old ex-gangster buddy Edmond Dinant was driving. He had pastored the church there for nearly thirty years. Dinant had come up when I came up (Harding, Coolidge, Hoover, et al.). He, like I, had survived World War II, Korea, and Vietnam and all the things you find chronicled in this autobiography. Up around seventy, Dinant was now a white-haired saint: just a faint trace of the "mobster" would flit across his visage at times. His wrist bones were as big as my thighbones, and his two hammer fists had had the knuckles on them broken so many times, from smashing faces in, that they looked like two pink bowling balls.

Dinant and I had always been close. We had met at Camp Chatauqua way back around 1958 somewhere. We liked to "compare notes." He understood my past, and I understood his. Unlike him, I had never wound up in the slammer; he had. In addition to that, he had survived a life of deadly hit-and-run episodes with "revenue agents," and had been in every kind of a fight a man can get into: fist fights, cue stick fights, knife fights, razor fights, pistol fights, rifle fights, broken bottle fights, and God knows what. He had operated under three aliases as a "mobster," and the night he was saved, way back in the hills, he gave the wrong name to the church clerk. Edmond Dinant was French. I was Austrian (an Austrian is just a German in 3/4 time). He had been raised in the bushes in the mountains (Adirondacks) while I had been raised in the "flats" (Kansas) in a city. But somehow we always had a rapport—a meeting of minds that not even married couples have.

Dinant once said to the "godly" members of the Baptist Bible Fellowship (they were all *teachers*): "If I believed about this Book [Dinant was "King James" from head to foot] what you fellows believe, I would never have become a preacher. I would have stayed a gangster." I never heard it put to the faculty of Bob Jones, Tennessee Temple, PCC, Wheaton, Fuller, Moody, Cedarville, BBC, Dallas, or Denver any better than THAT.

Well, the car moved slowly through the icy intersections. There was a lot of unmelted snow lying around. We had driven about two miles into the night and had been "reminiscing," as usual. Then a quietness settled over the car, and we drove on about a mile with no sound but the slushy "squishing" of the tires on the snowy pavement. Suddenly both of us turned to face each other, and then both of us said the same words (identically) in perfect unison. We said, "You know, Brother, you and I . . . ." And then we broke down laughing. Whatever we were going to say, it certainly would have matched word for word to the end. I know what we were going to say: both of us knew it. Without one signal or one bit of collusion, the two of us at the same time, in unison, were going to say, "You know, Brother, *you and I have had the best of it.*" After the laughter we both confessed that that is how the sentence was going to be finished.

There are probably not many Christians who would understand what I am about so say. You have to be like Edmund Dinant to understand it. He and I were closer than brothers. Neither of us ever had to even guess what the other had on his mind. We understood not only each other's motives and methods, but each other's strengths and weaknesses. It was like that relationship between Jonathan and David: **". . . he loved him as his own soul,"** (1 Sam. 18:3). When God took brother Dinant home, I lost one of the closest friends, if not the closest, I ever had on this earth. I have had friends who were more helpful and just as faithful, and just as loyal, but none with that inner understanding, that automatic perception that made our comradeship so flawless.

I will say what I had in mind (I usually do).

What Dinant and I meant was this:

1. God had given us everything in life that He could have given *any* sinner—both bad and good. He had let us not just "taste", but wallow in filth on the "seamy side" of life and live like the very devil himself, *without killing or crippling us.* Conversely, He allowed us to live in good health until He could reveal Himself to us, and then

gave us what we REALLY had been looking for, *without knowing it.*

2. He then had opened the windows of heaven and poured out a blessing so great that neither of us could receive it. Not being worthy of it, and knowing we had done nothing to deserve *anything*, every honor, every blessing, every dollar, every convert, and every answer to prayer came as a gourmet's feast worth a hundred dollars a plate. Having spared us nothing in the *old life*, He had spared us nothing in the *new life*. **"He that spared not his own Son, but delivered him up for us all, how shall he not with him also freely give us all things?"** (Rom. 8:32). We had not just tasted "life": we had quaffed the cup and drained the dregs—*on both sides of Calvary.*

"You know, brother, you and I have had the BEST of it."

How true. Behind us lay those rows and rows of corpses (more than *twenty-two million* in World War II, more than *three hundred thousand* in Korea, more than *one hundred thousand* in Nam), those marble slabs row on row (Hollywood stars, gangsters, authors, painters, musicians, millionaires, politicians, and military leaders). Behind us now lay not only the years and years of sin, but years and years of *fruitful ministries*. Ahead, for us, lay hospital beds and graves, if the Lord tarried, but in the END, nothing lay ahead for us but GLORY. Edmund Dinant is in that Glory now. I will see him again when I see my Saviour "face to face." And when I do, perhaps both of us—between shouts of praise and roars of holy laughter—will say (at one time), *"You know, brother, you and I had the best of it."*

I believe it. **"My cup runneth over."**

Epilogue

As I sit down to write this postscript on *The Full Cup,* I am aware of the fact that it is seven years later, and the cup has been "flowing over" throughout the entire time. The only change has been a doubling of the pace with more ministries added, more adult men saved in a year than were saved in any three years preceding it, a son called to preach, and five overseas trips to five different mission fields after ministering in Odessa in the Ukraine, instead of Romania.

For the last two years there have been 200 students a year coming to PBI, and since 1991, at least ten more young men have left for the mission field: Christopher Rue, Tom Johnson, Jason Hines, Brian Higgins, Joe Melvin, Edward Keough, James Tomzak, Mike Roberts, Tracy Elwood, and Pete Dickens.

If that were not enough, the Lord decided that an acre of wooded land near the Gulf (see p. 332) was not enough, so he gave me *five acres of wooded land near the Gulf,* and with it a grape arbor, bass pond (with catfish and bream in it), an acre of ground to garden (I grew 21 different vegetables in it last spring), and a house *twice the size* of the one that I had lived in for twenty-eight years at Rawson Lane, surrounded by Pensacola Christian College. Then as if that were not enough, the Lord chose this piece of land so that it was *less than 150 yards from the school and the church.* This ended thirty-two years of driving seven miles up and back Palafox during the rush hour (4:30–6:30) and after 10 P.M. at night.

In went Pam and I and the boys (Jeremy, Brian, and Michael) into a three bedroom, three full bathroom house with two dining rooms, a den, two offices, a living room, a sauna, and an art studio. Unlike 5420 Rawson Lane, it had a front porch and a back porch, lights that could be dimmed on switches, air-conditioning that was hooked up to water in the pond; and the pond was rigged so it could spray the garden through nine sprinklers. The fireplace had an automatic hot air blower in it, and there was room on the walls to mount thirty of my paintings. Along with this load of luxuries, my people in the church bought us a year-old Suburban with less than 30,000 miles on it.

The overflow from "the cup" is now forming in a *large lake.*

Adam's "last will and testament" (Rom. 5) continued to be administered by the Death Angel (Heb. 2:14). I lived to see *Richard Nixon's* funeral. *Kurt Cobain* headed for the White Throne Judgment (and the Lake of Fire) after pretending he had found "nirvana" (see p. 122). *Dotty West* hit the skids; *Stevie "Ray" Vaughn,* the blues singer, popped off; *Tupac Shakur* kicked the bucket; *John Candy,* the actor-comedian, croaked; and the Grateful Dead handed *Jerry Garcia* over to the funeral director. God spared Peter S. Ruckman again: again and again and again. He saw *Allen Ginsburg,* the poet, conk out; *William Buroughs,* the writer, hit the skids; *Sam Kinison* expire; and *John Denver* cash in his chips. Along with the multitudes and masses, went the walking gin barrel *Dean Martin,* living and dying as a drunken sot.

"And where are the snows of yesteryear?"

The "paths of glory" led where they always have led: straight to a hole in the ground—the grave.

"It is appointed unto men once to die and after this THE JUDGMENT."

While they continued to tumble into Hell, right and left, the Lord continued to save their souls right and left under my ministries. I wasn't going to have to go home "empty handed."

In 1995, I wound up in Mexico preaching to the people who had been given more than $20,000,000,000 in American tax money. They were as bankrupt as ever. Every time we gave a handout, it was to a Communist nation (Russia, Somalia, Mandela's South Africa, Haiti, etc.) or a Catholic country (Mexico, Nicaragua, Croatia, Eire, etc.). The press got 400 peacekeeping forces (English) out of Ulster to encourage Gerry Adams' Catholic terrorists to move in (March 12, 1995).

Mike (the computer boxer: "two bytes and no memory") spent three years in prison for raping another black; Mohammedans in Algeria continued to murder writers, artists, and journalists who were anti-Mohammedan; two Japanese banks (Mitsubishi and Tokyo) joined to form a bank three times as large as the largest bank in America (Citibank); and Slick Willie turned Haiti over to the UN after making sure a *Roman Catholic priest* would take over the government (Jean Bertrand Aristide).

More Mohammedans killed Jews on the 10th of April (eight of them); Clinton decided that the Freedom of Information Act was a joke, so he passed a rule that no highly classified documents could be examined till twenty-five years (April 17). Up went the Federal Building in Oklahoma City, killing 167 people—only fifteen children were killed in comparison to Waco (17). Timothy McVeigh was arrested. Instead of a "speedy trial by jury," he was shuttled into a complete blackout from all contacts with the news media and the TV for more than a year, and not even *fifteen minutes of his trial* was shown on TV: wrong color. O. J. Simpson got more than *500 hours exposure:* right color.

When McVeigh was finally convicted, all of the information about his presence, his confession, the planting of the bomb, his examination, the building of the bomb, the nature of the bomb, the time of evacuation of Feds before the bombing, and the locking out of all observers from the story in the building that had the Waco records in it, *was withheld from ALL news media outlets.* To this day, not one line of evidence has ever been printed that shows that McVeigh built any bomb, carried any bomb, or planted a bomb in any building. He was subject to drugged experiments the entire time he was held back from public exposure, as are all criminals today that are behind bars. The FBI created a patsy for themselves like Lee Oswald.

The Mohammedans murdered five more Jews on August 21st; a bloody war broke out in Rwanda and Zaire—400,000 casualties. The UN did nothing. Instead, Slick Willie threatened to bomb the Greek Orthodox Serbs (Aug. 27). Ten UN planes promptly dropped *bombs* to "keep the peace." They then flew 200 sorties over Greek Orthodox territory. The Serbs were told to give up 70 percent of the land they had gained back, after World War II, to the Mohammedans and Catholics. They were *bombed* into meeting the UN demands (Sept. 1995).

After Hillary tried to straighten the Chinese government out on civil rights, they gave Slick several hundred thousand dollars to get reelected, and in return, he gave them "favored trade status" to help with their heroine and cocaine traffic: "an insane asylum run by the inmates."

Pope John Paul II went to South Africa (Sept. 1995) to give his blessing to the new Communist government which has (since then) bankrupted the country, increased the rape and murder rate by 500%, and is preparing to wipe out the "whites" that still own property in South Africa.

And so time marched on. Yitzhak Rabin got his brains blown out after trying to give half of Palestine back to the Mohammedans. Madeline Albright turned against Israel and backed up Muhammad and the PLO, and so on and so forth. On January 16, 1995, 2,000 people got killed in an earthquake in Kobe, Japan.

I still survived. When 1998 showed up, I was still "running the race" and ignoring every major news event going on all around me on all sides, including the Communist uprisings in India while I was preaching there (Dec.–Jan., 1996–1997). In South Korea, 100 students were killed by a North Korean bomb explosion (April 28, 1995).

God gave this old "junk yard dog" seven more years *beyond* the allotted "three score and ten" (Psa. 90), and looking back over the trail, I realize that if I had fulfilled my own ambition to be a "thirty-year man"—following the military footsteps of my forbearers—I would now be twenty-four years PAST retirement. My "thirty years" would have been 1944–1974; from 1974 to 1998 I would have been sitting around on my "behunkus," like my father had done after his retirement (1950–1966) in Rehoboth Beach, Delaware.

Ah, the goodness and mercy of God! Ah, the FULL CUP! Whereas my poor, earthly father had to sit around and waste the last sixteen years of his life playing bridge, walking the boardwalk, watching movies and TV, attending a liberal church under an unsaved "Modernist," and occasionally swimming in the ocean, my "wasted time" had been occupied with traveling around the world (literally), leading scores of grown men to Jesus Christ, turning out books that reached the ends of the earth (and have been translated into as many as seven foreign languages), raising two more families of boys, and then training more than 600 young men and women for the ministry of THE BOOK. It was the Book that I first stole from a "flop house" in Pensacola in 1949 (p. 145).

Man! What a Book!

In the next eight years, I finished seventeen more books: *The Mythological Septuagint, The Christian Liar's Library, The Scholarship Only Controversy, Black is Beautiful, God is Love, Ruckman's Bible References, The Anti-Intellectual Manifesto, The Clownsville Carnival, Art and Artists, Music and Musicians, Discrimination, the Key to Sanity, The Damnation of a Nation, Why I Am Not a Calvinist, Why I Am Not a Charismatic, Why I Am Not a Seventh-day Adventist, Why I Am Not a Campbellite,* and *Why I Am Not a Catholic.*

And while this was going on, I continued to play

hockey four hours a week in the summers of 1992, 1993, 1994, 1995, 1996, 1997, and ice hockey in Michigan during the winters of the same years. I even attended a week of "grass drills" for hockey goalies at the Rick Heinz School for Goalies in Chicago (1993). I lost twenty pounds in five days. We were on the ice from 2:30 P.M. to 8:30 P.M., Monday through Friday, with a one-hour break each day for "supper" and "sports."

They gave me a book on professional hockey goalies as a prize for the goalie who had put out the most effort in the week. I was seventy-two years young at the time (1993), but I have only played 130 games of hockey since then.

And how did the old *"kosmos"* (Greek for "the organized world system") conduct itself throughout 1991, 1992, and 1993? Can't you guess? Did you read the last 296 pages? While I "pressed forward" for the prize of the "high calling" (Phil. 2:14), the UN, FBI, EPA, FEMA, ACLU, ECC, UNESCO, NBC, ABC, CNN, HRS, IRS, both houses of Congress, *Time, Life, Newsweek,* and "International" Public Radio went right on at the same clip they had been hot-rodding for ninety years: war, lying, crime, fraud, terrorism, rape, embezzlement, disasters, etc.

Bush promised to bail out Russia again (this was the *fourth* time) in 1990, and then sent 400,000 troops, 1,500 aircraft, and 65 warships into the Persian Gulf to bomb out some rag-heads who didn't have enough equipment to keep 89,000 tons of explosives from ravaging their country. The Americans got off with *144 casualties,* after murdering more than 200,000 civilians and troops. They didn't get Hussein, although Bush declared, "We are only after *one man,* not the Iraquis." After spending $20,000,000,000 to bomb out the camel jockeys, Saddam was alive and well.

Between January 17 and February 23 (40 days of war), *400 Americans lost their lives in the town of residence of the Commander-in-Chief of the U.S. Armed*

Forces—a fornicating draft dodger. Washington, D.C. boasted three times as many casualties during the "Desert Storm" operation as "the military" did in Iraq. In D.C. they were killed at the rate of *ten a day. This was the base of the U.S.A.'s "Commander-in-Chief."*

In 1992, Boris Yeltsin decided the UN had been sufficiently communized to where it could control American foreign policies, so he ended the "cold war." Following the beating of a dopeheaded, convicted criminal (driving more than 95 m.p.h. through a 55 m.p.h. speed zone), blacks in Los Angeles succeeded in killing fifty people and injuring 2,000 more and destroying more than $1,000,000,000 of property. This was done to blackmail a judge into giving the convicted criminal $3,000,000. A little later, *another* black criminal (O. J. Simpson) cost the taxpayers of Los Angeles $8,000,000 because of a "double suicide case" where one of the "suicides" *got her blood on him as she was committing "suicide" with her boyfriend.*

During the Rodney King riots, a white truck driver, passing through Los Angeles, was mobbed and beaten to within an inch of his life: *he is still crippled today.* He didn't receive *one penny* from the Feds for his hospital bills; the Federal bureaucrat who tried his case said the *black thugs* who beat him up were *innocent* because "during times of mob violence people lack self-control, especially after being aggravated for a long time." *The police who beat up Rodney were the wrong color.*

Then while God was opening up the mission fields for me in Russia (the Ukraine), Korea, and the Philippines, Hurricane Andrew killed thirty-two people and caused *almost* as much damage in Florida and Louisiana (Aug. 24–26) as the blacks did in downtown Los Angeles ($1,000,000,000). Bush proceeded to escalate a war in Somalia, pretending that he wasn't sending "relief" supplies to just ONE side in the conflict. In went 28,000 U.S.A. troops to kill anyone *on the other side.* This came to be called "peace keeping" in the next few years, and finally produced a case where a patriotic young American Army volunteer was given a *dishonorable discharge* for *not* donning a FOREIGN UNIFORM *after pledging allegiance to the United States of America.*

While I was preaching in KGB prisons and former government buildings in the Ukraine, where they had tortured hundreds of Christians between 1950 and 1980, Slick Willie gave his boss (Hillary) a business office in the White House as chairman of a committee on the Health Care System (1993), and Janet Reno gassed (and later BURNED) seventeen *unarmed minor children* in Waco, Texas on the grounds that a religious fanatic had been "abusing" them (Feb.–April, 1993). After lying about David Koresh's compound *attacking* the FBI, and lying about the *child abuse* and child neglect, and lying about *illegal arms* being present, and lying about "thousands of rounds of *ammunition*" being stored, the FBI committed a felony *by erasing all of the evidence of their crime* and refusing any pictures to be made of the murdered children, including any autopsies on ANY of the dead bodies.

When the government building in Oklahoma got bombed, the news media had a six month orgy of pictures of dead children and their weeping parents. At Waco, no one in America got to see the picture of one mother whose *unarmed child* was gassed (and then *burned*) before being buried *without an autopsy or a report.* The news media had declared Koresh guilty *before* the slaughter; they had declared O. J. innocent *before* the trial; and they had declared Timothy McVeigh guilty *the day he was arrested.* All juries and judges in charge of all four criminal cases (Ruby Ridge, Waco, R. King, and O. J.) were BLACKMAILED *before the court proceedings took place* and were threatened with black riots or prosecution by the IRS if they didn't bring in the right "verdict."

I went on down the road. I believe I saw twenty minutes through a six month period of O.J.'s "double suicide" and about fifteen minutes in a four month period of Rodney's escapade. I do not take a newspaper, and I listen to less than fifteen minutes of radio news daily. I was writing six books during this time and ministering to more than 500 students while pastoring more than 500 church members.

In 1990, Pam and I headed out for the Ukraine. I preached in a KGB prison and eleven prisoners walked down to the front, before 400 of their buddies, and openly accepted Christ as their Saviour. The warden asked us to stay for dinner, which we did, and then invited us to come back "any time." I preached in government buildings that had been used to interrogate (torture) Christians when Stalin and Lenin were running things. We had about forty-two first-time conversions to Christ in several other meetings, including preaching services on the streets. I did not count any "raising of hands after prayer" for conversions; otherwise the total would have been well over 400. I only counted those who called upon the name of the Lord Jesus *for the FIRST TIME*. (This is also my practise in the prison ministry in the United States. Many times in the last three years when I knelt to lead in prayer at the end of a service and showed the men how to receive Jesus Christ by "calling on His name," I have heard the *whole room* following me in prayer; sometimes this would be *over 100 prisoners*.)

And this brings me to the final filling of the "full cup." For in the summer of 1994, I made a contact through a Southern Baptist chaplain in a prison "Unit" near Beeville, Texas, through one of my graduates (Bevins Welder, pastor of the Bible Baptist Church), that opened dozens of prisons in Texas for me. Shortly after that, the Captain of the Jacksonville Police Force (David Peacock) got me into the city jail in Jacksonville, Florida, and brother Womack got me into the county jail located in Tallahassee. *These three contacts produced sixty evangelistic services in forty different prisons.*

The total number of adult men who received Christ as their Saviour for the first time was somewhere around

290 clear-cut conversions. Of these, about 200 were
blacks, 70 were whites, and 20 were Catholic Hispanics.
This brought the total of prisons I have preached in since
my conversion to fifty-five prisons; they include the Federal Penitentiary of Atlanta, the Federal Prison for Women
at Wetumpka, Alabama, the State Farm at Atmore, Alabama, and the Maximum Security Prison at Riker's Island in New York City. I am praying to get into
Lewisburg, Pennsylvania; Attica, New York; and Marion,
Indiana.

This opened *another* whole full-time ministry which
is now requiring answering more than twenty letters a
day (personally) and mailing out more than 500 pieces of
free literature every month. The Bookstore is now a missionary "outlet" that is donating more than $1,000 a month
in free books to prisoners, native pastors, and foreign
missionaries.

But the overflow keeps overflowing. *"Life begins at
70!"*

I still use a $150 electric typewriter and a $45 cassette recording machine. But these two handy, cheap little
"aids" now have to handle 200 pastors in the Philippines,
950 pastors in India, 41 of my own young men on the
mission field, and more than 185 prisoners in 30 different "Correctional Institutions" (jails, slammers, prisons,
coolers, etc.), plus the mail from the TV program which
is now on Satellite.

Koresh's building was set on fire by Reno's "jack-
booted thugs" because the military gas was *flammable.*
Since the electricity had been cut off, all the Davidians
had was *kerosene lamps* and *Coleman lanterns.* Unarmed
fathers were murdered trying to get *into* the compound,
and not one firecracker even "popped" in a conflagration
that was supposedly burning more than 5,000 rounds of
ammo. No bureaucrat killer was arrested. No bureaucrat
felon was charged with *anything.* A handful of Davidian
survivors were arrested and charged with being "in the
presence" of illegal weapons, since they didn't *have* any

or *carry* any or were *armed* with any.

Well, the same year (1992), 104 people were killed March 13, in a storm; and a car bomb killed 7 people (and injured 1,000) at the World Trade Center. A flood in the Midwest did away with 50 more, while 70,000 people were left homeless. (They couldn't find enough *dikes* to stop the flood because "all of the dykes were in Washington.") The fornicating, draft dodger (Slick Willie) sent 4,000 more troops into Somalia to escalate the "peace keeping process" (Oct. 3–6) in preparation for bombing Greek Orthodox Serbs (see p. 340) who tried to move back into the lands that the Catholic Croatians and Mohammedans (Muslims) *took from them during World War II.*

To round out a typical year of nutty madness in the "Insane Asylum run by the inmates," the Pentagon decided to let fairies, fruits, faggots, and "butches" into an Army that had women officers and was one-third black. No one bothered to get a "racial balance" or "affirmative action QUOTAS" on the Army, which is evident by the fact that America would have to be 33 percent BLACK to have an Army that was 33 percent black: *America is less than 15 percent black.*

"BACK TO THE BIBLE OR BACK TO *THE JUNGLE.*"

In 1994, as God began to open the prison ministries to me (which eventually led to correspondence with more than 185 prisoners in more than thirty prisons), the world went on as usual: straight down into the starless midnight of a Global Police State in the hands of Atheistic Humanists who professed to be *monkey men,* literally, as postulated by Charles Darwin before A.D. 1900 and Pope John Paul II after A.D. 1990.

As we said, Rodney King, the doped-up reckless driver who endangered the lives of scores of pedestrians and drivers, was awarded $3,800,000 *on the grounds of his color;* the truck driver (p. 343) was the *wrong color.* He got nothing; *the taxpayers didn't even pay his hospi-*

tal bill. At the same time, another man of the *RIGHT* color ("black is beautiful") tried to escape the scene of a "double suicide." When the police ran him down he had the blood of his dead wife on his clothes. He was tried and found innocent. Both the judge and the jury were blackmailed with a threat of mob violence if they charged either felon with murder. The black mobs controlled the courts. Paul J. Hill (*the wrong color*) killed an abortion doctor in Pensacola (July 29); and instead of his trial lasting six months, it lasted less than two hours, and he was found guilty in twenty minutes. *Wrong color.*

In 1994, Pam and I took off on a junket that put us in Hawaii with one of our graduates (Brother Fred Hernandez) and then in Seoul, Korea, with Brother Song Lee, to teach at *The Pensacola Bible Institute of Korea* (all kiddin' aside; that is the name of the Bible school), and to preach to the Koreans on the street. From there we went down into the Philippines and taught 130 Filipino pastors on the island of Panay, near Iloilo. We came back with only a handful of conversions (12) because 90 percent of the time we were teaching Koreans, Hawaiian, and Filipino Christians the word of God. Then in 1995, Pam and I spent a week in Guadalajara with Weldon Jones (another of our graduates), who has been there twenty-six years and founded three Bible-believing Baptist churches.

And then last December, we slipped off to teach the Bible in Bombay and Hyderabad, India. Nine hundred fifty pastors assembled to hear me teach two hours every morning, take questions ("cold turkey"), answer them with Scripture two hours every afternoon, and then draw chalk talks two hours every night.

The last three years (1994, 1995, and 1996) ran true to form without one deviation from the format followed between 1900 and 1910, 1910 and 1929, 1929–1933, 1933–1945, 1945–1955, 1955–1965, 1965–1975, 1975–1985, and 1985 to 1993: murder, rape, war, independence, loss of national independence, loss of constitutional rights, more Federal control, more unemployment, crime increases, disaster in foreign policies, the ascendancy of Communism as a world government, the ascendancy of the pope as the world's greatest religious leader, perversions and corruptions of Scripture, apostasy in the Body of Christ, an increase in terrorism, witchcraft, cannibalism, and pornography, and an ignorance of Scripture as deep and profound as that in the Dark Ages (A.D. 500–1500).

Reagan was taken with Altzheimer's Disease. The Catholic notebook of the Roman Catholic DeVinci was sold for $30,800,000 (good press). A federal judge overruled *all of the citizens of California* by saying that they had to support all *illegal immigrants* with their tax money (welfare, workers compensation, free school lunches, etc.). Boris Yeltsin threatened an all-out war against his own people (Chechnya) for "seceding from the Union." Slick Willie sent 25,000 troops to Bosnia to kill Greek Orthodox Serbs so the Catholic Croatians would not be threatened. Janet Reno said the FBI "made a mistake" when it "mistakenly shot" an unarmed WHITE mother with a baby (Ruby Ridge). The killer was a *TRAINED MARKSMAN* with a scope, shooting in *broad daylight,* at a range of *LESS THAN 100 YARDS.*

A Federal judge decided to give loggers in the Pacific Northwest a break *after putting several thousand of them out of work* with a "Spotted White Owl" routine. This judge (William Dwyer of the District Court in Seattle) caused the depression when BUSH was president. But when Slick Willie got in, *the same judge reversed his decree* so that Slick could get credit for a "revival" in employment (Dec. 21, 1994). To add to his prestige as a great deliverer and "friend of the worker," the fornicating draft dodger handed over several billion dollars to Mexico after giving them $6,000,000,000 "credit" to finance their drug traffic. The traffic (1995–1996) immediately took over all aspects of the government, including all of the police forces. When Congress refused to

give Mexico ANOTHER $40,000,000,000, Slick over-
ruled both houses and personally gave away $20,-
000,000,000.

Then, further stripping the American taxpayers of
their assets, Willie put up $9,000,000,000 of the taxpay-
ers' money for a loan of $18,000,000,000. It is *now* en-
abling the Mexicans to get about $80,000,000,000 a year
(1998) in drug deals across the border.

Nothing changed in Israel between 1990 and 1996.
The pope continued to back up the Muslims in Bosnia
and the Muslims in Palestine (the PLO). He used the UN
as a "sounding board" to assist the PLO in getting Jews
out of the "West Bank" and Greek Orthodox Serbs out of
Bosnia (Moslem territory). While he did this, Mohammedans (all Moslems and Muslims are *Mohammedans*)
killed nineteen Jews and wounded sixty more (Jan. 25,
1995). Later (1995–1997), they murdered 200 more and
injured 4,000. A Texas Republican threw the whole news
media cult and Washington, D.C. into a psychotic spasm
of Heterophobiac Paranoi when he ALMOST referred to
Barney Frank, the sex pervert from Massachusetts, as a
"faggot." Speech had to be censored now to protect *sex
perverts* as well as *black murderers.*

The "slump" in "savings" by the nation's population
was blamed upon Americans fifty-five years old and older
(Feb. 20, 1995). The blame should have been placed on
the Justice Department, the IRS, the news media, the
Welfare State, and the Federal Reserve bankers. No
WHITE man over fifty-five, in his sound mind, would
think of keeping money in a "Savings and Loan" or stocks
or a "bank" in view of what was shaping up: *MARTIAL
LAW UNDER A POLICE STATE.*

In line with Roman Catholic foreign policy, as dic-
tated by the Vatican State (the pope), Clinton encouraged
a *Roman Catholic terrorist* (representing the *Catholic*
Republican Army—often miscalled "IRISH") to make a
tour of the U.S.A. to raise money for weapons for the
Catholic terrorists in Eire. The Catholic killer was Gerry
Adams.

In order to convince Americans that they needed to surrender to the USSA (Unified Search and Seizure of Assets), the BATF put out a news item that stated that the "Brady Bill" law had stopped 45,000 felons from *obtaining guns* since that law was passed. They lied. They meant to say it stopped them from *buying guns across the counter of a gun shop.* All of the felons continued to obtain guns, while the biggest professional killers—the ones who killed seventeen unarmed minor children in Waco, Texas—all obtained guns easily, including "assault weapons" and machine guns. The "Brady Bill" accomplished nothing. *Typical.*

They tried to trick you into pushing further gun control bills so they could handle you like they handled the unarmed woman in Ruby Ridge and the unarmed children in Waco, Texas. Typical: *absolutely typical.*

As I sit here now, I feel backslidden. I have invitations to come back to five mission fields and ten more invitations to come to fields that I have not visited. I must confess that, at 76, "the old gray mare ain't what she used to be many long years ago." I feel like I must get up and go, but as the Hamite once said, "Mosta mah git up and go has already done got up and went."

I am afraid I am getting to be a "homebody." When I sit on this large front porch, in these reclining lawn chairs, and sip iced-tea, while gazing out across my pond (it has a bridge over it) and into the matted forest behind it (no houses or roads are visible on the south side of my land, and the nearest house is 200 feet behind my house with the next one 400 feet), I actually feel cowardly and backslidden. My wife and my church members try to tell me "God is letting you get some rest, at last," and "God is giving you a long needed rest," or "You've been going at it tooth, claw, and toenail for so long it is about time you sat down and rested." I believe they must be right, but . . . ! How can a man retire at 76 when he is in good health?

I remember Bob Jones Sr. saying many years ago:

"I thought when I got to be 60 I would sit down and rest, but when I got to be 60 I found out I had been kicked around for so long I was too sore to sit down!" My problem is that I have been in "the saddle" (with my boots on) for so long, galloping at 45–500 miles an hour, that I feel like I'm dying when I stop to get a drink of water.

And as sure as I "lived and breathed," my contemporaries continued to die, ten thousand on one side and ten thousand on the other (see p. 338). That bloody monster (the UN) continued unabated, with war after war after war, totalling more than eighty-five before 1996. Five thousand killed in Georgia; 1,000,000 in Afghanistan; 200,000 in Nigeria; 8,000 in Mongolia; 40,000 in Angola; 2,000 in Bosnia; 400,000 in Cambodia; 100,000 in Rhwanda; 1,000 in Haiti; 200,000 in Kuwait; 80,000 Kurds; 500 Croatians; 90,000 in Liberia; another 4,000 in Bosnia, etc., etc. Again, I was spared; spared through eighty-five bloody engagements beginning with World War II.

Looking out over my congregation I saw the pitiful "remnant" that had accompanied me through World War II, Korea, Vietnam, the Falkland Islands, Thailand, Cyprus, Lebanon, Pakistan, Bangladesh, Iraq, Iran, Hungary, etc. All of us—there are four of us—were over the "threescore and ten": *Brothers Robert Mitchell, Noble Boyette, Malcom Dickman,* and *Roy Clipper* were all that were left of the "Big Parade" (1939–1945) that took on Japan and Germany.

By now, I had more friends on "the other side" than I had here. Since 1991, *Brother Hauenstein* would soon die (a wounded vet from Vietnam who handled a Bible correspondence school for years: Xenia, Ohio); *Maze Jackson* and *Curtis Hutson* had gone home to be with the Lord; *Victor Sears* and *Fred Brown* (a pastor and evangelist) had departed; *Buddy Cargill* and *B. R. Lakin* had gone home; *Truman Dollar* and *Claude Bonam* were "absent from the body and present with the Lord"; *Tom*

Woodward and *Jack Prather* (two of my graduate students) had died; *Harold Sightler* was gone, my brother (in the flesh) Johnny was gone; and Bob Jones Jr. was "on the way" (Oct. 1997).

"Oh, the friends that now are waiting in the cloudless realms of day; they are calling me to follow where their steps have led the way! They have laid aside their armor and their work on earth is done. They have kept the faith with patience and the crown of life they've won! They are calling, gently calling, sweetly calling me to come; and I'm looking through the shadows for the blessed lights of home!"

Ah, the goodness and mercy of God!

I will close at 76 and trust the Lord will call all of us out here before I can add another ten gallons of overflow to "the cup." I will close with the greatest spiritual experience I have had in my own personal life since 1991. Going through this was like going through a time warp, backwards, during a fainting spell.

You see, I had always had a bad conscience about my military days in the "land of pork and beans" (p. 111). It is true that the Blood of Jesus can purge a man's conscience from such dead works (Heb. 9:14), and even when I remembered the past, I knew all of those sins were covered and atoned for (Heb. 10:2). My sins, unlike the sins of my Roman Catholic buddies (Tony Bertini, Nick Trelizzi, Pete Chiccine, Al Alois, Joe Zaza, et al.), had been "taken away" (Heb. 10:11). But when old memories came floating back through my mind, I always had an urge to do something to atone for **"the sins of my youth"** (Psa. 25:7).

When one of our young men took off for the Philippines, back around 1991, and wound up marrying a Filipino girl named "Bing-Bing" (they have two beautiful children now), I began to get letters from Filipino pastors asking for free books. I was overjoyed to be able to mail them. Quickly this mailing list doubled and then tripled.

I began to think about going back overseas and visiting the old "haunts" (1 Sam. 30:21) and passing out some tracts and trying to help some of the native pastors; especially after Pam and I had gone to Germany (p. 317). The money problem naturally arose. My problem was I was simply getting "old and crotchety." I could no longer "take" five and six hours inside an airplane. For that matter, three hours driving in a car, at one time, would just about give me the "jerks" (an expression from the Clownsville revival in Pensacola: 1996–1997). After four trips to Germany, *tourist class,* I paid a fortune for Pam and I to go *first class.* It made a tremendous difference.

When I thought of fifteen to seventeen hours in a trans-Pacific flight to Manila, it "rattled my cage." I remember how Beauchamp Vick died within about seven months after his return from Seoul, Korea. He had been back in that "cabin" for *seventeen hours* when he was over 75. He died victoriously, slumped by his desk in his office where he had been praying. One of his last acts in his life drama was to win several hundred Koreans to Jesus Christ.

So I told Pam we would not go unless we could buy first-class, round-trip tickets. The astronomical price we were given was about $7,000. I took one look at that "tab" and said, "That's too much money. It would be wasting God's money." She said, "Well, if the Lord wants us there He'll send it in." I said, "If he sent in that much money I would *mail it to the native pastors;* they need it a lot worse than we do. Why go on a joy ride like a rich tourist when these people over there have such a need? I wouldn't go any 'class' if I couldn't take some money with me to give *them.*"

Several weeks passed. One day there comes a note from David Reese, an old Tennessee Temple graduate friend of mine from up around Montogomery, Alabama. He had resigned his work to become a full-time missionary to China, the Philippines, and (eventually) Mongolia. He says that if I can get to the Philippines he can set me up with a meeting to teach the Bible to *200 Filipino pastors.*

My wife is elated: answered prayer! She starts praying for the money. Before she starts she asks, "How
much money would God have to send you now to get you
over there?" I reply, stubbornly, "I wouldn't go if he sent
a *free* round trip ticket. Those pastors don't need me;
they need money. I wouldn't go unless I could give each
pastor $100." "Well," she said, "that would be $20,000
over the plane ticket, and the first class ticket for us
would be about $7,000. *Ask God to send in $30,000.*"

We began to pray.

Slam! Some character I did not know (and had never
met or even written to) sends in a check. *It is 20,000
bucks.* I had only seen one *check* like that in a lifetime.
"You see!" says Pam, triumphantly waving it in my face,
"now all you need is $10,000."

Slam! I am going back to my church office Wednesday night to pray during prayer meeting—in our church
all the women stay in the building and pray, and the men
disperse outdoors, anywhere they can get, till prayer time
is over—and as I go through the back hallway a stranger
steps up to me, puts a fat white envelope in my hand and
says, "I'm so and so. I used to be a hyper-Dispensation-
alist over in Mobile. I'm not anymore. I've never helped
you out financially before, but here is a little to start
with, and there will be more later." Exit. He is gone
before I can finish saying, "Thank you."

I go into my office and in one move turn off the
light and place the envelope on the bookshelf. I prostrate
myself on the floor to pray, *without opening the envelope.* Then, reviewing the blessings and goodness of God,
I find myself saying: "Lord, I don't know what is in that
envelope, but whether it is $100 or $200 or $500, this
time, I am going to tithe the whole envelope. You have
saved me already from so many doctor bills and lawyer
bills I owe you a fortune. You take 100 percent this time,
whatever it is. I don't care."

When I finished praying, I got up and turned on the
lights, picked up the envelope and opened it.

It contained one hundred $100 bills: *$10,000.*

I almost passed out. I have never even *seen* that much cash in my life, let alone *handle* it. I felt like an FBI agent in a "sting" dealing with "laundered" drug money. I informed Pam immediately, and we bought the round trip tickets. The cup overflowed again. As soon as we bought the tickets, ANOTHER check for $20,000 showed up out of thin air. Man, there are sometimes (and God knows they are rare enough) when the "will of God" is so plain to see a blind man couldn't miss it if he were walking in his sleep.

So we wound up going to Manila on Luzon, and then Iloilo on Panay, and before we returned we had placed $24,000, in American money, in the hands of saved, Filipino preachers whose maximum incomes were $20 a month.

Now (after returning) I am getting mail daily and weekly from more than fifty pastors. I had to add *this full-time ministry* to my *prison ministry,* AFTER I was 72 years old.

But that wasn't "the half of it." The half of it was when I got to Manila I had an extra day on my hands, so Pam and I and the Reeses got into a "Jeepney," and I directed them up the road to Angeles in Pampangan Province, where I had trained the Filipino Scouts forty-nine years before. The road we took ran parallel to the old narrow gauge railroad track that went up from Manila to Cabanatuan, Tarlac, etc. I was going to see if I could find one spot (about ten by twenty feet and about five feet deep) somewhere by a country road, going east from Angeles. How could I find such a spot after forty-nine years? Angeles was no longer *Angeles;* it was now Angeles *City,* nearly FIVE TIMES the size it was when I was stationed there with the old World War II 86th Infantry Division. But I had to find the spot. Forty-nine years ago, it was a dry Damulag hole (for Caribous). It was the *first place on this planet* that I had ever fallen on my face, in despair, and "called upon the name of the Lord," (p. 112).

There followed four miracles in less than an hour.

I found *the road* that led out of Angeles, but not only was there no longer a Military Depot on either side of it, the whole country had been returned to the Filipinos after 1948, so the huge drill field and "Post" were completely covered with three to four foot high crops. On its former 2,000 acres of land were five dozen wooden buildings and ten dozen Swahli huts. I never could have found it if it had not been a "chance" encounter stopping to ask directions from one of the natives. I had already had our driver stop four times to ask people, "Do you remember such-and-such?" or "Could you tell me where the old such-and-such used to be?" No one knew. Two generations had passed since I staggered down that dirt road east of Angeles on the way to my Quonset hut (p. 111).

Now, 1994, it was a paved road, and no "Depot" could be seen.

Miracle. We stopped a poor, old, broken-down Filipino who looked like he was blind in one eye. Through our interpreter he said, "Yes, the old Depot was right down there about 200 yards." (We had driven by it four times.) On further inquiry he said, "Yes, I was a Filipino Scout and trained there in *1946.*"

Slam! That is when I taught "unarmed combat" and bayonet to the 1st Battalion. I asked the Filipino what Company he was in. Slam! He said, *"Dog Company."* That was *my company:* Company D, 1st Battalion. I gazed at him in unbelief and asked: "Do you remember our C.O. (Company Commander)?" He said, "Yes. He had a long moustache and kept a pet monkey" (p. 107). "Get in, man! and show us where it was at!" I said.

So he guided us into the land where the Depot had been for training Filipino Scouts. It was absolutely unrecognizable except for the "main road" which still ran through the middle of it and one beaten-down, well-worn cement slab about eight feet square that no longer carried any "logo." All the letters had disappeared from it years

ago. Once the "Scout" pointed off to a clump of trees on
the northeast corner, which I recognized immediately. It
was where the officers' quarters had been: *the old metal
Quonset huts.*

We took him back to his house by the road, and then
I had the driver back up the road toward Angeles and
made him stop for about ten minutes. I wanted Pam to
take a picture.

I got out, crossed the road, found the exact spot
where I had turned right to go to the Depot. I then walked
through the growing crops (I don't know what they were
but they were about four to five feet high) and took about
ten regular strides through them and then stopped and
turned to face Pam's camera. *This would be the spot* (p.
109). Here was the "new creature" (2 Cor. 5:17), standing where he had fallen on his face forty-nine years ago
and cried out to God. Forty-nine summers and winters
had passed; seven children had grown up and gotten married; three Bible-believing churches had been started
"from scratch"; I had preached in more than 300 churches,
held more than 800 Bible conferences and revivals, paid
off four houses and seventeen automobiles, and put
1,840,000 miles on my speedometer (counting land, sea,
and air) since I had prayed in *that spot.* I cannot tell
anyone on earth what it felt like.

The chances of a man, in his *seventies,* going to a
foreign country more than *8,000 miles away,* forty-nine
years *after* he had been there, and finding *ONE MAN* out
of a population of over 100,000,000 who was in the same
Rifle Company with him (the TO of a World War II Rifle
Company was about 210 men), forty-nine years before,
is less, I am sure, than one out of 800,000,000,000.

But the Cup was not quite full yet!

We started out of Angeles City on the way back to
Manila, but as we turned a street corner we beheld a
large gospel sign erected on the top of a small house. The
house was a church, and the sign said—you are not going
to believe this—*"Bible Baptist Church, the Home of the*

King James Bible!" And of all things on this earth (God be merciful to me a sinner!), the sign was a six by ten foot painting of Christ knocking at a sinner's door. It was the one that I painted in my tract *Tell It Like It Is* (1972). It was a perfect reproduction. (See p. 383.)

We got out of the Jeepney again (Mr. and Mrs. Reese and myself and Pam), went into the little yard, came around to the back and knocked on the door. I had already taken 200 pesos out of my wallet to give to the pastor of this "Bible Baptist Church," whoever he was. A pretty young Filipino woman opened the door and stepped out. I asked, "Are you the pastor's wife?" She replied she was. I asked, "Could I speak to your husband, please." She looked at me and said, "He's not here right now. He's gone down to Iloilo to hear *Dr. Peter Ruckman teach the Bible."*

Now, there is no way to describe the effect these words had on me. This was the town where I had spent more than forty Saturday nights, while in the Army of occupation (1945, 1946), as a godless, depraved, licentious, young sinner. You cannot imagine the feeling that overcame me. For ten to fifteen seconds I didn't know who I *was,* what I was doing, or where I was *going.* The thought kept spinning through my head, "Dr. Peter Ruckman? Dr. Peter Ruckman? *Who is 'Dr. Peter Ruckman'?* Do you know any Dr. Peter Ruckman that 'teaches the Bible?' *The Bible?"*

"This is Angeles, Angeles, Angeles, Lt. Peter S. Ruckman MOS 0927153. You have the money in your hand. *Her husband is not at home.* Angeles, Angeles, 'Bible Baptist Church?' *Gone to hear WHO?* Dr. Peter Ruckman? WHO IS 'DR. PETER RUCKMAN?'"

I stood there speechless, and if she had not said something I am sure that my wife and friends would have begun to wonder whether or not I was suffering from heat stroke. Then the woman laughed and said, "Oh, you ARE Dr. Ruckman! I didn't recognize you from your picture right away!" We all shook hands, chatted awhile, and I gave her the money and told her to be sure and tell her husband about our visit.

Since that time I have mailed more than twenty books to that pastor.

When we returned from the junket that took us to Honolulu, Seoul, Manila, and Iloilo, we brought back twelve more precious souls—first time conversions, after initiating a King James Bible-believing movement in the Philippines that reached out into Leyte, Mindanao, Luzon, Panay, Negros, Mindoro, Cebu, Samar, Burias, Boac, Zamboanga, Bohol, and Lubang. In the years that followed (1994–1998), those 200 pastors I trained set up more than fifty King James Bible Conferences and reported the salvation of hundreds of natives.

The Lord had spared me long enough to pay my bill.

But to my dying day I will never forget the fifteen minutes I stood on "holy ground" (after standing on *unholy* ground), *helping a Christian pastor's wife* instead of paying money to an adulteress. I was still shaken from seeing the place where I fell into a Caribou wallow trying to find God, when I heard that native woman say, "My husband has gone down to Iloilo to hear Dr. Ruckman TEACH THE BIBLE." I heard it standing under a picture *I had painted* for a tract back in the U.S.A. in 1972. The picture was now a 6-by-10 foot Christian billboard in *Angeles City, Luzon* where I had lived a life that I would not describe to anyone.

That day I believe I came to know and appreciate my salvation more than any one day in my life since March of 1949. If ever I had an understanding of 2 Corinthians 5:17, I had it at that moment. *There were TWO DIFFERENT MEN standing in that Filipino pastor's doorway;* neither one had *anything* in common with the other one at all, except their *names.* They were both named Peter S. Ruckman, but beyond *that,* the differences between them, the credibility gap, the spiritual chasm that separated those two men, was wider than a dozen Grand Canyons. *One man didn't even know the other man,* and the feeling was mutual.

"Therefore if any man *be* **in Christ,** *he* **is a new creature: old things are passed away; behold, all things are become new"** (2 Cor. 5:17).

It is 1998. *I am past 76 and pushing 77.*

I am teaching 185 young men and women this year, four nights a week. The house is paid for, the car is paid for, the church is paid for, and the school is paid for; and my people are giving to foreign missions at a rate of 61–65 percent of the church offerings. I still travel more than 3,000 miles every month in Bible conferences and am still playing ice hockey and racquetball. My cup was *full* seven years ago; this is the *overflow.*

"MY CUP RUNNETH OVER."

Appendix

The Poems, Paintings, Books, and Drawings
Of Peter S. Ruckman

Published full length books:

1. *Problem Texts*: over four hundred pages dealing with "apparent contradictions in the Authorized Version."

2. *The Christian's Handbook of Biblical Scholarship*: over three hundred pages dealing with the methods, motives, and products of all of the opponents of the Authorized Version—especially the "godly Fundamentalists."

3. *The Christian's Handbook of Science and Philosophy*: over two hundred and fifty pages dealing with evolution, abnormal psychology, and philosophy from a Biblical standpoint.

4. *The Christian's Handbook of Manuscript Evidence*: over two hundred pages dealing with the basic problems involved in accepting any translation over the *Authorized Version*.

5. *The History of the New Testament Church*: two volumes, over seven hundred pages, giving a history of Christianity from the standpoint of the local New Testament assembly instead of the denominational organizations.

6. *The Mark of the Beast*: a definitive work on the "man of sin," giving his number, color, name, mark, sign, letter, religion, and eighteen types in the Old Testament.

7. *The Sure Word of Prophecy*: over two hundred pages dealing with the main subject of the Bible, "The Kingdom of Heaven versus the Kingdom of God."

8. *The Bible Believer's Commentaries*: Job, Genesis, Exodus, the Minor Prophets (Vol. I), Matthew, Acts, Psalms (Vols. I and II), Proverbs, Ecclesiastes, Galatians

through Colossians, Hebrews, the Pastoral Epistles, and Revelation. These commentaries run from three hundred to eight hundred pages apiece and present all of the critical material of higher and lower criticism (including the changes made by Hebrew and Greek scholars in ALL of the English translations) without changing one letter or word in the *Authorized King James* text.

9. *Theological Studies: Vol. I and II.* Volume one is a complete study on the doctrines related to God. Volume two takes up over thirty other subjects. Among which are The Inspiration of the Bible, Creation, Evolution, The Fall of Man, Justification, Christian Suffering, Worship, Soul Winning, Law and Grace, Heaven, Hell, Work and Fall of Angels, Demonology, The Victorious Christian Life, and many, many more.

10. *Rome, the Great Private Interpreter*: more than eighty pages dealing with the seven basic lies taught as Christian doctrine by Rome and demonstrating that every one is a private interpretation divorced from ANY Bible.

11. *The Last Grenade*: a study of apostasy: 342 pages.

12. *The Bible Babel*: the earliest work, which lays the foundation for *Manuscript Evidence* and *Biblical Scholarship*.

13. *The Unknown Bible*: over one hundred pages.

14. *The Damnation of a Nation*: 117 pages.

15. *The Anti-Intellectual Manifesto*: 157 pages.

16. *The Local Church*: 125 pages.

17. *How to Teach the Bible*: 89 pages.

18. *Memoirs of a Twentieth Century Circuit Rider*: 140 pages.

19. *How to Teach the "Original" Greek Text*: 150 pages.

20. *King James Onlyism vs. Scholarship Onlyism*: 130 pages.

21. *How to Teach Dispensations*: 90 pages.

22. *Ruckman's Notations of Life and Laughter in the Twentieth Century*: 161 pages.

23. *Full Cup*: 431 pages.

24. *The Mythological Septuagint:* 196 pages.

25. *The Scholarship Only Controversy:* 472 pages.
26. *The Clownsville Revival:* 312 pages.
27. *The Christian Liars Library:* 337 pages.
28. *Black is Beautiful:* 348 pages.
29. *God is Love:* 130 pages.
30. *Ruckman's Bible References:* 388 pages.
31. *Discrimination: The Key to Sanity:* 100 pages.
32. *Music and Musicians:* 248 pages.
33. *Art and Artists:* 129 pages.
34. *Satan's Masterpiece, the NASV.*
35. *E=MC²*
36. *How to Teach the Bible*: more than eighty pages.
37. *The Local Church*: more than eighty pages.
38. *Why I Am Not a Calvinist*

Published booklets:

1. *The Monarch of the Books*: a color cartoon booklet justifying the King James text as superior to any other publication, including all "Bibles" recommended by all Fundamental schools.

2. *Segregation and Integration*: a Biblical view of both political positions.

3. *Custer's Last Stand*: a critique of BJU's publication, *The Truth about the King James Version Controversy.*

4. *Differences in the King James Version Editions.*

5. *Five Heresies Examined*: Catholics, Charismatics, Campbellites, Jehovah's Witnesses, and Seventh-day Adventists.

6. *Eternal Security.*

7. *Marriage, Divorce, and Remarriage.*

8. *About the New King James Version.*

9. *The NIV, An In-Depth Study of Apostasy.*

10. *A Survey of the Authorized Version.*

11. *Bible Numerics.*

12. *The Alexandrian Cult*: a series of eight booklets.

13. *About the New Scofield Reference Bible.*

14. *The Restoration of Israel.*

15. *Hyper-Calvinism.*

16. *Hyper-Dispensationalism.*
17. *The Path of the Second Advent.*
18. *Fact or Fiction*
19. *The Professional Liars in Action*
20. *What Saith the Scriptures?*
21. *Roots and Methodology*
22. *Why I Am Not a Catholic*
23. *Why I Am Not a Charismatic*
24. *Why I Am Not a Seventh-day Adventist*
25. *Why I Am Not a Campbellite*
26. *Why I Am Not a New Age Global Citizen*

Published Sermons:

1. The Seven Sevens.
2. The Seven Mysteries.
3. The Seven Resurrections.
4. The Seven Baptisms.
5. The Four Judgments.
6. The White Throne Judgment.
7. The Mass.
8. The Judgment Seat of Christ.
9. Tongues, Signs, and Healings.
10. Where Do the Dead Go?
11. Body, Soul, and Spirit.
12. Fact, Faith, Feeling.
13. Heaven and Hell.
14. The Simplicity of Salvation.
15. The Tabernacle.
16. Why I Believe the KJV Is the Word of God.

Published Gospel Tracts:

1. Tell It Like It Is: German, English, Spanish, and Mandarin Chinese.
2. Does Anyone Love You?
3. What Every Young Man Should Know.
4. Of Course I'm a Christian.
5. Tomorrow May Be Different.
6. The Most Important Decision.
7. The Way to Heaven.
8. What to Do in Case You Miss the Rapture.

Baptistries Painted:
1. Milton, Florida.
2. Pensacola, Florida (3).
3. Mobile, Alabama (2).
4. Tallahassee, Florida.
5. Meridian, Mississippi.
6. Canton, Ohio.
7. Rochester, New York (2).
8. Toledo, Ohio.
9. San Antonio, Texas.
10. Dixon Mills, Alabama.
11. Hamilton, Ohio.
12. Baton Rouge, Louisiana.
13. Tampa, Florida.
14. Green Bay, Wisconsin.
15. Birmingham, Alabama.
16. Atlanta, Georgia.
17. Pomona, California.

Artwork—Earlier Period (1931–1941):
1. Cartoon strip (*Don Diego and the Aztec Jewels*).
2. Cartoon strip (*World War One*).
3. Cartoon strip (*The Time Machine*).
4. Cartoon strip (*The Great Opium Case*).
5. Cartoon strip (*Red Fox*).
6. Cartoon strip (*Commander Hell*).
7. Cartoon strip (*The South Sea Mystery*).
8. Cartoon strip (*The Rim Shot Murderers*).
9. Cartoons for college magazine.
10. Colored chalk drawings on the blackboard at Topeka High School.
11. Chalk talk in the assembly at Topeka High School.
12. Crayon landscapes of Kansas. Colored ink sketches in New Orleans. Pastel drawings in New Orleans.

Psychopathic Symbolism:
These were originally done in Luzon on eight by eleven inch sheets of very cheap construction paper, which

was the only thing available at that time in the Philippines. Most of these were later enlarged onto sheets of illustration board, two by three feet in size.

1. The Apathy of the Stars.
2. The Fear of Old Age.
3. The Fear of Death.
4. The Fear of Disease.
5. The Illusion of Security.
6. The Fear of Ridicule.
7. The Fear of the Unknown.
8. Vital Statistics.
9. Karma.
10. Subpoena.
11. Nervous Tension.
12. Nicotine Fit.
13. Chronic Alcoholic.
14. Human Nature.
15. Jealousy.
16. The Outsider.
17. International Situation.
18. False Saviour (Wrong Messiah).
19. Religion.
20. Peace.
21. The Wasted Life.
22. The Unanswerable Question.

Artwork—Middle Period (1942–1959):

1. Pastel portraits of students in Tuscaloosa, Alabama.
2. Pen and ink illustrations for magazines (University of Alabama).
3. Cartoon strip for John Carlyle to go with a radio series.
4. One hundred and twenty sketches of infantrymen in various colors of ink.
5. First watercolors in Pearl Harbor (the shore, men on deck, boxers, men loading freight, bancas).
6. Second series of watercolors (Philippines and Japan): barrios, plane wreckage, Rizal Stadium, bombed

out buildings, three churches, water buffalo, night scenes, Mt. Arayat, Filipino girls, meat markets, laundry workers, Manila harbor, troop transports, Iwo Jima, Corregidor, downtown Manila, drunk GI passed out in bar room, Japanese Kendo fighters, Karate fighters, Samisen and Koto concerts, Japanese farmhouse, juggler juggling firebrands, Dai Ichi Building, pagodas at Nikko and Katsura, snow on Fujiama, Judo fighters, Buddha at Kamakura, shrine at Katsura, the Emperor's bridge, Emperor's palace, a Koto choir, government buildings, and "honey buckets."

7. A forty-page color cartoon book done in watercolors and pen and ink, called *The Little Girl Who Had Everything She Wanted*. This was done for my firstborn daughter, Diana, who at the time was two years old.

8. Oil paintings: two churches, portrait of Janie Bess, self-portrait, portraits of David and Priscilla, the Crucifixion, pen and ink ads for radio programs in the *Mobile Press Register*.

9. Surrealistic portrait of a radio announcer.

10. Oil mural on the wall of radio station WEAR, depicting the history of music.

11. Oil portrait on a bar advertising drinks.

12. Twenty posters advertising dances. At this point, conversion took place (March 1949).

13. Four still lifes (flowers) done for relatives in Alabama.

14. Four oil landscapes.

15. Four large-sized watercolor landscapes.

16. Four large-sized Japanese style (Shibui) still-life in oil.

17. Ten posters advertising dances and "jam sessions."

18. Bird dogs painted in oil for a relative in Sawyerville, Alabama.

19. Baptistry painted in Dixon Mills; another one in Mobile.

20. Watercolors: North Carolina boy with dog and gun, Wall Street, Yosemite Falls, bass fisherman, boy on

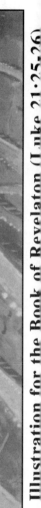

Illustration for the Book of Revelaton (Luke 21:25,26)

rail watching cows come home, man with dog, the shrimp fleet, boat at anchor, three sunset pictures, Brussels's Cathedral, two Grand Canyon pictures, Spring Street in Mobile, Bellingrath Gardens, four more flower arrangements, New Orleans French Quarter, interior of trailer, four mountain scenes, cow herder, and sixteen copies of Dettlefson's works.

21. Oil: night scene in the winter with Christ knocking for entrance into a frozen cabin.

22. Two swan scenes (water color).

23. Four autumn pictures in water color.

24. Four watercolors of streams and rapids.

25. Ten watercolors copied from Ideal magazine.

26. Ten watercolors copies from photos in Arizona magazine.

27. Three landscapes for a friend in Pensacola.

28. Two more landscapes (water colors) for a friend in Pensacola.

29. Four illustrated stories for DVBS (flash cards) and another twenty pen and ink illustrations for Sunday school material.

30. And here (1951) begins the "chalk talks" which eventually totaled more than two hundred different pictures. At least ten of these were drawn more than four hundred times, and another fifty were drawn more than a hundred times. The titles can be found listed in the catalogue of the Bible Baptist Bookstore.

31. One hundred and fifty watercolors painted to illustrate the cassette sermons.

32. Forty charts (two foot by three foot) drawn to use in teaching at PBI.

33. Seven portraits of Civil War Generals.

34. Portraits of wife and granddaughter.

35. Montage of twelve children's faces.

36. Watercolor pencil paintings of Japanese houses, mountain ranges, gardens, fall landscapes, and

37. Fifty pen and ink sketches of Generals, ice hockey players, still lifes, tanks, ships, and planes.

Artwork—Late Period (1960–1990):
    Oil Portraits:
1. Martin Luther.
2. Chrysostom.
3. Ignatius.
4. Polycarp.
5. Tertullian.
6. St. Patrick.
7. George Whitefield.
8. John Wesley.
9. Jonathan Edwards.
10. John Knox.
11. William Booth.
12. Balthasar Hubmaier.
13. John Bunyan.
14. William Tyndale.
15. John Huss.
16. Christmas Evans.
17. Mel Trotter.
18. David Livingstone.
19. John Wycliffe.
20. John Calvin.
21. George Fox.
22. B.H. Carroll.
23. J. Frank Norris.
24. Beauchamp Vick.
25. Dr. M.R. DeHaan.
26. W.B. Riley.
27. Peter Cartwright.
28. Gypsy Smith.
29. Billy Sunday.
30. Wilbur Chapman.
31. Mordecai Ham.
32. Dwight L. Moody.
33. Ulrich Zwingli.
34. Clay Hadley.
35. Sam Jones.
36. Twenty water color landscapes.

Classical Music: (Acrylics)
1. Beethovan's 9th Symphony.
2. Beethovan's 5th Symphony.
3. Schubert's 9th Symphony.
4. Schubert's Serenade.
5. Tschaikovsky's 6th Symphony.
6. Brahms' 1st Symphony.
7. Albinoni's Adagio.
8. Händel: Largo (Xerxes).
9. Liszt: Les Preludes.
10. Bocherinni's Minuet.
11. Dance of Blessed Spirits: Gounod.
12. Overture to Poet and Peasant: Von Suppe.
13. Scheherasade: Korsakov.
14. Theme of Pagannini: Rachmaninov.
15. Bach's "Air" on G-string.
16. Enesco's Romanian Rhapsody.
17. Händel's Water Music.
18. Ravel's Bolero.

Miscellaneous:
1. One hundred and forty-four oil and acrylic illustrations for the book of Revelation.
2. Ten Bible charts for missionaries to use in street work.
3. Sixteen illustrations for Christian books and jacket covers.
4. All the illustrations for *Manuscript Evidence, Bible Babel, Biblical Scholarship, Monarch of the Books, Science and Philosophy*, and *The Last Grenade*.
5. Twenty landscape watercolors (1976), plus thirty more between 1970 and 1988. Germany, Austria, and Switzerland.
6. Color illustrations for *So You Want to Be a Man?*
7. Forty foot dispensational charts fully illustrated.
8. Portrait of *Robert E. Lee* (acrylic).
9. Three landscapes in acrylic for personal friends in Michigan, Ohio, and California.
10. Five surrealistic oil paintings illustrating symphonic pieces.

11. Two pastel landscapes, twenty by thirty-two inches.

12. Three "storybooks" done for BJU (films). This was back in 1950–1951.

13. Four acrylic paintings for friends in Pensacola (Germany, Switzerland).

14. Four acrylic landscapes for friends in Alabama and Tennessee.

15. Four church posters advertising meetings.

16. Twenty illustrated cartoon chalk talks for use in DVBS.

17. Twenty watercolor landscapes for Priscilla (Germany, the South).

18. Large-sized acrylic illustrating *The Last Grenade*.

19. Portraits of Laura and Rachel.

20. Ten billboards, 12 foot by 24 foot, illustrating Bible verses.

This does not exhaust the list, as at least two dozen more water-color landscapes were done between 1985 and 1989, which were done just for pleasure. The number of pen and ink sketches and pencil sketches from 1928 to 1990 would be incalculable. Every school textbook from 1933 to 1945 (and then again from 1949 to 1953) was covered with sketches, and so were all of the notebooks for all of the subjects. Somewhere is a complete notebook of pen and ink sketches on karate and judo, and somewhere is a book-length "novel" called *Can Spring Be Far Behind?*, which is an illustrated cartoon strip on the Russian campaign (Barbarossa, 1942). In addition to this there has vanished at least eight hundred pen and ink sketches done "on the field" while traveling up and down between 1960 and 1980.

Poems (pre-conversion):

The first set (1940–1945) are missing, but they might be found somewhere. The poems were written in lined notebooks of about forty pages each. They were written in the last year of high school and while in college. The second set were written overseas and were titled *Bamboo*

Anthology. I burned those when I got saved.

Poems (post-conversion):
   The third set are these, written between 1962 and 1982.

The Rose of Sharon
Once there grew a rose so fair beyond the crystal sea.
It was pure and spotless white and bloomed eternally.
But one day God plucked that rose and planted it on earth.
It grew a root from driest ground, a red rose at its birth.
Oh, Rose of Sharon! who died for me!
Oh, Rose of Sharon, by the crystal sea!
Who knew Thy heartache? Who knew Thy loss?
As the blood red petals fell down from Your Cross?

Once there grew some ugly thorns, enshrined in mud and mire.
They were twisted, hard, and sharp, and fit for nought but fire.
But men made a thorny whip and then a thorny crown.
They lashed the rose and slashed the rose,
and cut Him to the ground.
Oh, Rose of Sharon, whose petals fell!
Oh, Rose of Sharon, who loved so well!
How sweet Thy fragrance, how kind Thy grace!
Despised by sinner, dying in their place.

The thorn, the rose, grow side by side, beyond the crystal sea.
There the thistle and the thorn are from the curse set free.
No more curse and no more mire; what joy God only knows!
For I am saved! I was the thorn, and Jesus was the rose!
Oh, Rose of Sharon, by the crystal sea!
Oh, Rose of Sharon, who died for me!
How can I praise Thee for Thy great love?
Till I enter heaven and Thy home above?
(Sung to "Heide Roslein")

Sailing with Jesus

The dawn has come, the tide moves out,
and we must sail the open sea.
We'll leave the shore, we'll leave the bay,
and sail off to eternity.
In Christ my Lord I've put my trust.
With Him on board, it's "Home or Bust!"
Farewell, farewell to all His foes, on land or sea,
who Him oppose.
Farewell, farewell to sin and shame! we've set our sails
in Jesus's name! (Ahoy!)

Cast off the lines, no ties with earth, for we must ride
the ocean waves.
We've dropped the world with its advice and now obey
the One who saves.
With Christ our Lord in full command,
We'll anchor yet, in His homeland.
Oh, comrade true, just feel that breeze! God's
Spirit moves the rolling seas!
Farewell, farewell to every claim. We're sailing now
in Jesus's name. (Ahoy!)
(Sung to "Wir fahren aus den Meer hinaus!")

The Death of a Nation

Now I will sing you of the death of a nation.
Now I will sing you of its grief and pain.
Once blessed by God, but now desolation,
Boasting in sin, rotting within, dying in shame.

Once they were free men who lived by the Bible.
Now they are bondmen with no heavenly calling.
Gone are God's blessings; there's no revival.
They followed Rome, losing their home, night now is
falling.

Why did they listen to bishops and priests?
Why did they worship science and learning?
Forsaking Christ, who delivered their souls,
God's Book and God's Spirit spurning.

Now Rome controls them with lies and seduction.
Man worships man, and death now is calling.
Hell beats its drums, Antichrist comes!
Night now has fallen.

What a Day!

What a day when I met Christ my Saviour!
And He took away my sin and shame!
What a day when Jesus paid my ransom,
And then He placed His Spirit deep within!
While the world prepares to worship Satan
And the nations faint and fall,
I will rest and hope in Jesus' promise,
And will rise to meet Him at His call!

Christ the Lord is still my God and Saviour,
Though my youth has slowly passed away.
And He's still my constant guide and helper,
Though I've often sinned and gone astray.
Though the coming years may bring me pain and sorrow, He will keep me all the way.
I shall live to see His holy city,
To shout and sing, "Oh, Saviour, what a day!"
(Sung to "So ein Tag")

Gold and Silver

Gold and silver cannot pay for my soul's redemption.
Kindly words and noble deeds I shall never mention.
Precious Blood alone can tell of God's grace and power,
And His Son who died for me, in His darkest hour;
And His Son who died for me, in His darkest hour.

Gold and silver cannot heal heartaches of a nation.
Work and hope cannot replace the joy of true salvation.
Christ alone can bind the wounds when He comes with power,
Coming back on earth to reign, in His glorious hour;
Coming back on earth to reign, in His glorious hour.

Acrylic Illustration for the Book of Revelation (Psalm 2, 110)

The King of Books

When this age has run its course of madness,
and its writers lie dead, one and all,
We'll still have the Book that causes gladness,
for God's words can never fail or fall!

When the books of men throughout the ages perish,
molding in their filth and dust,
When the Lake of Fire consumes their pages,
We'll still read the Book God gave to us!

Though the ASV was quite impressive
And the NIV was made for looks,
Still Satan could not steal our Bible,
For our Book will outlive all the books!

When our Saviour comes to earth in glory,
And brings down man's proud and haughty looks,
Darwin, Freud, and Marx will then mean nothing,
For our Book will judge ALL other books!
(Sung to "Wenn die Alpen Rosen Wiederbluhen")
        CHORUS:
Come and look! Come and look! It's the one and only
Book.
Come and look at this, OUR Book. It's the King of all
the Books!

The Christian Seasons

When the SPRING of youth is in my bones, and my
heart for sinful pleasure groans,
I will plead with Christ my Saviour, who was tempted
just like me;
Let me not waste golden hours; Lord I give my youth to
thee.
When the SUMMER sun is shining high and I have the
power to sell and buy,
I'll give thanks to Christ my Saviour, for my wealth, and
health, and breath,
Knowing all these things were purchased through His
poverty and death.
When my friends fall as the AUTUMN leaves and my
spirit sits alone and grieves,

I'll remember Christ my Saviour, that dear One who
stands by me,
How His dearest friends forsook Him when He hung on
Calvary's tree.
When the WINTER winds of death have blown, and my
body lies as still as stone,
I'll go home to Christ my Saviour, that dear One who
died for me,
And I'll sing of death no longer, for I'll live eternally!

Flying Home

I once was a sinner, but now I am saved
By One who ransoms from Hell and the Grave.
He promised to come back; His coming is soon,
And I shall fly away beyond the farthest moon!

Our flight home is loading; our Captain is true.
He bore our sorrows, He'll carry you.
Your passage is paid for—your wages of sin,
So trust the Pilot and come fly with Him!

Chorus:
Come fly with me home to glory!
Out where the sea meets the sky!
No sickness, no death, all is life, joy, and rest,
Forever, in God's home on high!

Acrylic Illustration of Psalm 9:1-7

PHILIPPINES

Angeles City (see p. 361)
Island of Luzon

Bible Conference on the island of Panay.

**Dorm at Calvary Baptist Church
Iloilo City, Philippines**

**Missionary Roger Bayona outside entrance to
church he is helping.**

**Brother Dickman's sign outside church in
Iloilo City, Philippines**

The Caribou hole of 1946 (p. 112).

Mt. Arayat—Angeles (Pampanga)

Daily Vacation Bible School class.

Christian school—Iloilo, 1994

Man with hat was in Dr. Ruckman's Rifle company when he was in the Philippines as a lost man.

Kindergarten class.

Food cooking in the kitchen.

KOREA

Dr. Ruckman (right) and Pastor Song Lee interpreting.

Korean welcome to me and my wife.

Conference with three Korean preachers.

Students in "The Pensacola Bible Institute of Korea."

Above: Pam Ruckman with Indian friend.
Below: Playing the "mouth organ" for some waifs.

Typical village scene in more than 100,000 villages.

Hindu temples: 9,000,000 gods in India.

"Special" sung by an Indian "choir."

Bro. Garikapaty and pastors brought
to the Bible Conference from
Nellore, on the East Coast.

Left to right: Bro. Kumar, Bro. Ware, and Mrs. Ruckman

Praying for children after the service.

**Loaded up and traveling.
No charge for external seats.**

**In Bombay, on my way to preach in a
poverty stricken area. Incomes are about
$5.00 a month in American money.**

Hindu gods: Hyderabad, India

A visit is made to the local Indian oprhanage.
Note four widows who also are supported.

No regular income, no government help,
no support from local churches.

**Church dedication service. Forty miles
from nowhere.**

An
**"Open Bible
Forum"
before 950
preachers.**

(Hyderabad)

Good attendance (950) at Bible Conference in Hyderabad.

Our "cooks" for the conference.

**Preaching to "pariahs." Whole congregation
illiterate—could not read or write.**

Indian choir at the conference.

Village 50 miles north of Hyderabad.

**A "sikh"
doorman
at the
motel.**

Welcome to Hyderabad, India

**The lowest caste kids playing in a village.
Bombay, India**

**Streetside altar to Kali—goddess
of destruction.**

Preachers at the Bible Conference.

Preaching of the gospel brings a crowd.

Baptizing takes place in a local canal.

Along the highways and in the market.

More orphans.

"Street" preaching.

Preaching in a Hindu locality.

Preaching in a tribal village.

Preaching among the "tribals."

**My Sunday morning congregation
in Bombay. Three saved.**

MEXICO

BEHOLD, THE FEAR OF THE LORD, THAT IS WISDOM:

Riding the van to church—Mexico

Passengers praising God.

**Witnessing
to store
keeper
in the
mall**

(Guadalajara)

**Going to preach somewhere S.E. of
Guadalajara.**

Weldon Jones' son "in action."

Weldon Jones' local church which he established and built.

Weldon Jones' "hometown" in Mexico.

Street preaching near Guadalajara.

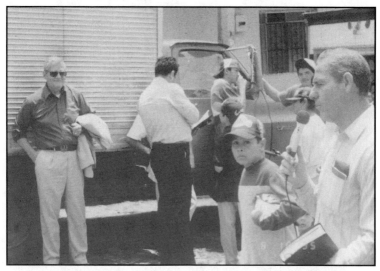

Watching Weldon Jones street preaching.

Dr. Ruckman and Bro. Jones in a local church

U K R A I N E

**Above: Me with Ricky Bolick, one of my graduates.
Below: Odessa in the Ukraine.**

Getting ready for baptismal in the Ukraine.

**Christian family at baptismal service.
Odessa, Russia.**

NEW YORK

In the Mafia Museum.

Touring Little Italy

A window full of gods and no help.

A Jew being witnessed to (Bro. Miletello)

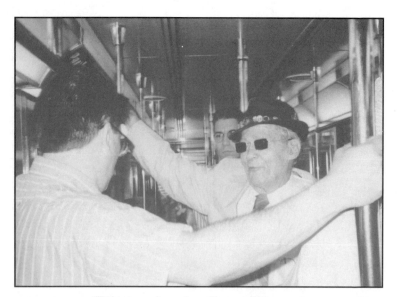

Witnessing in the subways.

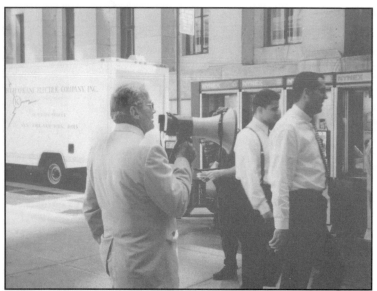

Street preaching on Wall Street.

One of the Mafia "families."

**Dr. Ruckman (left) and Pastor Miletello
visit birthplace of John Gotti.**

**Services in a Presbyterian Church,
New York City.**

Chinatown in New York City.

HAWAII

Pam and I at the "Dali" (Oahu).

Dr. Ruckman (right) and Bro. Hernandez
This room was the beginning of Bro. Hernandez's
present church.

Pot O' Gold Ranch

Every summer from 1967 to 1998

**Chow time is a favorite time at camp.
Comfort, Texas**

**Huisache Baptist Church, San Antonio, Texas.
The man on my left is Claude Bonam who was
J. Frank Norris' visitation director.**

MARCHING BAND

MISCELLANEOUS

**The "old homestead"—28 years.
5420 Rawson Lane**

**"Suiting up" in the motel (10 p.m.) for a
midnight ice hockey game.**

Greta, Rebel, and Chief: the security system.

**Playing on the ice in Detroit from
11 p.m. to 1 a.m.**

**Married in church, April 30, 1989
Rev. Lawrence, presiding.**

My Taekwondo class: Master Song.

My garden at 8808 Chisholm Road.

**Preaching to 200 soldiers at Ft. Knox.
Fourteen got saved.**

Part of the brass section in the church orchestra.